EXPLANATION:
NEW DIRECTIONS IN PHILOSOPHY

EXPLANATION: NEW DIRECTIONS IN PHILOSOPHY

by

THE FACULTY IN PHILOSOPHY
AT
THE AMERICAN UNIVERSITY

MARTINUS NIJHOFF / THE HAGUE / 1973

To Our Graduate Students

ISBN 90 247 1517 2

PRINTED IN THE NETHERLANDS

PREFACE

This volume initiates a series of American University Publications in Philosophy. It is expected that, as occasion permits, volumes will be added to the series, contributing to the dialogue that is contemporary philosophy. The essays in this volume were written by the faculty in philosophy at The American University during the academic year 1970-71 and appear here for the first time.

In a variety of modes the essays cluster around epistemological problems collateral with theories of explanation. In view of recent attention to such theories, this volume explores several new directions in the explanation of behavior, language, and religion.

We are especially appreciative of the secretarial assistance of Mrs. Madaline Shoemaker, whose magic turned many an unreadable manuscript into an intelligible essay. We are also grateful to Miss Maria Wilhelm for the final typing of the volume, and to the Office of the Dean for Graduate Studies, The American University, for encouragement and for a financial grant toward typing expenses.

Barry L. Blose
Harold A. Durfee
David F. T. Rodier
Editorial Committee

TABLE OF CONTENTS

CONTEMPORARY DIRECTIONS

THE SPIRIT OF CONTEMPORARY AMERICAN PHILOSOPHY

by

ROGER T. SIMONDS

In 1963, John E. Smith published a study of Peirce, James, Royce, Dewey, and Whitehead, entitled *The Spirit of American Philosophy*. The title itself is an act of homage to the great forgotten idealist of the American "golden age," Josiah Royce, whose ghost hovers over the pages of the book. It is consonant with the idealist tradition to say, as Smith does, that there is such a thing as the "spirit of" a philosophical movement; that it is something more than a set of doctrines because it is "a style, a stance toward life in the world" (*i.e.*, a moral sensibility and a *praxis*); that it is something less than a set of doctrines because it is an unwritten philosophy rooted in the life of the people (*i.e.*, a *Volksgeist*). According to Smith, the essence of this unwritten philosophy lies in three convictions: (1) "that thinking is primarily an *activity* in response to a concrete situation and that this activity is aimed at solving problems;" (2) "that ideas and theories must have a 'cutting edge' or must *make a difference* in the conduct of people who hold them and in the situations in which they live"; (3) "that *the earth can be civilized* and obstacles to progress overcome by the application of knowledge." [1]

The lives of Smith's five philosophers stretch over an enormous period of time, from the birth of Peirce in 1839 to the death of Whitehead in 1947. During that time, many other American philosophers lived and died, and an evaluation of Smith's theory of the American ideology would have to take them into account. There was Santayana, whom Smith deliberately excludes from consideration because he does not fit into the ideological picture. There were men like Perry, Hocking, Mead, Urban, Parker, Woodbridge, Montague, R. W. Sellars, Lovejoy, Jordan, and Brightman, men whose names are at most barely mentioned in survey courses today, but who exerted direct and powerful influence on the American philosophers who came of age and began professional careers between World Wars I and II.

[1] *The Spirit of American Philosophy* (New York, 1963), p. 188.

World War II brought profound changes to American philosophy, as it did to so many other aspects of American life. Leading European artists, scientists, and intellectuals came to this country during the late thirties and early forties, to escape the nightmare of totalitarian regimes, in a migration of talent such as the world had never seen. The American intellectual lost some of his provincialism. He became more aware of European problems and achievements, and after the war he expanded this awareness to include Asia and Africa. In philosophy, the expanding horizon brought into view the positivistic and Neo-Kantian philosophies of science, the phenomenology movement, existentialism, Neo-Thomism, and the English analytic schools; it brought increasing awareness of traditional Oriental philosophies and of the variety and flexibility of modern Marxism. There has been a great surge of interest in philosophy generally. The English-language professional journals in that field have increased from a mere handful before the war to some three dozen or so, with no end in sight. One may well ask, therefore, what the spirit of American philosophy is today.

In the first place, who are the leading American philosophers now? Professor Andrew J. Reck of Tulane has recently published a book, *The New American Philosophers* (1968), in which he identifies them as follows: C. I. Lewis (now dead), Stephen Pepper, Brand Blanshard, Ernest Nagel, J. H. Randall, Jr., Justus Buchler, Sidney Hook, F. S. C. Northrop, James K. Feibleman, John Wild, Charles Hartshorne, and Paul Weiss. All of these men have produced substantial book-length works in many different fields of philosophy during the post-war era. All of them except Nagel were born in the United States. All were educated primarily here and became professors at leading universities. Although their interests and involvements in foreign philosophy and inter-cultural issues generally are much broader than were their predecessors', they have all been heavily influenced by American philosophy, and especially by Peirce, Dewey, and Whitehead. Although these men are clearly at the head of their profession by virtue of the quantity, quality, and range of their works, their views are by no means representative of the profession as a whole. For they have practiced philosophy in a manner thoroughly unfashionable among English-speaking professionals today. And this is so in three ways: (1) they are fiercely individualistic, (2) they are difficult because each one has created his own technical language, and (3) they are unashamed system-builders. Among themselves they appear to be so diverse that one is hard pressed to say what common theme or spirit, American or otherwise, might be present in them. Professor Reck, indeed, after reviewing them one by one, concludes that there is no common theme. They are as diverse, he says, "as the forces and factors in American culture." [2]

Should we conclude, then, that the spirit of American philosophy is no more?

The current situation in philosophy brings out more sharply than ever before a problem which has always been important and difficult for scholars, which is itself a philosophical problem, but which has not received the attention it deserves, namely: How should one go about comparing the philosophical views or systems of different writers? This question becomes pressing at a time when the writers of philosophical books no longer stick to a familiar terminology, and when there is as much disagreement as there seems to be today over the very basic issue as to what sort of thing philosophers should be doing. It becomes pressing if only because we want to know how much philosophers really do disagree about what they should do. Modern schools of thought, violently opposed to one another, claim to be the legitimate heirs of the same classical philosophers. Such claims involve interpretation and comparison; surely they can't all be right. Or can they? When existentialists and "ordinary language" analysts, for example, claim to represent the true tradition of Plato, are they really giving different interpretations of Plato?

The first hurdle to cross is what seems to be a typical misunderstanding of what comparison demands. This is very noticeable among students, but one finds it occasionally in the more exalted regions of scholarship. Ask the average undergraduate to compare the views of philosopher A with those of philosopher B with respect to a question Q, and he will usually tell you that A said X about Q while B said Y about Q; and then he will stop. It does not occur to him to ask whether X and Y are really different answers to Q, or how they are related if different. Yet this is what you hoped he would ask. I fear that Professor Reck is open to criticism on this score when, after describing twelve philosophers, each in terms of that philosopher's own technical language, he concludes that they are all different. An agreement or disagreement in words does not always amount to an agreement or disagreement in ideas.

Along with this goes another common attitude, that writers who use different words cannot really be compared at all. This attitude, at any rate, is one not shared by the leading philosophers themselves, whether they are speculative system-builders or critical analysts. The system-builder thinks that his ideas are more adequate than those of his competitors, past or present, and in order to show this he defines every other system of philoso-

[2] *The New American Philosophers* (Baton Rouge, 1968), p. 348.

phy as a fragment or subsystem of his own. The analyst thinks that his critical methods have general validity not dependent on the choice of some systematic standpoint; hence he applies those methods without hesitation to the writings of any philosopher. When he encounters a system to which his analysis seems inapplicable for some reason, he simply declares it to be nonsense. To abstain from comparison, then, is not necessarily to vindicate the integrity of the philosopher. On the contrary, it is more apt to be grossly unfair to his own conception of what he is doing.

Assuming that comparison is legitimate, the next question is whether there is such a thing as *objective* comparison, in other words, comparison which does not depend for its validity on the choice of some philosophical standpoint. Can one compare, say, Whitehead with Pepper, without *ipso facto* subscribing to the views of Whitehead, Pepper, or any other particular philosopher? Is there a philosophically neutral ground for the comparison of philosophical ideas? I believe that there is, and in what follows I shall outline my views on that subject and illustrate them by reference to some of the contemporary American philosophers.

Please note that the "objectivity" I have in mind is not the objectivity of some standpoint *outside* every philosophy but is rather the objectivity of a standpoint *within* every philosophy and common to every philosophy. Thus my position depends on the idea that there is such a common standpoint. In this common standpoint I find at least four elements: a conception of truth-value, a conception of generality, a conception of logical proof, and a conception of thought or experience.

Every philosopher, speaking or writing *qua* philosopher, makes assertions for which he claims truth and which he presents to his audience for evaluation as such. This may not seem very important as a characteristic of philosophers. But the claim to make true assertions, as one finds it in philosophical prose, is already sufficient to set it apart from some other sorts of writing, such as poetry, drama, and fiction. It is not that true statements do not occur in poetry, etc., but only that there is no reason to demand them or expect them. But one who presents himself as a philosopher is in the truth-telling business, although he may not be as good at it as some amateurs are. In any case, he is committed to the idea that there are truth-values just because he is in that business. Some people are fond of saying things like "There are no absolutes," or "Everything is relative," in the manner of the ancient Sophists; and sometimes one is tempted to think that they really believe that there are no truth-values and hence no truths or falsehoods. But the only way to take them seriously, as one would have to do if one took them for philosophers, is to attribute to them just such a belief in truth-values as they ostensibly reject.

Philosophy differs from other sorts of inquiry in that it is absolutely general. It is not limited, as the various empirical sciences are, to some special subject matter. It is true that some writers claiming to be philosophers have tried to restrict the field of philosophical discourse to, say, the analysis of language. The question then is whether this restriction is to be construed as a philosophical commitment, that is, as part of their philosophy. If so, then clearly their philosophy is inconsistent, because an assertion forbidding reference to some class of things, in some theory, cannot itself belong to the theory in question, since it refers to the forbidden things. If, on the other hand, the assertion is construed as *not* belonging to the philosophy, then it must belong to some still more general discipline. But traditionally philosophy has always been regarded as the most general of all disciplines, and a writer who thinks there is something more general should tell us what it is. The reason why scientific discourse, on the other hand, can be successfully limited to particular kinds of subject matter is that such limitations are regarded as metascientific or philosophical and need not be expressed in the language of science itself.

The fact that philosophy enjoys (or suffers from) an unrestricted sort of generality has some interesting consequences which are quite independent of any particular choice of viewpoint. One consequence is that philosophical theories contain their own semantic rules: in other words, they lay down the conditions for translating the language of the theory into that of any other theory. Otherwise, philosophical semantics would have to be expressed in some metalanguage richer than philosophical language itself; but this is impossible if philosophical language is already the richest possible language. Another consequence is that any and every system of logic is expressible in philosophical language (although the converse is not true). Still another consequence is that philosophical theories are not, in the ordinary sense, amenable to empirical or experimental tests. The "logical positivists" of the Vienna Circle made a great deal of this point and tried to use it as a weapon against traditional metaphysics. But experimental tests work only for theories with carefully limited subject matter, because the validity of such tests must be established independently of whatever theory is to be tested. Philosophical theories, with their unlimited generality, can never meet this requirement; they define their own relationship to experience in their own terms. If this lack of experimental "objectivity" is a weakness of philosophy, as the positivists thought, it is largely compensated by the fact that philosophy has to meet a more stringent test of logical consistency than the empirical sciences do. Unlimited generality carries with it the dangers of self-reference and the obligation to maintain self-referential consistency as well as ordinary consistency. For example, suppose the philosopher asserts that every meaningful statement is either empirically testable or logically decidable (which was essentially Ayer's position in *Language, Truth and Logic*). Such assertion may be consistent enough in the ordinary sense, *i.e.*, in that it does not contradict any other statement belonging to the same system; but it may be self-referentially inconsistent if (as happens in this example) it does not conform to its own edict.

In one sense it is up to the individual philosopher to decide what importance logical theory has, if any, for his system. He might decide that it has no importance at all, since he might regard the "system" as consisting merely of a number of assertions or propositions, some of them extremely general, to which he subscribes. Thus he might assert that the sky is blue, that all men are mortal, that only declarative sentences have truth-value, and so forth. But these assertions would not, I take it, immediately confer the status of "philosopher" on one who makes them. We expect the philosopher to do something more than merely hold or assert generalizations, just as we expect the scientist to do something more: namely, we expect him to offer reasons or arguments in support of his assertions, and we expect these arguments to conform to certain standards of validity which do not depend on accepting the generalizations they are designed to support. To the extent that he argues, as we expect him to, the philosopher makes at least tacit use of some logic or other. *What* logic it may be, I care not for the moment. My point is simply that some concept of logical reasoning or proof is involved in any philosophy.

Moreover, the philosopher's activity always involves some recognition of the presence of consciousness, awareness, thought, feeling, experience, or the like. It involves this recognition, whether explicitly or not, the moment the philosopher gives his thoughts utterance. The philosopher may have only himself for audience, of course, and he may even believe that there is no other audience. In saying this, I do not necessarily suppose that every philosophy recognizes a distinction between thoughts and expressions of thoughts. The Italian idealist Croce, for instance, denied this distinction.[3] But the important point to notice is that in so doing he did not actually dispose of either thoughts or expressions. Likewise the behaviorists, who want to reduce thoughts to physical-chemical events in the bodies of organisms, have not thereby disposed of them either.

To clarify this point somewhat, one might compare it with the famous

[3] In "Aesthetics," in *Encyclopaedia Britannica*, 14th ed., vol. 1, p. 266.

problem of nonexistent and impossible objects. It has been argued occasionally (as by Meinong) that in some sense chimeras and square circles must "be," or subsist as objects of thought, if it is possible to assert truly concerning them that they do not exist. Against this, one can invoke Russell's theory of descriptions, or perhaps Frege's doctrine of "reference," and one can argue that statements ostensibly about nonexistent objects need not be construed as referring to such objects at all. Conceivably, some philosopher might want to hold that thoughts are nonexistent like chimeras, or even impossible like square circles. In that case, could he dispose of them in the same way, namely by saying that the expressions which *seem* to refer to thoughts do not really refer to them at all? No, for the trouble is that any claim as to what "seems" is already an admission of thought. Few of us will be disappointed if an exhaustive inventory of the universe fails to turn up any nonexistent objects; but we will be rightly indignant if it fails to turn up any thoughts, as if a census were taken in such a way that the census takers themselves were not counted.

Some recognition of truth-value, generality, logical proof, and thought is involved in every philosophy regardless of its particular character. Hence these four conceptions, at least, may provide a philosophically neutral ground for the comparison of one system with another. To every philosopher we can pose the question, not whether he has these conceptions, but how he relates them to one another. More specifically, I would pose two pairs of questions, as follows:

Group I. (a) Are any truth-values decidable by logical proof? In other words, is there at least one assertion for which a proof exists? (b) If the answer to the first question is affirmative, then is every truth-value logically decidable? In other words, is there a proof of the truth or untruth of every assertion that has a truth-value?

Group II. (a) Are there any assertions which are true strictly if and only if the speaker thinks that they are true? In other words, are there any intuitively decidable truth-values? (b) If the answer is affirmative, then is every truth-value intuitively decidable? This second pair of questions can be regarded as a generalization from Bishop Berkeley's famous dictum, that with respect to "sensible things" to *be* a thing is to be *perceived* as such. But I regard this dictum as an elliptical way of saying, with respect to a thought or experience, that to be such a thing is to be apprehended or thought as such.

The point of the questions in Group I is that they deal with the fundamental relationship between the concepts of truth-value, generality, and

[4] See Melvin Rader, *The Enduring Questions* (New York, 1956).

logical proof. It does not seem possible to express any relationship between two of these concepts without invoking the third at least tacitly. In logical theory, the "propositional calculus" makes no use of quantification devices and thus ostensibly makes no appeal to the concept of generality. But in fact the variables in the propositional calculus are all universally quantified, although the standard notation does not call attention to the situation. The questions in Group II introduce the concept of thought or experience. This concept does not appear to be necessarily involved in the notion of an "assertion," which could be understood in some purely formal way.

It seems to me that we can put these questions to any philosopher without thereby taking some position for or against his views. Obviously they are related to traditional issues in philosophy which have been formulated in various ways; and one may feel that the information they would provide is very limited, so that perhaps many more questions would have to be asked in any serious attempt at comparison. The problem of relating my comparison questions to traditional terminology is complicated, and I must by-pass it here. As to the limited scope of the questions, I would say that they are not really so limited as they appear, and that most of the further questions one wants to ask are apt to be quite closely related to the ones I have posed. But I must by-pass this problem also.

Now let us see what happens when we put these comparison questions to some of the "new American philosophers" whose views are discussed by Professor Reck in his recent book. I shall consider only the views of Brand Blanshard, Justus Buchler, James K. Feibleman, and F. S. C. Northrop. These particular men are interesting because of their apparently extreme individualism, and because the results of analysis of their views are somewhat surprising.

The name of Brand Blanshard is well known to the profession, even if his works are not, and in particular he is known for his "coherence theory" of truth. An excerpt on that subject from his *The Nature of Thought* has been reprinted in anthologies.[4] Blanshard is the leading contemporary representative in this country of the British Neo-Hegelian idealistic school, and especially of Bradley, Bosanquet, Joachim, and T. H. Green. On questions of logic and metaphysics, at least, he declares himself to be their disciple. In many ways, however, Blanshard is more of an analyst than a speculative philosopher, and the great bulk of his work has been devoted to analysis and criticism of modern theories in the philosophy of mind, the philosophy of language, and meta-ethics. His *Reason and Analysis* (1962) is the most penetrating and comprehensive study of the contemporary English analytic movement so far published.

Blanshard uses a notion of "coherence," as is well known, both for a test of truth and for a definition of it. To say that something is true, according to this definition, is to say that it is coherent with everything else that is true. The definition is obviously circular, but this is not a problem peculiar to Blanshard's theory. Frege points out in one of his essays, in connection with the attempt to define truth as correspondence, that this attempt fails because, as he puts it, "the question of truth would reiterate itself to infinity." [5] It is hard to see how any explicit definition of truth could succeed, because the notion of truth operates as a logical and philosophical primitive; and an attempt to reformulate logical theory, for example, on some other basis would require the use of rules of inference in which the notion of truth appears. Hence it is curious that Blanshard thought that some definition of truth was appropriate. I shall come back to this point presently.

Ordinarily one is inclined to read "coherence" as meaning logical consistency or possibility. If this is what Blanshard means, then he is saying that anything is true if and only if it is consistent with everything that is true. Unlike the definition, this offers no special logical difficulties. Any logician would admit that a true assertion is consistent with every true assertion. Conversely, any assertion consistent with every truth must be true (if it has truth-value at all). On this interpretation, Blanshard's "coherence" rule is surely correct. But as a "test" for truth it is clearly useless. The only need we might have for such a test is to help us decide whether or not some assertion is true, and until we know every truth we would have no way to carry out this "test." Hencc one is tempted to think that Blanshard's position really is that we do, in principle, know every truth or have the capacity to discover it on demand. And in virtue of his definition of truth in terms of "coherence" or consistency, his answers to my first comparison questions would be clear. He would say that there are logically decidable truth-values, and indeed that every truth-value is logically decidable.

But this interpretation of Blanshard will not stand up. In *The Nature of Thought* hc makes clear that "coherence" has a very special meaning for him. He applies the term "coherent" to just those systems, or sets of "judgments," in which every judgment in the system logically implies every other judgment in the system. But then it turns out, according to Blanshard himself, that there really are no systems satisfying this condition.[6] Mathematics approaches it more nearly than anything else; but even there, as in Euclid for example, it is always necessary to take certain judgments for granted

[5] Gary Iseminger, *Logic and Philosophy*, (New York, 1968), p. 7.

[6] *The Nature of Thought* (London and New York, 1939), vol. II, pp. 264-66.

as axioms, and these axioms do not logically imply each other. Hence he is led to speak of degrees of coherence and degrees of truth.

But if there are no systems actually satisfying Blanshard's standard of coherence, there are no particular judgments or assertions satisfying it either. If we have no completely coherent system, we can hardly claim to make some assertion that logically implies every assertion in such a system. Hence we have no way of knowing the truth-value of any assertion. This perhaps accounts for his attempt to offer a definition of the notion of truth itself. For he could not admit that notion as a logical primitive without also admitting laws or axioms in which it appears. For Blanshard, it seems, there are really no decidable truth-values at all, and his answers to all four of my comparison questions are negative. This result is confirmed by two salient features of his position: (1) that he refuses to recognize any but a relative notion of logical necessity (*i.e.*, necessity relative to some given set of assumptions),[7] and (2) that he refuses to admit any notion of self-evidence or any notion of incorrigible judgments (*e.g.*, sense data).[8] Thus the analysis of his position in terms of my comparison questions gives a result quite different from what his rather innocently traditional language leads one to expect. One could hardly wish for a clearer example of the dangers of reading chunks of philosophical prose – even when they are as extensive as Blanshard's chapter on "coherence" – apart from the context of the works in which they are embedded.

With Justus Buchler we enter a completely different world of discourse. Although he is best known, perhaps, as co-author (with Randall) of an introductory text in philosophy, he is one of the most original and speculative living philosophers. Buchler has almost none of Blanshard's intense interest in critical analysis. He is intent on building a comprehensive philosophical system based on a novel theory of human judgment. The system has taken shape so far in four short but difficult books: *Toward a General Theory of Human Judgment* (1951), *Nature and Judgment* (1955), *The Concept of Method* (1961), and *Metaphysics of Natural Complexes* (1966). What Buchler wants to do, I think, is to get a satisfactory philosophy of mind, without a reductive behaviorism, in the context of an essentially naturalistic viewpoint in the tradition of Peirce, Dewey, Woodbridge, and the "new realism." His *modus operandi* is like Whitehead's in that he redefines the concept of "nature" for this purpose. His style is also like Whitehead's in that he uses neologisms at crucial points and makes startling use of ordinarily humdrum words. As a result, Buchler is probably the most

[7] *Ibid.*, pp. 428 ff.

[8] Blanshard, *op. cit.*, vol. I, pp. 52 ff.

difficult and obscure writer in American philosophy today. It is possible to read page after page of his prose, recognize every word as familiar, and not have the slightest idea what he is talking about.

Everything in Buchler's terminology depends on certain key words, but these words are only vaguely defined. Here is how he defines one of his most important key words, the neologism "proception."

The interplay of the human individual's activities and dimensions, their unitary direction, constitutes a process which I shall call *proception*. The term is designed to suggest a moving union of seeking and receiving, of forward propulsion and patient absorption. Proception is the composite, directed activity of the individual. Any instance of his functioning, any event in his history enters into the proceptive direction. Reciprocally, and perhaps more significantly, the way that an individual will act at any time, and the way in which his intellectual and moral character will be modified, depends on his proceptive direction. Proception is the process in which a man's whole self is summed up or represented. On this idea that the whole individual is the cumulative representative of the moving individual I should like to lay the major stress. To say that the human animal is a proceiving animal is to state the most general or pervasive attribute of his being, and at the same time the most distinctive attribute.[9]

Clearly the obstacles to interpretation and comparison here are staggering, and for this very reason Buchler's work is a useful test of the method of analysis I am using. Buchler says very little about truth, falsehood, logic, or experience. He wants to avoid identification with historically recognizable positions, although he rather freely criticizes other philosophers for not seeing this or that (to him) obvious truth about the world. He does not like to argue, so he cannot be pinned down to any particular theory of logical proof. He is articulate, however, about his own conception of the philosopher's task, and in various places he emphasizes the aesthetic values of categorial schemes and tends to play down the discursive and descriptive values. In his first book, for example, he asserts that philosophy consists of definitions rather than of assertions, and that these "appeal to a sense of satisfaction or to approval of the combination as a structure."[10] He goes on to say that there are two phases of what he calls "philosophic perspective."

In one of these, a philosophy constructs; in the other, it comments on the construction. On the one hand, it brings together a number of categories and develops them by analogy and metaphor and definition; in the other, it examines alternatives, excludes supposed implications, and justifies the categorial con-

[9] *Toward a General Theory of Human Judgment* (New York, 1951), pp. 4-5.
[10] *Ibid.*, p. 122.
[11] *Ibid.*, pp. 122-23.

figurations in terms that do not make use of the categories.... A philosophy – and the same applies to a theory of science or a work of art – is not simply an aggregate of judgments but an order of interrelated judgments. The process of construction lays emphasis on "seeing" the meaning and "feeling" the impact of the conceptual configuration. Inevitably it is suggestive in character.[11]

It is not easy to reconcile Buchler's statements, in his four major books, on the subject of logic. In the first book, he deals with this subject in a chapter on "compulsion," as follows:

Logical compulsion – the compulsion imposed by the laws of logic – is the elemental framework within which proception and communication occur. Consistency is a condition of survival in utterance, exhibitive and active as well as assertive. While questions of consistency are not so frequently applied to the non-assertive modes of utterance, there can be nothing in any judgment that actually refutes the law of contradiction. Inconsistent signs may be physically juxtaposed and even systematically manipulated by conventional resolution, but they achieve the status of meaningful entities in the system only through consistency or order in the manipulation. The laws of logic exercise the most basic compulsion: we cannot reject them and still retain intelligibility. They are the conditions of discourse, for discourse cannot, as Aristotle showed, reject them without assuming them. We cannot conceive the circumstances under which they would be inapplicable, for they are conditions of conceivability.[12]

Later on, however, he suggests that sceptical doubts can always arise, even in pure mathematics and logic.

We can have no final proof that our rules and systems have been consistently employed. The laws of logic ... represent the maximum compulsion in all query, but the question whether we are employing them properly, or even whether at some point the very compulsion to which we are subjected may not lead us astray in some sense, can always be asked significantly.[13]

Notice how Buchler's characterization of logical "compulsion" seems to have shifted in this latter passage. Where in the first passage the laws of logic are defining conditions for conceivability, so that the very possibility of denying them significantly is ruled out, here that very possibility is entertained. There the compulsion of logic was apparently absolute; here it is only maximal, the suggestion being that no compulsion is really absolute. In his last two books, Buchler indicates a certain hostility toward what he calls "formal logic." He deplores the modern tendency to demand clarity and literalness in philosophy, and he traces these demands in part to "developments in formal logic." [14] And he writes:

[12] *Ibid.*, pp. 69-70.
[13] *Ibid.*, p. 164.
[14] *Nature and Judgment* (New York, 1955), p. 184.

> To link philosophic ideas by weaving a formal inferential apparatus around them, is not to be philosophically systematic. Selecting a word that has had something of a philosophic history – "value," for instance – then erecting a purely syntactic and deductive framework for it, accomplishes an exact elaboration of intended meanings; but it is not a philosophic "theory of value." It is a complex definition that may prove to be useful when certain categorical or ready-made formulations are sought. With or without a formal apparatus, every philosophic system is a broadly inferential structure: certain implications, after all, are present, others are not.[15]

Here it seems clear that Buchler wants to distinguish between logical relations as being "simply present," *i.e.*, as being something in themselves, and logical relations as embodied in a "formal apparatus." Most logicians would agree that logical principles are not to be identified with the way they appear in this or that formal apparatus. But in what sense is any implication simply present if it is not formally present? Ordinary language, surely, is just as much a formal apparatus as any technical language is; it can say anything a technical language can say, if one is patient enough to spell out what the technical language abbreviates. The sense in which implications are present, without being formally present, as far as I can see, is the sense in which they are present to someone's mind. When Buchler uses the word "implication," it is really, I think, *inference* that he is talking about. On that interpretation, in any case, everything he says about logic makes coherent sense. The fact that Buchler so often speaks of logical laws as "compulsions" confirms this reading. There is no basis in logical theory itself for saying that the concepts of formal proof or logical necessity involve some notion of compulsion. The rules of proof may be understood as justifying or permitting various types of inferences, but there is nothing in logic to compel anyone to make some inference he does not want to make. One thinks of logical necessity as compulsion to the extent that one psychologizes it. And the judgments one is compelled to make, in this sense, are not thereby guaranteed to be true. Buchler's long discussion of the concept of possibility, in his last book, again confirms this reading. It is clear there that he recognizes no such thing as absolute possibility or consistency but only possibility or consistency relative to some "order of natural complexes" (*i.e.*, some given system of relations or set of postulates). The more traditional concept of possibility as an eternal rather than a temporal order he explicitly rejects.[16]

To come back to my comparison questions: It seems to me that Buchler must deny that there are any logically decidable truth-values. For him,

[15] *The Concept of Method* (New York, 1961), pp. 123-24.

[16] *Metaphysics of Natural Complexes* (New York, 1966), p. 142.

logical decisions are ultimately relative and provisional expressions of underlying "natural" compulsions. As to the other questions, whether there are any intuitively decidable truth-values, his answer is also negative. There is little doubt about his position at this point, in view of his lengthy attack on the distinction of the "mediate" from the "immediate" in experience and his rejection of incorrigible judgments.[17] But I must omit the details of these views here.

What my analysis suggests, then, is that in certain fundamental ways the philosophy of the "naturalistic" Buchler and of the Neo-Hegelian idealist Blanshard are alike even though their styles and vocabularies are far apart. With two fairly striking exceptions, a study of the other "new American philosophers" to whom Reck refers would show (I believe) that they too share the essentials of this outlook. The exceptions I have in mind are James K. Feibleman and F. S. C. Northrop.

Feibleman, who is Chairman of the Department of Philosophy at Tulane, is probably the most prolific author of all time among American philosophers. His formal education ended halfway through freshman year at the University of Virginia, and as a philosopher he is almost completely self-taught. He is also an accomplished poet and novelist. His first serious efforts in philosophy arose from problems in his early career as a businessman. Specifically, it was the financial crisis of 1929 that started Feibleman and a fellow businessman, Julius Friend, on a joint quest for diagnosis and cure, and hence ultimately philosophy. As Feibleman tells it in his autobiography, they started by reading the literature on the theory of business enterprise, discovered that many of the problems associated with business came from the technology of power tools and automation, realized that this technology was simply a natural outcome of developments in physical science, and traced the ideas of physical science back from Einstein through Newton to the ancient Greeks. "Then suddenly," he writes,

> as if a veil had been lifted from our ignorance, we felt clear about our vision. We studied philosophy swiftly, feverishly, eagerly. We studied modern philosophy first, as was our custom, beginning with Whitehead, and reading backward through the German dogmatists, the English empiricists, the medieval theologians, and the neo-Platonists, until we came to Plato and Aristotle.... Thus from our start in the most practical kind of problem conceivable, that of how to remedy the shortcomings of the conduct of business in the United States in 1929, we finally emerged into the abstract and eternal air of Greek philosophy.[18]

[17] In *Toward a General Theory of Human Judgment*, pp. 25, 85-88.

[18] *Philosophers Lead Sheltered Lives* (London, 1952), p. 142.

The upshot of these labors was that Feibleman and Friend wrote a book, *Science and the Spirit of Man*

In it we showed the subjectivity of physics and the physical elements, and the objectivity of the aesthetic, the moral and other normative elements. We went into the writing of that book humanists and emerged from it realists, in the medieval and Platonic sense of the latter term.[19]

Although Feibleman no longer subscribes fully to the position of this early work, it does announce what turns out to be the main theme in his philosophy: "the independent and underived rediscovery of the independence of values."

Feibleman's system has been described (by Reck) as an axiological realism.[20] It is an attempt to define a richly metaphysical (or, as Feibleman would say, ontological) philosophy which will meet all of the strictures and antimetaphysical critiques of the modern analytical schools. Feibleman thinks that the analysts have been right in criticizing the obscurantism, occultism and linguistic sloppiness of much traditional philosophy, and he locates the prime source of traditional problems in what he calls the Platonic "crypto-materialist reification of essence." [21] Hence, in order to avoid this, he constructs what amounts to a nominalistic theory of classes (universals). That is, classes are sets of finitely many individuals based on observed similarities; thus they are abstractions, for him, not part of the world's furniture. But values are real. Nevertheless, values and universals are not ultimately distinct, but are just the same things considered from different standpoints.[22] What makes Feibleman's ontology tick is his assumption that the realm of being is divided into actualities (or existences) and possibilities (or essences). Universals are possibilities; they are beings, but they do not necessarily exist. Values are universals in so far as universals are, as Feibleman says, "powerful" (*i.e.*, actually exemplified). In other words, a value is a class considered as a set of actually similar individuals; a universal is a class considered as a potentially infinite extension of such a set. In all this there are echoes, on the one hand, of Whitehead's theory of subsistent beings. So it is no surprise that Feibleman takes Russell to task for having unnecessarily abandoned realistic metaphysics.[23] But Feibleman's brand of realism, at any rate, does not seem to commit him to universals or essences except as pure possibilities. Hence logic, the exploration of the realm of

[19] *Ibid.*, p. 143.
[20] Reck, *op. cit.*, ch. 7.
[21] In *Ontology* (Baltimore, 1951), pp. 279, 600.
[22] *Ibid.*, pp. 232 ff.
[23] In *Inside the Great Mirror* (The Hague, 1958), pp. 114 ff.

essences, is only an exploration of possibilities. This perhaps accounts for his view that logic has ontological presuppositions: that is, to take the laws of logic as actually true is to assume that some pure possibility is actualized, and this is to assume something more than what logic itself can provide.

To the question whether there are any logically decidable truth-values, then, Feibleman must answer "No." But to the other question, whether there are any intuitively decidable truth-values, he would have to answer "Yes." For his whole strategy is based on meeting positivistic objections by conforming to a principle of parsimony (Ockham's Razor), and hence ultimately on the acceptance of certain data as that with respect to which parsimony is defined. But by recognizing a realm of pure essences, or possibilities, he avoids saying that every truth-value is intuitively decidable.

If Feibleman is an extreme example of the self-taught philosopher, F. S. C. Northrop is at the opposite extreme. Northrop took to formal education and its milieu like a duck to water. Beginning with an interest in religion that took him through divinity school and a brief career as a missionary in China, he was forced to return for reasons of health and launched himself into philosophy with two M.A. degrees and a Ph.D. from Harvard. His dissertation was an interdisciplinary study of the philosophical foundations of biology which later became his first book, *Science and First Principles* (1931). Northrop's tastes are catholic and his curiosity insatiable. He studied with such diverse leading philosophers of the pre-war period as Hocking, Sheffer, McTaggart and Whitehead. He worked in higher mathematics under G. H. Hardy at Cambridge and at Weyl's Mathematical Institute at Göttingen. He met Albert Einstein in 1927 and was strongly influenced thereafter by Einstein's views on the philosophy of science.[24] His residence and travels in the Orient bore fruit in his best-known book, *The Meeting of East and West* (1946), an astounding synthesis of Eastern and Western philosophy which attracted world-wide attention. In his later works, Northrop has concentrated on problems of jurisprudence, diplomacy, and intercultural relations.

The best introduction to Northrop's thought, and the most comprehensive statement of his whole philosophy, is his *The Logic of the Sciences and the Humanities* (1947). Everything in that book depends on a basic epistemological dualism of "concepts by intuition" and "concepts by postulation." A "concept," as he uses that term, is any word, symbol, or expression that carries meaning; it is not itself an idea or a meaning. Thus he defines a concept by intuition as one "the complete meaning of which is given by

[24] See his *Man, Nature and God* (New York, 1962), Introduction.

something which can be immediately apprehended." [25] "A concept by postulation is one the meaning of which in whole or part is designated by the postulates of some specific deductively formulated theory in which it occurs." [26] Naturally it often happens that the same word or expression may function ambiguously as a concept by intuition or as a concept by postulation. For example, the adjective "blue" is a concept by intuition when it refers to a certain kind of observed visual quality, but it may also be a concept by postulation when it signifies a certain range of frequencies of electromagnetic radiation, or when it characterizes certain pigments or surfaces which reflect radiation of that frequency range. The noun "electron," on the other hand, has no meaning as a concept by intuition but is a concept by postulation implicitly defined by the postulates of the Lorentz version of electromagnetic field theory; it also occurs in a different theoretical context, and hence with a different meaning, in the theory of quantum mechanics. Thus Northrop's distinction of "concepts" is a functional one, a distinction of uses, not a division of expressions into mutually exclusive classes.

Northrop's views on logic are somewhat obscured by his terminology in this book, and as a result of certain misunderstandings he has changed that terminology in at least one striking way in his most recent work. He now prefers to speak of "relationally analytic concepts" rather than of "concepts by postulation." [27] The choice of the earlier phrase was unfortunate in two ways: (1) It suggested that certain concepts (or rather meanings) are created, brought into being *ex nihilo* as it were, by the mere act of postulating or laying down arbitrary sets of general assumptions. (2) It seemed to encourage the inference that any and every set of postulates define concepts in that they define a purely logical relatedness in which these concepts play a certain role. But that such a relatedness is possible or intelligible at all is a formal logical question. In "defining" it, the postulates do not create it but only point it out as one of the many possible forms of relatedness given by logical and mathematical theory.

Northrop's realism goes much further than Feibleman's. For him, logical possibility and necessity are absolute, not merely relative to some choice of axioms. While Feibleman recognizes only universals of a sort that Northrop calls "concepts by abstraction," Northrop also insists that there are purely logical universals, "concepts by intellection," which are entirely imageless but which designate real objects of knowledge. In this connection, he quotes

[25] *The Logic of the Sciences and the Humanities* (New York, 1947), p. 36.
[26] *Ibid.*, p. 62.
[27] Northrop and Helen H. Livingston, eds., *Cross-cultural Understanding* (New

with approval [28] some sentences from G. H. Hardy's *A Mathematician's Apology*. Hardy writes:

(T)here is probably less difference between the positions of a mathematician and a physicist than is generally supposed, and ... the most important seems to me to be this, that the mathematician is in much more direct contact with reality. This may seem to be a paradox, since it is the physicist who deals with subject-matter usually described as "real"; but ... neither physicists nor philosophers have ever given any convincing account of what "physical reality" is, or of how the physicist passes, from the confused mass of fact or sensation with which he starts, to the construction of the objects which he calls "real" ... It is plain that he is trying to correlate the incoherent body of crude fact confronting him with some definite and orderly scheme of abstract relations, the kind of scheme which he can borrow only from mathematics.

A mathematician, on the other hand, is working with his own mathematical reality. Of this reality ... I take a "realistic" and not an "idealistic" view.... It may be that modern physics fits best into some framework of idealistic philosophy –, I do not believe it, but there are eminent physicists who say so. Pure mathematics, on the other hand, seems to me a rock on which all idealism founders: 317 is a prime, not because we think so, or because our minds are shaped in one way rather than another, but *because it is so,* because mathematical reality is built that way.[29]

Northrop leaves no doubt that he agrees wholly with this position, as many passages in his later books testify. So it is clear how he would answer my comparison questions. For him there are truth-values decidable by logical proof; and there are truth-values, namely of propositions containing concepts by intuition, that are intuitively decidable. But there is also a third class of truth-values, those belonging to the freely chosen postulates of deductively formulated theories, which are hypothetical in character and hence nondecidable. Northrop stands almost alone in American philosophy today as a champion of logical truth and of a realistic theory of universals. In this respect he is, like his former pupil the logician Frederic B. Fitch, an unashamed and unreconstructed Platonist. And this is so in spite of his very pragmatic and empirical emphasis on natural and social science, and his interest in concrete human problems.

To come back to my initial theme in this paper: It seems to me that there still is such a thing as the spirit of American philosophy. The writers I have discussed are just as much activists, pragmatists, and optimists as (according to John Smith) their predecessors were in the American "golden age." But these qualities are surely not the exclusive property of American

York, 1964), *passim.*

[28] *Man, Nature and God,* pp. 222-24.

[29] *A Mathematician's Apology* (Cambridge, 1967), pp. 128-30.

philosophers; one can see them in various forms at every stage in the development of Western thought. If Americans seem to show them more than others do, perhaps it is only because America herself is a sort of incarnation of Western activism, pragmatism, and optimism; not something radically new on the face of the earth, but a natural outgrowth of an important part of the European tradition.

To come back to my initial theme in this paper: it seems to me that there possible a more precise and objective assessment of the character of that tradition and of its continuing influence. It is important for us today to understand, I think, that the concepts and problems of philosophy do not completely change or disappear with changes of time, place, and circumstance; that certain concepts are present in any philosophy regardless of its specific character; and that in terms of these concepts we have an objective means of comparison.

ŚANKARA'S EPISTEMOLOGY: A NEW DIRECTION FOR THE WEST?

by

CORNELIA D. CHURCH

Genuine rapprochement between Indian and Western thought today is yet in its infancy. In the study of philosophy both sides have often manifested a sense of superiority toward each other that is probably inspired by a certain defensive ignorance. Are these two styles of thought in fact compatible in any way? A brief study of the thought of one Indian philosopher of unquestioned genius – Śankara, the 9th century systematizer of the *darśana*[1] called Vedānta[2] – can exemplify the fact that the main concerns of at least one branch of Indian philosophy have not been radically different from those of Western philosophy since Descartes. They differ in point of departure, and in where each assigns highest value, in what appears, however, to be essentially the same analysis of the nature of Being. In short, a clear structural compatibility can be found between Vedānta and Western philosophy of the past 400 years that may provide a new starting point for greater mutual respect, understanding, and exchange of ideas between them.

Both Eastern and Western traditions of thought have defined Being, or the subject of philosophical inquiry, in roughly the same way. Being, which is a unity, is understood and discussed in four major dimensions: God (or the Absolute), world, man, and mind. These are the four main categories of Śankara's investigations, and they are also the four main dimensions into which Western philosophical inquiry has traditionally been divided: Metaphysics, focusing on God, or the Absolute understood as a reality unper-

[1] *Darśana* means literally "seeing; perception, observation." It commonly refers to any of six major Indian philosophical systems, all of which are usually understood to be different views, or *darśanas*, of the same single reality.

[2] Vedānta means literally "the end of the Veda," the Veda being the oldest and most sacred Indian literature. This system of philosophy claims to be the final and truest interpretation of these ancient liturgical and inspirational texts. Śankara's viewpoint is commonly called *advaita*, or "non-dual," because he sees no essential duality between God and the world, and is opposed to the dualist point of view or *dvaita* which does. For an excellent and concise presentation of the structure of Advaita Vedanta, see Eliot Deutsch, *Advaita Vedānta: A Philosophical Reconstruction* (Honolulu, 1969).

ceived by the senses; Ontology, focusing on the essential reality of the natural world; Ethics, focusing on man's nature and the appropriate actions he should take in life; and Epistemology, focusing on the activity of the mind, how it is able to know, what knowing means. In the West, the philosopher's search for truth has most often started from the point of view of the seeker himself, on the assumption that the only certainty for the thinker is determined by the activity of the human mind. For Śankara, the strongest premise of human thought is the reality of God (understood personally), or the Absolute (understood impersonally). Thus whereas the circularity of Western thought has characteristically led from man, or mind to world, to God and back to man again, Śankara's process of thought characteristically begins with the Absolute as the condition of all things, moving therefrom to man, world, and mind as functions or modes of that Absolute, and finally resolving them into the Absolute again.

Where the final aim of thought in the West is self-realization via truth, or realization of truth via the self, in Śankara's thought it is self-annihilation via truth, a shifting of dimensions from the apparent reality of the self to the final reality of the Absolute. The differences between these two philosophical thought styles result largely from their differing points of departure within the similar fourfold structure of Being discerned by each (Figure 1).

In addition, whereas epistemology is one of several separate approaches to the study of Being in Western philosophy, knowledge or knowing is the key to Śankara's entire system of thought, wherein man and world exist at

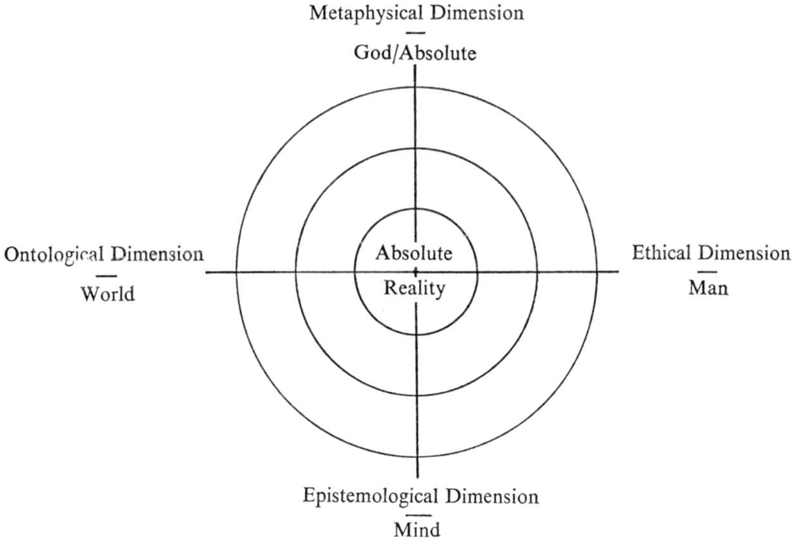

all only on account of a cognitive error, and wherein full realization of truth, an epistemological event, transforms the knower into the Absolute.

The review of Śankara's major ideas which follows will show clearly not only the fourfold structure he assigns to Being and its similarity to the outline of Western philosophical inquiry, but will reveal a remarkably clear and systematic account of what is commonly called "mysticism." Śankara holds the way open for every man to know truth, insisting not only on man's power to know, but on his obligation to do so. When the Absolute and truth are understood to be identical as they are by Śankara, and when man is understood to have the power to know this Absolute completely, with a kind of knowledge that includes all other kinds of knowledge, the search for God and truth become one and the same quest. To grasp one means to grasp the other. It is a new and exciting prospect for Western philosophy to consider seriously the implications presented by Śankara for the proposition that to know is to become.

PART I: ŚANKARA'S FOUR PREMISSES

Historical Introduction

The Philosopher Śankara lived in southwestern India probably from 788 to 820 C.E.[3] As an interpreter of the Brahma Sūtras of Bādarāyaṇa (*ca.* 2nd century C.E.), which themselves form a commentary on the Upaniṣads,[4] Śankara is part of the religio-philosophical tradition of Vedānta, one of its most prominent spokesmen. Śankara in fact systematized the thought of the Upaniṣads, whose aim was to instruct men in the proper path to personal salvation from the eternal round of rebirth. Their central teaching according to Śankara was "know that you are that (*tat tvam asi*);" that you, the seeker after truth, *are* truth; that you, the seeker after God, *are* God. The cryptic commentary on this literature by Bādarāyaṇa called the Brahma Sūtras is the actual subject of Śankara's own commentary. A *sūtra* (literally, "thread") is a shorthand sentence, or sentence fragment, unintelligible in itself, a

[3] M. Monier-Williams, *A Sanskrit-English Dictionary* (Oxford, 1964), p. 1055. See also S. N. Dasgupta, *A History of Indian Philosophy* (Cambridge, 1963), vol. I, p. 418.

[4] Upaniṣads are treatises on the meaning and purpose of life composed in northern India in the first millennium B.C.E. by unknown sages in poetical, metaphorical, and devotional language.

[5] Several examples of Bādarāyaṇa's Sūtras will make this point clear:

I.1.1 Then therefore the enquiry into Brahman.

I.1.2 From which the origin etc. of this.

I.1.4. But that because it is connected as their purport.

See *Sacred Books of the East*, ed. M. Müller, vol. XXXIV: *Vedānta Sūtras*, trans., G. Thibaut (Oxford, 1904), pp. 9 ff.

teaching device requiring the elaboration of a teacher to become fully meaningful.[5] Śankara provides this elaboration, claiming no originality for himself, but claiming only to show that there was a coherent and systematic philosophy in the Upaniṣads, as taught by Bādarāyaṇa. But it is clearly due to the genius of Śankara's systematization that the Vedānta has continued to be a living force in Indian thought for a thousand years and is now one of India's chief exports to the West. In the Indian philosophical tradition, every new thought was referred to the authority of Vedic literature (*śruti*), a varied collection composed between *ca.* 3000 and 500 B.C.E., for substantiation.[6] But it is also clear that this was a device of legitimation that did not materially hamper original thinking because vastly different views trace their origin to the same sacred texts.

Method

Śankara's method of argument reflects this strong Indian dependence on tradition. The three principal *pramāṇas*, or means of true knowledge, that he respects are testimony (*śabda*), perception (*pratyakṣa*), and the equivalence of that which is called reason in the West, inference (*anumāna*).[7] Testimony is the prime authority in Indian thought, both religious and philosophic. It means that the experiences of the Vedic sages as to life's meaning and purpose are of most importance in man's search for truth. Testimony in this sense means certain specific *śruti* literature supposedly embodying these experiences. For Śankara, one specific experience stands in highest place: the intuition of the true nature of the Absolute, or Brahman as it is called in Indian texts. Thus, for Śankara, testimony implies the validity of intuition. And his philosophy is an attempt to draw out and systematize the implications of those original intuitions whose witness is found in the Upaniṣads.

Perception for Śankara is the valid means of knowledge of external objects. It is valuable for knowledge of the world, irrelevant for the knowledge of Brahman. Finally, Śankara also felt that what was true could never contradict human experience, and thus could be demonstrated by reason as well as by reference to the authority of scripture. In fact, reason, which includes inference is in some ways superior in value to testimony as a means of knowledge.

[6] *Śruti* means literally "hearing," and signifies literature that records what was heard or directly known to be true by early sages of India, as opposed to *smṛti*, or what was remembered, secondhand knowledge learned from the teachings of others. *Śruti* is usually understood to include literature entitled Veda, Brāhmaṇa, Āranyaka, and Upaniṣad.

[7] A more complete listing of *pramāṇas* considered valid by different branches of Indian philosophy includes the following six: perception (*pratyakṣa*), inference (*anumāna*), analogy (*upamana*), testimony (*śabda*), nonperception (*anupalabdhi*), and inference from circumstances (*arthāpatti*). See Monier-Williams, *op. cit.*, p. 685.

Reasoning, which enables us to infer something not actually perceived in consequence of its having a certain equality of attributes with what is actually perceived, stands nearer in perception than *śruti* which conveys its sense by tradition merely.[8]

Thus Śankara's method is twofold in aim: to prove his assumptions by reference to Upaniṣads and Bādarāyaṇa's Sūtras, and to demonstrate their mutual implications by a process of reasoning. He seems to have felt that "so long as the reasoning faculty of man is not fully satisfied and things are not explained by reasoning in the light of common experience, there is no possibility of man's acceptance of the intuitions of others, however high."[9] A final aim and method was to refute the contrary positions of numerous other contemporary schools of thought. To this end, both testimony and reason were used.

Premisses

The premisses of Śankara's thought are derived from intuitionally given texts. They include statements about the Absolute, called Brahman, the world, man, and mind. As noted above, the major concerns of Śankara's thought form a rough parallel with those of Western philosophy:

Śankara's Categories	*Categories of Western Philosophy*
Brahman/Absolute	Metaphysics
World	Ontology
Man	Ethics
Mind	Epistemology

In Śankara's system, there appears an identity among these four aspects of Being rarely articulated in the history of Western thought. A summary of the four major premisses of Śankara's thought and the implications of their interrelations follows.

Premiss I: Brahman is the only ultimate real

Brahman is described as "that omniscient, omnipotent Brahman, whose essence is eternal pure cognition and freedom, and which is ... the creative principle of the world."[10] Brahman is both source and multiform content of the cosmos:

the cause from which [proceeds] the origin or subsistence and dissolution of this world which is extended in names and forms (*nāmarūpa*), which includes many

[8] Vedānta Sūtra II.1.4, *Sacred Books of the East*, vol. XXXIV, p. 299.

[9] S. Chatterjee and D. Datta, *An Introduction to Indian Philosophy* (Calcutta, 1968), p. 375.

[10] Vedānta Sūtra II.1.22, *op. cit.*, vol. XXXIV, p. 344. See also I.1.4, p. 45.

agents and enjoyers, which contains the fruit of works specially determined according to space, time and cause ....[11]

Brahman is the ultimately real seen under two aspects: both devoid of all qualities and full of attributes. "Qualities in which lower and higher degrees can be distinguished belong to the qualified Brahman only, in which plurality is admitted, not to the highest Brahman raised above all qualifications."[12]

As the essence, or Self of all things, Brahman is described as *sat*, or being, *cit*, or intelligence, and *ānanda*, or bliss.[13] The nature of Brahman is consciousness, not materiality. Yet the intelligent Brahman is the cause and substance of this world: "... Brahman is acknowledged as the cause of the world, all attributes required in the cause are seen to be present, Brahman being all-knowing, all-powerful."[14] In sum, all that is real in the world is Brahman; there is nothing in world, self, or mind that is not Brahman. Brahman is not, however, exhausted in material forms, yet he is eternally present in them.

Premiss II: The world is illusion

The world springs from Brahman as do tricks from a magician, or dreams from a dreamer; the former are produced by the latter in each case without altering the producer in any way. They are equally illusory.[15] The world is caused by Brahman both materially and efficiently: "the world springs from Brahman by way of modification."[16] Given Brahman as the source and essence of all things, even though nonmaterial, Brahman is still however "the operative cause, because there is no other substance from which the world could originate."[17] Brahman is both potency and material, yet pure consciousness, unextended. Brahman's relation to the world is exclusively one of immanence; Brahman is eternal subject, never object. In the Kena Upaniṣad, one of Śankara's sources, Brahman is described as "that which is the hearing of the ear, the thought of the mind, the voice of speech, as also the breathing of the breath and the sight of the eye."[18]

In short, Śankara asserts the identity of cause and effect in Brahman (*satkāryavāda*); the world and its source are essentially identical. The apparent world of change is, therefore, unreal, illusory (*vivartavāda*). The

[11] Vedānta Sūtra I.1.2, *ibid.*, p. 15.

[12] Vedānta Sūtra III.3.13, in *Sacred Books of the East*, ed. M. Müller, vol. XXXVIII: *Vedānta Sūtras*, trans., G. Thibaut (Oxford, 1904), p. 203.

[13] S. N. Dasgupta, *op. cit.*, vol. I, p. 438.

[14] Vedānta Sūtra II.1.33, *op. cit.*, vol. XXXIV, p. 360.

[15] Vedānta Sūtra II.1.7, *op. cit.*, vol. XXXIV, p. 302.

[16] Vedānta Sūtra II.1.14, *ibid.*, p. 322.

[17] Vedānta Sūtra I.4.23, *ibid.*, p. 285.

[18] Kena Upaniṣad I.2, in *The Thirteen Principal Upaniṣads*, trans. R. E. Hume (Lonon, 1965), p. 335.

originative model for the world's existence is *vivarta*, or manifestation. The world is related to Brahman as wave to ocean, or sound to drum; essentially the same, apparently other. As Śankara explains it,

> The omniscient Lord of all is the cause of the origin of the world in the same way as clay is the material cause of jars and gold of golden ornaments, that by his rulership he is the cause of the subsistence of the magical illusion; and that he, lastly, is the cause of this emitted world being finally reabsorbed into his essence.[19]

The world has neither necessary nor real existence.

Premiss III: Brahman is the Self of man

"... The Lord is the Self of all of us."[20] Man's self or soul is at its center the eternal changeless Brahman. There is no real personal individuality. The apparently individual Self is "known to exist on account of its immediate (intuitive) presentation ...."[21] But man's chief error is to assume that his limited Self is other than Brahman.

> The soul is of eternal intelligence. ... [It is] not a product, but the unmodified highest Brahman, which, owing to the contact with its limiting adjuncts [the apparently real body], appears as individual soul.[22]
>
> ... And that individual soul is to be considered a mere appearance of the highest Self; like the reflection of the Sun in the water, it is neither directly that, nor a different thing. ... As that "appearance" is the effect of Nescience (ignorance) it follows that the *saṃsāra* [world of names and forms] which is based on it is also the effect of Nescience, so that from the removal of the latter there results the cognition of the soul being in reality nothing but Brahman.[23]

As the world is a function, or illusion of Brahman, so is the Self. Man shares with Brahman his full unlimited nature, consisting of both existence and intelligence, or consciousness. Man is Brahman; "he, verily, who knows that supreme Brahma, becomes very Brahma,"[24] or rather perceives the truth that has always been there. His apparent individuality has neither real nor necessary existence.

Premiss IV: The world and the Self exist by virtue of a cognitive error

Śankara finds the existence of the phenomenal world to be due to a perceptual error on the part of perceiving beings. In his discussion of the Self of

[19] Vedānta Sūtra II.1.1, *op. cit.*, vol. XXXIV, p. 290.

[20] *Idem.*

[21] *Sacred Books of the East*, vol. XXXIV, p. 5.

[22] Vedānta Sūtra II.3.15, *op. cit.*, vol. XXXVIII, p. 34.

[23] Vedānta Sūtra II.3.50, *ibid.*, p. 68.

[24] Muṇḍaka Upaniṣad III.2.9, in *The Thirteen Principal Upaniṣads*, p. 377. For Śankara's discussion of this passage see Vedānta Sūtra I.1.4, vol. XXXIV, p. 34.

man, he comes to grips with the problem and provides a solution. He says that "there is a Self ... which rules the body and the senses and is connected with the fruits of actions."[25] It is "of eternal intelligence; for that very reason that it is not a product, but nothing else but the unmodified highest Brahman which ... appears as individual soul."[26] An objection could be raised that if Brahman and the Self of man are one and the same, and that if "Brahman is of the nature of intelligence and therefore not different from the individual Soul, it follows, that Brahman also has the same fruition of pleasure, pain and so on."[27] Or in other words, that Brahman is changeable and limited as man is. Not so, says Śankara, because "fruition [good and evil and their consequences] on the part of the individual soul has wrong knowledge for its cause, and Brahman as it truly exists is not touched thereby."[28] The cause of the world's appearance and man's sense of individual Self is simply wrong knowledge, a perceptual error.

> There is a difference between false knowledge and perfect knowledge, fruition being the figment of false knowledge while the unity [of the Self and Brahman] is revealed by perfect knowledge.[29]

Man's Self *is* Brahman, and one need only realize this truth to have perfect knowledge. Fully knowing Brahman is thus the same as fully becoming Brahman; only the language of ordinary grammar is unequal to the task of expressing this simply. By this perfect knowledge one knows one's true Self and the nature of all things at once. There is no Self apart from Brahman; hence, the idea of "the entire phenomenal world ... having an independent existence is likewise to be set aside. ... For him who has reached the state of truth and reality, the whole apparent world does not exist."[30] All distinctions between things are illusion, all objects false including the embodied, individual Self.

The connective link between Brahman and world and world and man is a mental function depending on consciousness only. Śankara uses two common Indian metaphors to demonstrate this point: 1) As a man supposes a coiled rope in the dark to be a snake, thereby experiencing fear and running away, so does man suppose the world to have real existence and acts accordingly; his error and his actions consequent on that error do not make it true; 2) A dreamer creates an entire world of forms and relationships, yet

[25] Vedānta Sūtra II.3.17, *op. cit.*, vol. XXXVIII, p. 29.
[26] Vedānta Sūtra II.3.18, *ibid.*, p. 29.
[27] Vedānta Sūtra I.2.8, *op. cit.*, vol. XXXIV, p. 115.
[28] Vedānta Sūtra I.2.8, *op. cit.*, vol. XXXIV, p. 116.
[29] *Idem.*
[30] Vedānta Sūtra II.1.14, *ibid.*, p. 322.

they have no substantial reality, or permanent effect, and can in an instant be eclipsed.

By the doctrine of illusion (*māyā*), or mental error, Śankara avoids compromising Brahman's changeless unity. The world whose nature is a function of ignorance (*avidyā*) likewise has its continued, if relative and illusory, existence. Śankara declares: "the changeless Brahman cannot be the substratum of varying attributes. [However] for as long as a person has not reached the true knowledge of the unity of the Self [and Brahman] ... there is no reason why the ordinary course of secular and religious activity should not hold on undisturbed."[31] All distinctions are relatively valid from the point of view of the ignorant world, invalid from the standpoint of perfect knowledge. The epistemological issue in Śankara's thought is not the knowability of the relative world, but the complete relativity of the knowable world, which is not what is enduring, changeable and ultimately real. And this reality, or Brahman, is knowable in a different sense entirely.

From Śankara's first premiss that all is Brahman, his other three premisses follow by reason; if Brahman is all, then Brahman is world, man, and mind. Since it contradicts ordinary reason to assert that there is no real difference between these four, Śankara holds that by definition, the really real is that which is permanent and does not change. Thus Brahman is that aspect or way in which world, man, and mind are unchanging. And so all apparent differences are entirely false. How can the changeless Brahman be manifest in the world and man as modifications? Because, says Śankara, both world and man are illusions, like dreams. Their difference from Brahman is totally eclipsed by that perfect knowledge that renders knowledge itself unnecessary.

Śankara's problem, then, is to account for the arising of apparent existence due to illusion (*māyā*) in the first place, and of the ignorance (*avidyā*) that causes this illusion. Why is there any kind of differentiation from Brahman at all? Śankara merely states the fact, that as soon as "the consciousness of difference arises in one, so does the whole phenomenon of plurality."[32] It is as if Brahman dreams the world. As explanation of this event, Śankara offers play (*līlā*): "the activity of the Lord [in creating the world] may be supposed to be mere sport, proceeding from his own nature, without reference to any purpose."[33] Thus there is no necessary reason for the existence of world, man, and mind, nor any reason for their nonexistence. Śankara has outlined the fourfold structure of an only apparent reality; a four-level dream in

[31] Vedānta Sūtra II.1.14, *ibid.*, p. 324.
[32] Vedānta Sūtra II.1.22, *ibid.*, p. 345.
[33] Vedanta Sūtra II.1.33, *ibid.*, p. 357.

which only the dreamer is real. The world is a fruit of totally nonpurposive activity, whose existence, in the greater sense of what is real, makes no difference at all.

If the four major poles of Being are for Śankara as they are for Western philosophy: God, world, man, and mind, then the core question of all human inquiry into truth remains unresolved for Śankara as it does in Western thought: Why is there anything at all? And why does Being appear fourfold to man if it is not in fact quadrangular, but unity? Where the West offers God's nature, or necessity, as answer, Śankara suggests play. As long as man needs to feel important, none of these are satisfying answers.

Conclusion

In Śankara's thought there is fundamentally no difference between Brahman, world, Self, and mind. They share real existence which is composed of consciousness. The ordinary world of *saṃsāra*, or *nāmarūpa*, is an illusion like a dream or magic trick, having no permanently real nature, no ontological status independent of Brahman. So for man the issue of knowledge is a critical one; to know the truth is to become the Absolute, or rather to realize that one has always been God. Yet what kind of knowledge is this liberating and transforming knowledge? It is clearly not the same as ordinary knowledge. A summary of Śankara's three-dimensional analysis of the four poles of Being, ending with his epistemological views will provide an answer to this question.

PART II: DIMENSIONAL PARALLELS

Each of Śankara's four categories can be understood on three levels: 1) the Absolute, 2) the Relative, and 3) the Erroneous. Each level is immanent in the subsequent ones. As depicted visually in Figure 1, the three levels are to be understood as three dimensions of a single reality, made up of four aspects, whose essence is unity.

Brahman – Metaphysical Aspect

First, Brahman itself is understood in two ways by Śankara: Absolute, without qualities (*nirguṇa*), the Self of all things, the knower of all knowledge, eternal subject. Brahman is also understood relatively as Lord (*īśvara*), full of qualities (*saguṇa*). As such he is omniscient, omnipotent, creator, sustainer, and destroyer of all phenomenal forms.[34]

[34] Vedānta Sūtra III.3.39, *op. cit.*, vol. XXXVIII, p. 248.

The Lord's being a Lord, his omniscience, his omnipotence, etc., all depend on the limitation due to the adjuncts whose Self is Nescience; while in reality none of these qualities belong to the Self, whose true nature is cleared, by right knowledge, from all adjuncts whatever.[35]

In the third dimension, that of error, Brahman is not perceived to exist at all. The material world is understood to be the ultimate real, and the Self of man to be the body with its intelligence or consciousness, which is only a function of the material body.[36]

Man – Ethical Aspect

Again there are three levels of ethical behavior open to man. On the highest level, man is aware that the object of life is to realize or know Brahman, to know that the Self is the Absolute, or *nirguṇa* Brahman. This knowledge is a fruit of meditation, following on the testimony of the Vedas (*śruti*), not the result of action, effort, nor simply reason alone. "If the object of the knowledge of Brahman were something to be accomplished there would be no reference to intuition."[37] Brahman is subject, never object; man comes to realize that there are no objects and that he himself is the subject of all things. The highest ethics in life, therefore, require man to undergo a disciplined effort to deepen his powers of intuition, not to perfect and refine perception and reason; but rather to shut off both external sensations and reasoning processes in order better to perceive the inner source of true ideas, Brahman itself. In this view, man is essentially nonmaterial. A contemplative life is hereby implied, one that will enrich mental powers at the expense of active involvement in the human condition, or indeed any action at all.

Śankara admits also of a second kind of ethics, comprised, according to his cultural milieu, of household and family duties of certain kinds, and religious rituals enjoined in the sacred texts (*śruti*), largely centered on the worship of *saguṇa* Brahman, the Lord of attributes. For most men, this kind of life, whose central assumption is that the Lord is creator, sustainer, and destroyer of all, is most appropriate; their response is one of worship and appreciation. This kind of ritual-centered ethics, where the good is defined by the injunctions of the sacred texts of the past, is for the man who does not realize the true nature of God. Śankara states clearly that there are two kinds of holy texts, those recommending action and those teaching the essence of Brahman; each requires of man a different response. Actions lead to merit, and a heavenly reward after death. Knowledge of Brahman brings a transfor-

[35] Vedānta Sūtra II.1.14, *op. cit.*, vol. XXXIV, p. 329.
[36] Vedānta Sūtra I.1.1, *ibid.*, p. 14.
[37] Vedānta Sūtra I.1.2, *ibid.*, p. 18.

mation within life, and a release from rebirth altogether. Rewards of a relative kind accrue to the relatively virtuous path of worshipping *saguṇa* Brahman; total and eternal freedom is the fruit of the cognition of *nirguṇa* Brahman. The latter virtue is purely mental, not depending directly on deeds, actions, or achievements; it is realized, not accomplished. Good deeds are appropriate only to the second dimension of life, wherein the qualified Brahman is worshipped in form.[38]

Finally, a third kind of ethics is supposed for the man who is ignorant of Brahman altogether, who holds there to be no reason for action beyond the determinations of his own wholly individual mind. This self-sufficient attitude toward life, and its implications for action are not of interest to Śankara, who does not discuss appropriate ethical consequences to it.

World and Mind – Ontological and Epistemological Aspects

As in Śankara's metaphysics and ethics there were found three dimensions, so too are there three dimensions in his ontology and epistemology. The three orders of reality according to Śankara are

1) the Real, or *pāramārthika*: the Absolute, unchanging and eternal;
2) the Relative, or *vyavahārika*: the ordinary world of human experience;
3) the Illusory, or *prātibhāsika*: the dimension of common error, or mis-perception.[39]

These three aspects of the real are related to one another dimensionally; and that which is responsible both for their separation and for their ultimate unification is simply knowledge, or the ignorance-knowledge polarity. In Śankara's thought there is no fundamental separation or difference between being and knowing. In Brahman, he declares, "existence is thought and thought existence; ... the two do not exclude each other."[40] And this is true, also, of both man and world. Their apparent separation is due only to the illusive power of thought.

Knowledge, or cognition, thus holds a key position in the thought of Śankara. It is the key to the very existence both of the world and of man, and the means to man's discovery of this key. The three dimensions Śankara discerns in knowledge are

1) Perfect Knowledge: the knowledge of Brahman that liberates man from his separateness, giving him total knowledge of the nature and unity of all things;
2) Relative Knowledge: ordinary knowledge of the apparent objective world

[38] For a discussion of the two aspects of Brahman and the ethical duties of man, see Vedānta Sūtra I.1.3, *ibid.*, p. 15.

[39] Dasgupta, *op. cit.*, vol. I, p. 485.

[40] Vedānta Sūtra III.2.21, *op. cit.*, vol. XXXVIII, p. 160.

(*saṃsāra, nāmarūpa*), dependent upon the *pramāṇas*, or testimony (*śabda*), perception (*pratyakṣa*), and reason made up of inference (*anumāna*) and confutation (*tarka*);

3) Error: the mistaken identity of external objects in the world, as rope for snake or seashell for silver.

A discussion of these three epistemological dimensions will expose the central structure of Śankara's thought as it is found in the previously discussed four poles of Being.

1. *Relative Knowledge* – Although for Śankara only perfect knowledge has any final validity, it is with relative knowledge that the philosopher must start, the knowledge which concerns the ordinary world of *nāmarūpa*. Śankara maintains this knowledge to have only a relative value: "the relation of consciousness to its objects cannot be regarded as real but as mere illusion. ... It is not possible to determine the relation between knowledge and its forms."[41] This is so because such forms do not really exist. However, a relative knowledge of the world's apparent forms can be acquired by the *pramāṇas*. As valid means of mediate knowledge, Śankara emphasizes in particular testimony, perception, and inference. *Testimony* means the witness of others to certain intuitive truths, as recorded in certain literature regarded as sacred (*śruti*).[42] *Perception* is understood to be "the union or nondifference of the subjective consciousness comprehending sensible objects through specific mental states (*vṛtti*)."[43] These *vṛtti* arise corresponding to external objects. They may be correct or erroneous as far as they conform to objects or not. What one knows, then, are the mental states and not the objects; one can never have certain knowledge of the actual existence of these objects. External objects, thus, are equivalent to the differentiated consciousness of the knower at the moment of perception. As for *inference*, Śankara appears to follow standard Indian logic, which depends on the comparison of a certain present situation with a concrete past event to determine validity. Valid inferential knowledge is acquired by a three-step process, traditionally schematized as follows:

1. *Inference*	*pratijñā*	The hill is fiery.
2. *Reason*	*hetu*	Because the hill is smoky.
3. *Example*	*dṛṣṭānta*	As in the kitchen.[44]

This differs from Western syllogistic logic principally on the ground that the Indian proposition is always referred to the truth or falsity of its actual claim

[41] Dasgupta, *op. cit.*, vol. I, p. 445.
[42] See note 6.
[43] Dasgupta, *op. cit.*, vol. I, p. 472.
[44] *Ibid.*, p. 474. For a detailed discussion of Indian *pramāṇas*, see K. Potter, *Presuppositions of India's Philosophies* (Englewood Cliffs, N.J., 1963), chapter 5.

for final validation. Thus every inference is ultimately tested against the knowledge of the thinker. There are no truths inferred in Indian thought, as there are in Western logic, that have logical consistency but not intuitive acceptance. Thus as in the *pramāṇa* of testimony, personal conviction derived intuitionally lies finally behind the means of knowledge called inference.

Śankara explains that these two realms of knowing and being are related to one another, each with its own rules.

> The entire complex of phenomenal existence is considered as true as long as the knowledge of Brahman being the Self of all has not arisen, just as the phantoms of a dream are considered to be true until the sleeper wakes.[45]

All the common distinctions between objects, people, etc. are valid from the point of view of the phenomenal world.

Yet ultimately this kind of knowledge has no force since there is really no difference between the knower of knowledge and what he knows. "If there is no knowing agent [Self separate from Brahman] the means of right knowledge cannot operate."[46] Thus all objects of ordinary knowledge depend on ignorance (*avidyā*). "The mutual superimposition of the Self and non-Self ... [is] the presupposition on which there base all the practical distinctions ... between the means of knowledge, objects of knowledge, etc. ...."[47] This superimposition is the original ignorance responsible for all other ignorance.

Śankara hopes to teach man that he can be free of the essential error involved in relative knowledge. The self-acknowledged aim of his writing is "freeing one's self from that wrong notion which is the cause of all evil ... such as Nescience, the seed of the entire *saṃsāra* ... and attaining thereby the knowledge of the absolute unity of the Self."[48] And for Śankara there is no question that such perfect knowledge is attainable by man.

2. *Perfect Knowledge* – The knowledge of Brahman is of a different order than the relative knowledge of the world.

> As Brahman is not an object of the senses [but the subject of all things], it has no connection with those other means of knowledge. For the senses have, according to their nature, only extended things for their objects, not Brahman.[49]

Thus sensual perception and the other ordinary means of knowledge cannot lead to the knowledge of Brahman, which is of an intuitional nature, neither

[45] Vedānta Sūtra II.1.14, *op. cit.*, vol. XXXIV, p. 324.
[46] *Sacred Books of the East*, vol. XXXIV, p. 7.
[47] *Ibid.*, p. 6.
[48] Vedānta Sūtra I.1.1, *ibid.*, p. 9.
[49] Vedānta Sūtra I.1.3, *ibid.*, p. 19.

sensual, inferential, nor deductive. Brahman is immaterial, neither an object to be known nor something to be attained."[50]

Dasgupta points out that "the validity of knowledge is sometimes used [by Śankara] in the sense of the faithfulness of knowledge to its object, and sometimes in the sense of an inner notion of validity in the mind of the subject."[51] There are clearly two kinds of knowledge discerned by Śankara. If mediate knowledge of the relative world is understood by the first kind, it is in the latter sense that Śankara understands the highest form of knowledge, the perfect knowledge of Brahman; it is the result of immediate intuition of an inner sort. Śankara makes a clear distinction between conventionally derived knowledge of the world and meditatively derived knowledge of Brahman: "through [which] all things become known."[52] This latter self-sufficient knowledge is of a qualitative difference from relative knowledge and is sometimes called by Śankara "perfect knowledge" relative to which conventional knowledge is error.

> There is a difference between false knowledge and perfect knowledge, fruition [the results of good and bad actions] being the figment of false knowledge while the unity (of the Self) is revealed by perfect knowledge.[53]
>
> The true nature of the cause of the world on which final emancipation depends cannot ... become the object of perception because it does not possess qualities ... It does not lend itself to inference and the other means of right knowledge.[54]

It is only this perfect knowledge that can effect the final release of the soul. Release simply means the removal of mediate knowledge by perfect knowledge. All boundaries and differences between Self, world, and Brahman no longer are perceived; the whole cosmos is known to be an immaterial unity.

This perfect knowledge is effected through meditation, an inner development of consciousness whose specific processes are well attested to in Indian texts on Yoga and the object of almost complete scepticism in the Western world.[55] Suffice it to say that knowledge so derived has not yet adequately been explained in the language of Western philosophy, so it cannot yet be fairly assessed to the satisfaction of Western thinkers.

Śankara summarizes the power of this perfect knowledge:

[50] Vedānta Sūtra I.14.1, *ibid.*, p. 32.
[51] *Op. cit.*, vol. I, p. 406.
[52] Vedānta Sūtra III.1.17, *op. cit.*, vol. XXXVIII, p. 111.
[53] Vedānta Sūtra I.2.8, *op. cit.*, vol. XXXIV, p. 116.
[54] Vedānta Sūtra II.1.11, *ibid.*, p. 314. See also II.1.27, p. 350.
[55] Vedānta Sūtra III.2.24, *op. cit.*, vol. XXXVIII, pp. 171 ff. See for examples and further bibliography on Yoga, M. Eliade, *Yoga, Immortality and Freedom* (New York, 1958).

This whole apparent world – which springs from Nescience – is characterized by actions, objects, and results of actions, and is the cause of all qualifications for works, is essentially destroyed by the power of knowledge.[56]

The phenomenal world exists only as a function of ignorance; correct knowledge eclipses it altogether. As the cosmos is an illusion, its relative reality depends on the embodied Self whose original error is to confuse permanent Self and bodily form. This event occurs "not because the connection of the Self with the world ceases, but because the appearance of the world process does not represent the ultimate and highest truth about it."[57] We can, in fact, only really know Brahman, for the world of *saṃsāra* is false.

3. *Error* – The third dimension of knowledge is error. Error stands in the same relation to relative knowledge as mediate knowledge stands to perfect knowledge. Once the illusion is dispelled, the truer knowledge is revealed. Again, one mistakes a rope for a coiled snake and runs; one mistakes a seashell for a piece of silver and picks it up. In each case actions follow from perceptual error, yet a more accurate perception reveals the original falsehood.

The same is true of dreams. "This world of dreams ... is mere illusion and there is not a particle of reality in it ... because it does not manifest itself with the totality of the attributes of [relatively] real things ... the conditions of place, time and cause, etc. ...."[58] As relative knowledge is false before the knowledge of Brahman, so are dreams false in relation to knowledge of the waking world.

The world connected with the intermediate state (dreams) is not real in the same sense as the world consisting of ether etc. ... The entire expanse of things is mere illusion. ... [It] remains fixed and distinct up to the moment when the soul cognizes that Brahman is the Self of all; the world of dreams on the other hand is daily sublated by the waking world.[59]

In sum, the three dimensions of knowledge Śankara discusses provide the key to his ethics, metaphysics, and ontology. They are all focused on a single event: the moment of perfect knowledge when the soul of man perceives intuitively that it is Brahman, the world is Brahman, all things are Brahman, all things are one. In the absence of this knowledge, the cosmos is seen to be structured in four aspects, the three dimensions of the real cutting across each of the four aspects, Absolute, world, man, and mind (see Figure 1). For Śankara, this fourfold division is essentially unreal, only a function of

[56] Vedānta Sūtra III.4.16, *op. cit.*, vol. XXXVIII, p. 294.
[57] Dasgupta, *op. cit.*, vol. I, p. 440.
[58] Vedānta Sūtra III.2.3, *op. cit.*, vol. XXXVIII, p. 134.
[59] Vedānta Sūtra III.2.4, *ibid.*, p. 138.

ignorance, not a description of the essential structure of Being. Brahman, he asserts continually, is a partless unity. Thus both the four aspects and the three dimensions characteristic of Śankara's analysis of the world are finally dependent on a cognitive error for their very existence, and on a cognitive event for their final resolution. In short, for Śankara all Being is dependent on thought, and thought is a function of Being. Or simply, being is thought and thought is being. There are ultimately no valid distinctions or separate reals. There is only one Brahman.

Conclusion

In what way is Śankara's philosophical system compatible with Western thought? On the surface, the differences appear to be considerable. First, Śankara's strong reliance on the testimony of revealed scripture contrasts with the primacy of man's reason, however defined, as means of valid knowledge in the West. Secondly, whereas Śankara's first premiss is the primacy of the Absolute, Western thinkers have tended to start philosophical inquiry with man, the knower. Thirdly, Śankara's main value is assigned to the dimension of the Absolute, denying reality to the world except as it manifests Brahman. Main value in Western thought is given to the reality of the world and of man's power to know this world. Whereas for Śankara, only God is real, for the West, only what the senses and reason prove can be said to be demonstrably real. Fourthly, where Śankara discerns three dimensions in Being itself, the Absolute, the Relatively Real and the Erroneous, focusing most of his attention on the first dimension, Western philosophy has emphasized the second and third dimensions and their interrelatedness. And finally, where metaphysics, ontology, ethics and epistemology often appear as distinct philosophical pursuits in Western thought, the four are indivisibly welded in Śankara's system, all four being finally dependent on epistemology, since Being is finally understood to be thought, and thought, Being.

After the foregoing summary of Śankara's thought, however, it should now be clear that there exists a structural parallel between his overall system and the main outline of Western philosophy. As shown in Figure 1, in both styles of thought a quadrangular structure has been assigned to Being itself, and an intimate interrelatedness can be discerned among the four aspects of this Being common to both. The five major differences just delineated between Śankara's thinking and the concerns and method of Western philosophy can best be explained as being due to different points of departure within this same fourfold being; where Śankara starts with the Absolute and ends with the Absolute, Western thinkers start with man and end with man, both including the other three aspects in a circular motion of thought. All consequent differences, some of which appear to be considerable, between Vedānta and Western philosophy can be traced to these different points of departure, rather than to any profoundly different understanding of the nature of the world.

What are the implications of this compatibility so revealed between Śankara and the West? There are many; let us mention only two. First, Vedānta and Western thought may find a fruitful avenue of approach to each other by focusing on the interrelatedness of God, man, world, and mind. It has been seen that the structure and content of each system has been dictated by the particular aspect of these four given highest value: man by the West, God by Śankara. If value and emphasis are shifted rather to the interrelatedness of the four dimensions, to the questions of why and how they are interdependent, Vedānta and the West will not only have a basis for genuine interaction, but they will also have much to learn from each other. Secondly, Western epistemology may take on a new and productive direction if it revises its definition of knowledge to include Śankara's third dimension – perfect knowledge, that kind of knowledge that is capable of knowing fully the meaning of Being. The single greatest handicap Western philosophy has placed upon itself throughout its entire history – both scholastic and secular – is the limitations it has imposed on the power of human knowledge. These limitations have seemed to grow more stringent in the past century, and are partly responsible for the increasing irrelevance of the academic study of philosophy in the West. In this regard, Śankara has something important to say to the modern Western world. The possibilities he holds out for the universal scope of human knowledge are tremendously exciting, permitting to man in the pursuit of truth a refreshingly new approach. For him there are no limits to the power of human knowledge; there is a truth the knowledge of which includes all other truths, and that truth is accessible to man. Since the central structure of his thought and that of recent Western philosophy are not foreign to one another, but structurally analogous it would seem possible that the door might be opened by Śankara for the West to make a new evaluation of the meaning and power of knowledge. Such a new definition of knowledge would foster a new direction for Western epistemology; it would (1) permit to man himself full knowledge of the Absolute, or of Being itself, (2) allow to intuition the status of a valid means of knowledge, and (3) revalidate the pursuit of philosophy as the road to full knowledge of the essence of Being, which is, after all, the central and original quest of philosophy, no matter what its country of origin.

GLOSSARY OF SANSKRIT TERMS

anumāna	Inference; one of the *pramāṇas.*
avidyā	Ignorance.
Brahman	The Absolute.
darśana	View; any one of the six systems of Indian philosophy.
īśvara	The Supreme Being; *saguṇa* Brahman.
līlā	Play.
māyā	Illusion, deception.
nāmarūpa	Name and form; the objective world.
nirguṇa	Without qualities; adjective used to describe Brahman.
pramāṇa	Means of valid knowledge.
pratyakṣa	Perception; one of the *pramāṇas.*
śabda	Testimony; one of the *pramāṇas.*
saguṇa	Having qualities; adjective used to describe Brahman.
satkāryavāda	Philosophical doctrine that effect pre-exists in cause.
saṃsāra	Passing through; secular life, worldly illusion.
śruti	That which has been heard; sacred and authoritative literature.
tarka	Confutation; one of the *pramāṇas.*
Vedānta	End of the Veda; one of the six systems of Indian philosophy, systematized by Śankara.
vivarta	Transformation; manifestation.
vṛtti	Mental state.

EXPLANATION AND BEHAVIOR

ACCOUNTING FOR THE FAILURE OF BEHAVIORISM

by

PHILLIP H. SCRIBNER

When a young girl walking down Peachtree Street in Atlanta, Georgia, smiles at a stranger, mere friendliness is probably all she has on her mind. However on Main Street in Buffalo, New York, a stranger could reliably take a similar smile to suggest a more serious invitation.[1] As Birdwhistle reports, there is no reason to suppose there is a difference between the cases in the overt behavior of the girl, at least no difference which could be detected by the sorts of information which could be recorded on film. Yet the girl's intention in smiling in each case is probably different, and more significantly, the intentions attributed to the girl by the strangers she smiles at would probably be accurate. People occasionally mistake one another, of course, but that is not the norm.

Most of us find nothing very startling in such examples for we are all familiar with the diversity of social conventions. The case can stand, however, as an example of a general difficulty encountered by the social sciences in their attempts to realize the traditional empiricist ideal of scientific objectivity – a difficulty which is exemplified by the failure of the behaviorist's program. Grossly, the girl's intention is not unambiguously indicated by her behavior, even though in ordinary life we find no great problem in telling what her intentions are.

In what follows I shall assume that behaviorism, as it has been attempted, has failed. The major thrust of my argument will be that a now-fashionable way of accounting for that failure, while still preserving the objectivity of mentalistic ascriptions, will not work. Some have assumed that the difficulty with behaviorism lies in the fact that the mentalistic language is incommensurable with the behaviorist's physicalistic language. I shall argue instead that its difficulty lies in the fact that it has not recognized the full

[1] Ray L. Birdwhistle, *Kinesics and Context: Essays on Body Motion and Communication* (Philadelphia, 1970), p. 31.

extent of the information one needs and uses in determining the mental states of others.

After discussing the thesis of behaviorism and its purpose (in I), I consider an account of its failure which would preserve the objectivity of mentalistic ascriptions (in II). I then argue that this account, if true, would entail, on the basis of certain assumptions about the physical processes mediating perception, a form of behaviorism (in III). Finally I argue that the account is subject to the same difficulties encountered by behaviorism, and that these difficulties point to the insufficiency of information in the test situation rather than to the incommensurability of languages (in IV).

I

Behaviorism has been associated with various theses and has been defended for different reasons. I shall be concerned in this essay only with the behaviorist thesis that all nonlogical terms used to describe humans (or animals) be definable by, reducible to, or introduced as theoretical terms for a special set of descriptive terms which refer only to physical processes, such as movements of the organism, physical traits of the environment, etc. Other behaviorist principles, not directly relevant here, would restrict the sorts of laws and theories which can be used to explain behavior.

Descriptive behaviorism can be understood, then, as a restriction on the language which can be used to report what is happening in the world and on the basis of which psychological and social theories would be accepted, explanations given, and predictions verified. No mentalistic or intentional expressions, that is, no terms referring to the beliefs, intentions, desires, feelings, sensations, etc., would be part of the data language unless they were introduced by definitions, reduction sentences, or theories.[2] Although behaviorists included physicalistic expressions as part of the data language, they agreed to exclude descriptions of physiological or neurophysiological processes going on "beneath the skin" on the grounds that they were not

[2] Traditionally behaviorism has been thought to attempt to formulate definitions of mentalistic terms by expressions referring only to physical conditions and events. For the purposes of this paper there is no need to insist that the connecting rules between physicalistic expressions and mentalistic expressions be definitions, reduction sentences, or the more complex relations involved in introducing a theory on some data base. The connecting rules may have empirical content, as long as they are perfectly general and do not entail statements which are true only of some particular situation. Nor is there any reason to suppose they are not probablistic, for, as will be seen, it is the degree of reliability of ascriptions of mental states which is at issue.

normally observable. Consequently, descriptive behaviorism limited the data reports to information about observable physical processes.

Although in general behaviorists were interested in the restriction on the data language to insure objectivity, one can distinguish two narrower motives. By insisting that mentalistic expressions admitted to the science be defined in the behaviorist language, some hoped to clarify and tie down their meanings to specific behavioral traits in a way which would prevent semantic disputes from consuming their efforts. More modestly, others were more concerned to insure that acceptable mentalistic terms have a specified empirical content so that, regardless of what they were thought to mean, one could tell whether they correctly applied or not, in some particular cases at least, on the basis of observations rather than mere prejudice or preconception. For many reasons, including certain doctrines about meaning embodied in their positivistic views, these two concerns were not often carefully distinguished. In discussing the import of the denial of behaviorism for observation in the psychological and social sciences, the empiricist concern for objectivity, rather than the explication of meaning, will be relevant.

If descriptive behaviorism had succeeded, and they had been able to define, or otherwise introduce, mentalistic terms in a behavioristic language, a kind of empiricist objectivity would have been guaranteed. That is, the applicability of mentalistic terms would, at least in standard cases, be determinable, and the determination would depend on what could be observed to be going on in and about the person (or organism), rather than "smuggled in" by the biases of the observer. What they feared, after all, was that mentalistic terms were mere subjective interpretations projected onto the person by the observer.[3] And if they were mere projections, there would be no reason to expect that their applicability, as determined by the investigator, varied systematically with what was happening in the organism, and thus no reason to expect that they would be causally or scientifically relevant. Thus by insisting on observable conditions of application, stated in the behavioristic language, a special kind of objectivity – what I shall call "empiricist objectivity" – could be insured from the outset.

Descriptive behaviorism failed and before discussing the reason for the failure its significance should be noted. For some, of course, the inability to introduce mentalistic terms in the behaviorist language was a fulfillment of their expectations; they had believed all along that minds, consciousness, thoughts, etc., and even social roles, were mythical entities invented, perhaps, to serve some social, political, or religious interest.

[3] Charles Taylor, *The Explanation of Behavior* (New York, 1964), pp. 73-75.

For others the failure must be surprising, for in ordinary life the reliability of our ascription of mental states to others is a fact. By "reliability" I mean that at least two conditions are satisfied. First, independent observers of the behavior of someone generally agree, with respect to at least some of the questions at issue, about what the person believes, feels, intends, etc., in behaving as he does. That is, there is substantial intersubjective agreement. Moreover, that the agreement reflects more than shared dogma can be seen in the fact that predictions and retrodictions based on their assessment of the mentalistic state of another normally turn out to be true. Of course these predictions are often, indeed usually, made by employing mentalistic expressions, but the verification of the prediction can be established by independent observers unaware of the prediction, and done with substantial intersubjective agreement.

By these tests the ascriptions of mental states to others in ordinary life are, in fact, reliable. In some sense their objectivity may be insured by this fact, but for the empiricist the failure of descriptive behaviorism is puzzling because it becomes mysterious how our normal ascription of mental states to others could be reliable.

It may be useful at this point to recall the kind of considerations which led recent critics to conclude that mentalistic terms could not be reduced to behavioral or physicalistic terms.[4] In a classical example, suppose Skinner is looking for his glasses. Since "looking for one's glasses" is a mentalistic expression, the behaviorist project is to give a set of behavioral conditions which will enable us to determine that the person is, indeed, looking for his glasses, by observing, in this case or others, that the behaviorally described conditions obtain.

To indicate that his intention is, indeed, to find his glasses, one might look for those typical movements, including directing the eyes, groping about with the hands, which terminate in clutching the glasses, etc., which would occur when (or when and only when) one is looking for his glasses. The general problem, however, is that different accounts of his intentions are also compatible with those behaviorally described movements. For example, he might be stretching his muscles, making ritualistic obeisance to a god (or gods), or communicating a deep sense of gratitude to his host in a strange culture. Which of these intentions obtain could be singled out if we knew what his beliefs about the situation were. If we knew he believed he owned glasses, that he believed they were somewhere about, that they were

[4] *Ibid.*, p. 79. Michael Scriven also considers these arguments in "A Study of Radical Behaviorism," *Minnesota Studies in the Philosophy of Science,* vol. I (Minneapolis, 1956), p. 104.

the sort of thing whose presence could be detected by (even dim) sight and touch, and that he did not believe that such groping communicates great gratitude to another, etc., then we would be fairly sure that in groping around he was looking for his glasses. But to attribute such beliefs to him is to ascribe mental states whose behavioral reduction has yet to be given. A good behaviorist would take the challenge here and attempt to give a more complete behavioral description of conditions which would obtain when (or when and only when) the person had those beliefs in the context of which his movements would indicate he was looking for his glasses. But, unfortunately for the behaviorist, the sorts of behavior which ordinarily indicate that he has those beliefs do so only when we assume he has certain intentions. For example, that he believed he owned those glasses might be indicated by his repeatedly picking them up when departing from other places, but it would do so only if we assume that he intends to take what he owns with him. That intention has not yet been given a behavioral reduction, but providing behavioral grounds for attributing to him that intention involves us again in the problem of finding yet further behavioral grounds for ascribing to him the beliefs in the context of which we could safely conclude he intended to take with him what he owned.

In form, then, we face the following sort of problem. Certain behavior can be taken as a sufficient condition, or even as a probable condition, for having an intention of the prescribed sort only in the context of the person's having certain beliefs (that is, a description of the world as it appears to the person). But we can find kinds of behavior which would indicate with some reliability that the person has those beliefs only in circumstances in which we can assume that he has certain goals or intentions, as well as perhaps still further beliefs. The interdependence of beliefs and intentions seems to make any behavioral condition insufficient; we cannot select out which of the combinations of beliefs and intentions, compatible with the movements, holds. One can only hope to find other situations which allow one to infer he had then, and still has now, the same beliefs or intentions here as were behaviorally indicated in those other situations. But in other situations the same problem of interdependence of beliefs and intentions is faced and the prospect of an indeterminate regress is unavoidable.

On the basis of considerations such as these, many philosophers have been inclined to conclude that descriptive behaviorism is impossible. As I indicated above, however, this sort of argument is puzzling, because even though observable physical conditions for predicating mentalistic descriptions of people cannot be found, and the conditions of empiricist objectivity are not met, in ordinary life and as social scientists, we can and do ascribe mental states to others with considerable reliability.

II

In *The Explanation of Behavior,* after arguing that descriptive behaviorism is false, Charles Taylor offers an explanation of the reliability of our everyday ascriptions of mental states to others. His account, he claims, involves the rejection of certain basic empiricist principles. I shall argue that his account neither departs very seriously from empiricism nor, consequently, does it offer an adequate account of the reliability of mentalistic expressions in ordinary life.

Taylor locates the fundamental error behind descriptive behaviorism in its empiricist view of experience as the passive reception of impressions.

For if experience was the receiving of impressions, then any belief about the world must find its evidence in impressions received on the mind. Every "idea" which was empirically founded must have a corresponding "impression." And if a distinction between two ideas was to be empirically founded, there must be a corresponding distinction between the impressions.[5]

This notion is reflected in the belief that there is a privileged language for reporting what is happening in the world.

...we assume that there is only *one* data language, one which is common to and neutral between all theories.... Now this assumption follows from empiricist epistemology where the basic evidence for all beliefs is given in the impressions of primitive experience which sets the forms of the basic data language.[6]

The behaviorist's physicalist language became the privileged language for stating all the evidence for psychological theories, and any conclusions about mental states would have to be based on it.

Taylor explains why descriptive behaviorism is false by insisting that there is no reason to suppose there is one privileged language for reporting all observations. The physicalist language and the mentalist language can each serve as its own observational language.

We might ... assume that "primitive experience," or our ordinary perception of the world, is not a passive reception of impressions but is always accompanied by classification, a subsumption of the things and events seen under some description. There would thus be many ways of seeing a given set of things or events, many descriptions under which the seer could subsume them, depending on his interest, background, training, etc., one of which would be the basic way. That is, the division between "seeing" and "interpreting," between "observation" and "inference" would not be clear cut, for there would be no way of seeing

[5] *Op. cit.,* pp. 90-91.
[6] *Ibid.,* p. 96.

which would be considered, relative to the others, as pure seeing, without interpretation. Thus the notion of a specially privileged stratum of expressions, the data language, would have no basis; for seeing something under the description of an action would involve no more inference than seeing it under the description of a movement.[7]

If there is no neutral observational language, there is no reason to suppose all objectively attributable expressions must be defined in terms of it. Further, there is no longer any puzzle about the reliability of ordinary-life ascriptions of mental states to others. They are applied on the basis of observation, to be sure, but the mentalistic language like any theoretical language serves as its own observation language.

Taylor's solution relies on a more sophisticated view of language and meaning than positivists or behaviorists were accustomed to, and there should perhaps have been something initially suspect in the notion that one could cut out part of ordinary and scientific language and introduce all the remaining expressions in the language on the basis of that small part. In rejecting the crude theory of meaning embraced by positivists, however, Taylor is able to preserve a more basic empiricist doctrine. He still assumes that the applicability of the terms in the language to objects in the world can be determined after a limited period of observation of these objects, for the observation allows one to detect traits which evidence their applicability. Although Taylor is surely correct in his more sophisticated view of language and meaning, his retention of the more basic assumption of empiricism – namely, that mentalistic terms are objective because they are applied on the basis of observation limited to the situation in question – is sufficient to undermine his account. By developing the model of the robot observer I shall argue, first, that Taylor's account entails, given certain assumptions about the physical process involved in perception, that a form of descriptive behaviorism must be true, and second, that the very same considerations which led him to reject descriptive behaviorism in the first place count equally as well against his own empiricist view.

III

If the behaviorists had been correct, then it would be possible to program a computer with a translation formula so that when it is fed a sufficiently complete physical description of what is going on with and around a person, but not going "beneath the skin," the computer would be able to print out

[7] *Ibid.*, pp. 94-95.

which mentalistic expressions probably apply. More practically, we might imagine the computer asking us a series of questions about the person and his situation in a physicalist language, which, when we answer, also in a physicalist language, enables it to answer questions about what the person believes, feels, intends, etc., as well as any person encountering him in ordinary life could.

It makes no difference for the purposes of this argument whether the translation formula programmed into the computer represents operational definitions, reduction sentences, or general psychological and sociological theories, although it is not likely that anything less than a rather complete theory of psychology and society would suffice. The only restriction imposed on the program is that it not include any information about *particular* individuals or societies; all its information about particulars in the world will be fed to it in answer to its questions about the physical state of the world it is dealing with.

Taylor's rejection of descriptive behaviorism can be taken as the denial that there exists a translation formula which would permit the computer to answer as reliably as we do in ordinary life questions about the mental states of others. Taylor would explain why the behaviorist computer must fail, when observers in ordinary life succeed, by pointing out that the computer information is restricted to what can be described physically or behavioristically. Taylor seems to believe that the computer is thereby denied precisely the sort of information, observationally available in the situation, on the basis of which the ordinary human observer can reliably judge the mental state of another.

As Taylor sees it, the behaviorist language cuts up the world in different ways than the mentalist language. Neither language can be translated into the other. It is as if they were differently shaped nets casting shadows of figures on the same surface which crosscut one another irregularly. Neither is finer nor more basic than the other; they are simply different.

Having modeled Taylor's negative thesis about behaviorism by the behaviorist computer, it is possible as well to model his positive empiricist thesis that the mentalistic language can serve as its own observation language, if we make certain assumptions about the physical processes involved in perception. It should be possible, in theory at least, to program a robot so that it would be able to determine the mental states of humans as reliably as do human participants. If we equip the robot with sensors which are analogous to our sensory organs (a feat way beyond present technology), and provide it with the mobility to investigate situations on its own, it

[8] *Ibid.*, p. 96.

should be able, with the proper program, to determine the mental states of people as well as participant observers do.

Of course there are enormous practical problems here, for the mere presence of such a robot running around a person would be enough to alter the mental states of most people in ways which would give the robot observer skewed readings. It would be necessary to disguise the robot observer or hide it in clever ways that do not cause the subject to behave in special ways but which still permit the robot to make its observations. The robot may even need to be equipped to create special test situations. These are technical problems, and no doubt insoluble in practice. But they are beside the point to be made here. The issue is not whether this plan can be carried out in practice, but that there is no reason, on Taylor's account, to suppose the problems are any more than technical. The robot observer would have access to the same events as the participants in ordinary life, and unless one believes there are special ESP communications going on which account for the reliability in ordinary life of our ascriptions of mental states, the robot observer could conceivably do just as well as participant observers.

Likewise, of course, another computer could be equipped with sensors and a program for making behavioristic judgments about the movements of the person and the physical aspects of the situation. This second behavioristic robot observer should in theory be as reliable as human observers at answering questions about the physical aspects of the situation, just as the other, mentalistic robot observer is as reliable as human participants at answering questions about his mental states.

These mechanical models reflect Taylor's position. The impossibility of the translating computer is an alternative way of representing the failure to carry out the program of descriptive behaviorism, *i.e.*, Taylor's thesis that the mentalistic language is not reducible to the behaviorist's physicalist language. Taylor's own account of the reliability of ordinary-life ascriptions of mental states requires the possibility of the mentalistic robot observer. To say that such a mentalistic robot is possible, is equivalent in this context to saying that the mental language can serve as its own observational language. Further, since the physicalistic language can also serve as its own observation language, the physicalistic robot observer should also be possible. The falsity of descriptive behaviorism is explained, then, on this model by the fact that what the mentalistic robot finds out in its investigations of the world is different from what questions the behavioristic robot answers in its investigations. The translating computer cannot reproduce the results of the mentalistic robot from the results of the behavioral robot.

From this model, however, it becomes apparent that there is reason to believe that there is, after all, a privileged language in terms of which mentalistic expression can be introduced. If the mentalistic robot is possible, then there must be a level of description of the program of the robot, including how it deploys its sensors and records its findings, which enables it to determine the mental states of people. What it finds out by means of its sensors is dependent on the physical state of the object and situation it senses, for the sensors' readings can be given a purely physical explanation. The program can be no more than a systematic selection of readings from among these physical conditions, for the program which produces the mentalistic ascription, if it is deterministic, can be reduced to certain logical operations. There is no question that the program would be incredibly complex and the number of readings enormously large, but that does not alter the fact that if the mentalistic robot observer is possible, then there is a privileged level of description to which mental language can be reduced, namely the physical conditions it checks out to produce its conclusion.

For example, the robot in observing the actions of a person would presumably deploy its sensors to detect as much as is necessary to determine the mental state of the person. But, the sensors are physically explainable in the sense that whatever signals are given to the robot by means of its sensors, they can be explained either as a result of the physical conditions of the object in relation to the sensors or as noise from the sensor system itself. Therefore, what the sensors find out about the object can be no more than what could be determined by knowing the physical condition of the object and its relation to the sensors. But the mentalistic ascriptions it produces could be reduced to a physicalist description, since its program is merely a set of logical operations on the information it gains about the physical condition.

What holds true of the mentalistic robot observer is not a peculiarity of its robothood, but holds true as well of human observers. Unless our physical theories are wrong and something like ESP is the standard means of communication, we can get no more information out of an object than is physically transmitted to us by the senses. We know, in principle at least, that all our information about the particular situation can be stated in physical terms, since all the events going on in the object which can affect our senses are physically describable. Thus, whatever we can determine about the object, by means of the senses, can include no more information than could be derived, by some appropriate translation, from a sufficiently complete physical description of the object and the deployment of the sensory organs.

The principle to which this argument appeals, both for the mentalistic robot and for the human observer, is analogous to the medieval principle that there can be no more reality in the effect than in the cause. For any discrimination made by the observer, on the basis of his senses, there must be some difference in the object which accounts for it. But since the processes of perception are mediated by physical processes, a sufficiently complete physical description of the object will account for all possible discriminations by sensory means. And this is true regardless of the ways in which the physical inputs are processed to yield the mentalistic ascription, for whatever those processes are, if they are deterministic, they can be duplicated as operations on the physical description alone. Although such a duplication would be at least as complex as the mechanisms of our perceptual apparatus, there can be no more information derivable from the sensory input to the observer than could be derived from the sufficiently complete physical description.

There are at least two assumptions of this argument which need to be reemphasized. First, it is assumed that the processes mediating sensory perception are physically explainable. It is not assumed that there are no mental events ontologically distinct in some way from physical processes, but merely assumed that one person's knowledge of them, in so far as they are based on observation of the other, are mediated by processes which are fully describable and explainable by physical theories. Metaphysically, the mental state ascribed to another may not be itself a physical state, but our ways of observing it are limited to information which can be coded into the physical processes mediating perception. One might deny this, but then, beyond denying the truth of physical theories, one would seem to be committed to a special mentalistic channel of communication. And if this is what is involved in Taylor's position, it would seem to be very dubious indeed. Second, neither is it assumed that the human observer's mental processes, conscious or unconscious, by which he makes his ascriptions on the basis of observation are physical processes. It is assumed only that the final ascriptions are determined by the information gained from the physical processes of sensing. This was the reason for limiting the information programmed into the mentalistic robot, and also permitted to the human observer, to general truths of human psychology and laws of sociology. To allow either information about the particular situation, which does not hold equally of every other situation which it could be presented with, would violate the empiricist assumption that the final mentalistic ascription was based on the observation. Background information about the situation, not derived from observation, could conceivably allow the mentalistic robot or the human observer to ascribe mental states without any observation at all.

Once the importance of the assumption that there is no background knowledge about the particular situation in question is made explicit, however, it becomes clearer why Taylor is wrong and his view commits him to a kind of behavioristic reduction. Taylor assumed that if the observer were allowed to use the mentalistic language as his observation language, then we could account for the reliability of mentalistic ascriptions while denying that a behavioristic reduction was possible. If the above argument is correct, however, Taylor's implicit empiricist constraint, that the ascription be based on observation of the situation, entails that some (very complex, perhaps) physicalistic reduction must be possible.

A more likely explanation would deny that we are able to ascribe mental states on the basis of such limited information, that certain nontheoretical background information, such as familiarity with the conventions and institutions, knowledge of the social circumstances of the situation, is crucial to most if not all mentalistic ascriptions. Whether such information about the societal context of the situation observed can be given a physicalistic reduction is a vastly different question and one which I cannot settle here. But it would account for the impossibility of the behavioristic reduction when it is restricted to the limits of a set of test situations.

Therefore, given the impossibility of the behaviorist's physicalistic reduction (a position for which I have not argued, but assumed), one cannot account for the reliability of ordinary mentalistic ascriptions, as Taylor does, by supposing merely that the observer is allowed to employ a mentalistic language as his observation language. The argument suggests that the account might be made by looking to the background information about the particular situation which the observer brings. The argument of the next section accords with this account.

IV

If we look at Taylor's own example (cited from Tolman) of the difficulties in providing a behavioristic reduction of a mentalistic term, it is again clear that Taylor's account of mentalistic ascription will do no better and another approach is necessary.

Taylor cites Tolman's proposed behavioral definition of "the rat expects food at location *L*."

When we assert that a rat expects food at location *L*, what we assert is that *if* (1) he is deprived of food, (2) he has been trained on path *P*, (3) he is now put on path *P*, (4) path *P* is now blocked, and (5) there are other paths which lead away from path *P*, one of which points directly to location *L*, then he will run down the path which points directly to location *L*.

When we assert that he does not expect food at location *L*, what we assert is that, under the same conditions, he will not run down the path which points directly to location *L*.[9]

The problem with this analysis is that the test conditions, stated in behaviorist terms, could hold, and yet the psychological and mentalistic description not be true. Taylor suggests [10] that the rat may have also been trained to take any white path when hungry and the path leading directly to *L* was white. In that case the rat, in running down the path to *L*, might not expect food at *L*, but rather expect food at the end of the white path. In the reverse case, if there were a cat in the path leading directly to *L*, the rat would not take that path even though, contrary to the definition, it expected food at *L*.

How should we explain the failure of Tolman's reduction sentence? On Taylor's account we should expect that if we look more carefully at the situation, using the mentalistic language as our observation language, we could tell, with greater reliability, whether the rat expects food at *L*.

This view gains some plausibility when we look at Taylor's example in which the cat, sitting astride the path which points directly to *L*, prevents the rat from taking that path. Taylor would insist that if we had not limited ourselves to a behaviorist description we would have noticed the cat and not concluded that the rat did not expect food at *L*. But the point does not prove the case.

There is no reason why a behaviorist account could not take into consideration the presence of cats, for they are surely describable in a physicalistic language. Taylor might simply be saying [11] that there is no reason in a behavioristic reduction to anticipate that the presence of a cat would make any difference to the rat's behavior, that innumerable similar intervening factors cannot all be taken into account in a simple definition.

If Taylor's point is merely the complexity of the factors which must be taken into consideration in the behavioristic reduction, the point can be granted. But there is no reason to think that such complexity implies an incommensurability between the mentalistic and behavioristic languages, for merely using the mentalistic language as its own observation language does not simplify the number of things one must look at, or factors one must take into consideration. In other words, if the failure to take account

[9] *Ibid.*, p. 79.

[10] *Ibid.*, p. 80, following MacCorquodale and Meehl.

[11] *Ibid.*, p. 81.

of the presence of the cat is to count against the possibility of a behavioristic reduction, then it must also count as well against the possibility of reliably applying mentalistic expressions when they are used as their own observation language. The problem of noting the conditions is no different, in principle, whether one uses a physicalistic or a mentalistic language. It is not, after all, part of the meaning of "expecting food at *L*" that rats avoid cats.[12]

The kind of example which does begin to tell against behaviorism also begins to tell against the application of mentalistic expressions using the mentalistic language as its own observation language. That is, in so far as behavioristic reduction is impossible, so is it impossible to ascribe mental states even when one uses the mentalistic language as his observation language.

MacCorquodale and Meehl suggest that the rat may have been trained to go down white paths and the path leading directly to *L* was white. Thus, even though the rat would follow the path directly to *L*, it need not be correct that it expected food at *L*. It may instead have expected food at the end of the white path, wherever that might be. Thus the behaviorist reduction is not successful.

In this case, however, the person using the mentalistic language as his observation language would be just as unsuccessful given the same information. On Taylor's account, one would expect that if we were to observe the situation carefully using the mentalistic language instead of the behavioristic language to describe our observations, we would be able to determine more reliably the expectational state of the rat. But under these circumstances no more detailed observation of the rat's behavior as it runs down the path to *L* will help, regardless of one's observation language. Unless we know that the rat was trained to use white paths, or we can run some additional tests to see what the rat must do when forced to decide between direction cues and color cues, there is no way for the observer to decide. What is needed, in other words, is not a more motivated, theory-guided observation of the situation, as Taylor suggests, but more information having to do with earlier training situations and other choices by the rat under other circumstances.

Now I agree that the preferred behavioristic definition is false, and false

[12] Taylor seems at times to be arguing merely that by using the mentalistic language it is easier to remind oneself to take account of such factors (*e.g.*, p. 81). But what he portrays there as the complexity of the behaviorist's definition of the mentalistic term reappears as the complexity in applying the mentalistic term. In either case these intervening conditions must be taken into account and that involves having general knowledge about the psychology of rats.

because neither necessary nor sufficient. But I suggest that its falsity is not due to an incommensurability between the behavioristic and mentalistic languages as Taylor suggests. Rather, the difficulty in devising behavioristic definitions of mentalistic terms, as this case shows, stems from the difficulty in cataloguing all the different sorts of evidence, or sorts of behaviorist conditions, on the basis of which one could determine, in any case, that the rat expects food at *L*. The difficulty of defining, in this sort of case, is merely another way of characterizing the difficulty of telling whether the rat expects food at *L*.

The point of this rehearsal of Taylor's example is not that behaviorism is possible. Surely it is not. Rather, the point is that the difficulty encountered in trying to give behavioristic definition is not overcome by supposing, with Taylor, that if we just look more closely at any situation, with a more theoretically motivated set of observations, we can tell whether the mentalistic term applies. No more detailed set of observations of the rat in the test situation, regardless of the language we use, will allow us to determine whether or not he has been trained to white paths in the past; that information simply is not available in the test situation. Even the conditions of the test behavior in Tolman's reduction sentence refer to past events outside the test situation itself. That it was deprived of food and trained on path *P* are facts which cannot be ascertained by observation in this situation. They were included as assumptions about the test conditions and not observed in that situation. The problem is that many more such conditions, not observable in the situation, may also be relevant, and only by looking to them can one tell at all what the mental state of the rat is.

The conclusion of this argument supports the earlier conclusion. Taylor's account of the reliability of mentalistic ascriptions by supposing that the observer employs the mentalistic language as his observation language succumbs to the same difficulties which led him to think that the behaviorist's physicalistic reduction is possible. The problem with behaviorism is not that the physicalistic and mentalistic languages are incommensurable, for that account both entails a physicalistic reduction and falls ill to the same difficulties as behaviorism. Rather, the problem with behaviorism is that the information relevant to ascribing a mental state – information which normal observers often have when they make mentalistic ascriptions – is about conditions and circumstances which go beyond what is observed in the test situation.

The attempt by behaviorists to find a set of physical conditions in a situation which would entail, or indicate as reliably as human observers can, the mental states of people or animals has not succeeded. Taylor argues that the reason for their failure is the incommensurability of physicalistic and mentalistic expression. Consequently he suggests that an observer, employing a mentalistic language as his observation language, can determine much more reliably the mental state of a person in some situation than can a behaviorist on the basis of physicalistic descriptions of the person and his situation.

As opposed to Taylor I have suggested that the failure of behaviorism is due to the limitation on the information available to the observer of the person and his situation rather than to the fact that he states his information in a physicalist language. I have tried to show this two ways: By showing that if it is possible to determine the mental state on the basis of the conditions observed in the situation, then there must be, if our physical theories about how perception is mediated are not false, a (very complex) formula which will enable us to determine that mental state on the basis of a sufficiently complete physical description of the situation with equivalent reliability. And secondly, by showing that the difficulties in a behaviorist reduction which Taylor cites are not overcome by supposing that the mentalistic language is incommensurable with the physicalist language, but can be overcome only by additional information about the person (animal) and his situation.

The reliability of the participant's ascription of mental states to others would be accounted for, on this hypothesis, by the additional background information which human observers have about the situation rather than by the fact that they are using the mentalistic language as their observation language. Such information may include knowledge of the conventions of society, of the institutional system, of the typical beliefs of agents in the society as well as specific knowledge of the social situation. None of these can be ascertained in a limited test situation, but they surely play an important part in our ability to understand one another. Neither are they the general knowledge permitted the observer or the mentalistic robot, for they are conditions which vary from society to society. The failure of behaviorism, and the inappropriateness of Taylor's version of empiricism, result from underestimating the significance of the sort of information we have about the situations we observe but which are not detectable by observation of them. The intention of the girl smiling as she walked down the street is not detectable by the behavior she displays, regardless of whether one uses the mentalistic or physicalistic language to describe it. Rather it is detectable because we know the social situation in which she exhibits this behavior. How we have that additional knowledge, however, is a matter to be handled elsewhere. The behaviorist may not be correct in his account of our having that knowledge. The ideal of empiricist objectivity, however, cannot be shown to be attained in the social sciences unless it can account for the background knowledge. The conclusion that one cannot account for the reliability of mentalistic expressions, given the failure of the classical attempts to carry out the behaviorist reduction, may seem unduly negative, but it does point to the kind of analysis which would explain our ability to ascribe mental states reliably.

RITUAL: A WHITEHEADIAN INTERPRETATION

by

DAVID F. T. RODIER

Christening a ship or a baby, celebrating a birthday or a mass are all instances of a kind of action which, although not necessary in any usual sense of the word, are among the most basic facts of any society. Major rituals, the "rites of passage," are well-known objects of anthropological study, but the ongoing life of society is as dependent on more common, everyday ritual activities as it is on those rituals used in times of crises. In a family it is not only marriage and births which must be faced, but also the daily task of getting the children to bed. Both the crisis situation and the everyday activity go more smoothly because of routine patterns of activity. To the extent that some of these routine patterns seem to be nonfunctional in a strict sense, they may be called "rituals." The prevalence in our social life of ostensibly nonfunctional patterned activities, *i.e.*, of rituals, raises several questions which are not properly sociological or anthropological, but rather philosophical. These philosophical questions are primarily concerned with the relationship between the individuals and the ritual and with the value of ritual to a society.

If it is granted that ritual behavior is a common and pervasive aspect of life, then the inadequacies of the prevalent philosophic models of ritual become evident. These models are of two kinds: either ritual is viewed as a special way of presenting myth [1] or it is seen as a particular kind of performative language.[2] Despite their respective merits neither the model of myth nor that of performative utterance is satisfactory. In the first place, rituals are a far more pervasive aspect of social life than the interpretation of ritual as a way of presenting myth would allow. Although it may perhaps

[1] Adherents to this view often completely assimilate ritual to myth. For a balanced presentation which avoids this extreme see Clyde Kluckhohn, "Myths and Rituals: A General Theory," *Harvard Theological Review*, XXV (1942), 45-79.

[2] Perhaps the clearest attempt to interpret ritual in terms of a model of performative utterance is Margaret Macdonald, "Ethics and the Ceremonial Use of Language," in *Philosophical Analysis*, ed. Max Black (Englewood Cliffs, N. J., 1963).

be illuminating to distinguish a mythic form of consciousness from our more rational, everyday mentality, and to see certain public functions such as a presidential inauguration or a college homecoming analyzed in the same terms as a religious celebration, it is impossible for all ritual-like activities to be interpreted on this model. Most small children devise a number of activities which must be followed precisely if the child is to go to bed, and hopefully, to sleep with a minimum upset both to the child and to the parents. Similarly, many husbands dare not leave for work without a ritual farewell to their wives. In many families meals, as well as birthdays, have their set actions and formulas. But if these kinds of behavior are to be treated as celebrations of a myth, then there is no other form of consciousness than the mythic for most members of even an advanced industrialized society. Furthermore, the proper response to a question about why you send a child to bed with these specific actions rather than some other ones is not the telling of a tale which takes place in a mythic time. The normal response would be, "If I don't put him to bed this way, he'll be noisy and keep getting up."

The analysis of ritual as the representation of myth fails to account for a large number of ordinary rituals. The analysis of ritual activities as performative utterance fails not by excluding our ordinary ritual activities but by wrongly focusing on a single aspect of these actions.

A performative utterance is a statement like, "I promise to do it," or "I herewith bequeath," or "I pronounce you man and wife." In any statement like these to utter the statement is to accomplish what the statement intends. Therefore, when a ritual is analyzed as a performative utterance, it is no longer possible to speak of the meaning of the ritual as separate from the performance. Now while it is certain that the account of ritual as merely representing myth goes too far in assuming that every ritual must be interpretable, the analysis of ritual as performative utterance seems to go too far in the opposite direction and assumes that ritual is completely independent of interpretation. More important is the fact that in many rituals no verbal formula is at all necessary. One could say a prayer as one genuflects, but it is hardly the verbalization which is the ritual. Similarly, one might say something when shaking hands but the handshake, surely a ritual behavior, is quite independent of any verbal accompaniment and is quite often done apart from any.

Since both of the prevalent views seem inadequate as analyses of all the various kinds of ritual behavior, I should like to propose in this paper an alternative analysis of ritual. This analysis will interpret ritual in terms of the special categories provided by the process philosophy of Whitehead.

To accomplish this analysis I shall first state what I feel are four crucial problems which any theory of ritual must answer; then I shall develop Whitehead's theory of propositions as a possible model for ritual. Finally I shall state how the analysis of ritual in Whiteheadian terms provides solutions to the problems stated in the first section.

There are four problems with which any model for ritual must deal. These are (1) the relations of the individual to the ritual, (2) the element of spontaneity in ritual, (3) the meaning of symbolism in ritual, and (4) the value of ritual for society.

To begin, let us state each of these problems briefly. The first problem for any philosophic analysis of ritual is that of the relation of the individual to the ritual. The relationship between the individual participating in the ritual and his function in the ritual being performed is very unusual. There are situations in which the individual plays a role but retains his identity quite apart from the role. Ignoring the problems raised by "method acting," an example of this kind of role-playing can be seen in play-acting or storytelling. In daily life the individual is involved in role-playing of quite a different kind. This role-playing is essential to the individuality of the person concerned, so essential that a person may be almost exhaustively defined in terms of the roles which he plays in relation to the others. Both of these kinds of role-playing, although quite distinct from each other, must be distinguished from the way in which an individual is related to his role in a ritual. Unlike in play-acting the person and the role do not remain distinct. There is a sense in which during performance of the ritual, the person is the role which he represents. But unlike with the role-playing of daily life, the person, although identifying in some sense with his ritual role while the ritual is being performed, does not define his identity in terms of what he represents in the ritual. It is sufficient for the security of the individual, at least in most cases, that the ritual be performed, regardless of the part he is to play.

The second problem for a philosophic analysis of ritual is the element of spontaneity in ritual. Although a ritual, by definition, involves the repetition of similar actions on various occasions, the actual performance of a ritual has a certain element of spontaneity. The ritual must take place at a certain time and with certain actions, but the manner in which the actions are done is not predetermined. *What* must be done is set but not *how* it is to be done. The style of each occasion of performing the ritual varies to a greater or lesser extent from the style of performance on any other occasion. The style in which a ritual is performed is not simply an aesthetic element in the ritual. It is, of course, quite possible to criticize the performance of a ritual from an aesthetic point of view. However, the criteria in that case are not intrinsically relevant to the ritual. To appreciate an action aesthetically is not to appreciate it ritually. But from within the framework of ritual itself there is an appreciation of balance and harmony, which is very close to aesthetic appreciation of these elements. The distinction appears to be that the appreciation of style from within the context of ritual subordinates and integrates the appreciation of harmony and balance for a nonaesthetic end, rather than appreciating them as ends in themselves.

In addition to the element of spontaneity provided by the varying styles in which a ritual may be performed there may be a second kind of spontaneity in any particular ritual. This second kind of spontaneity is due to the evolution of any particular ritual. As a general rule a ritual will begin by being in no very significant way different from the everyday action of the participants, but successive repetitions will tend to accumulate other actions which will become an intrinsic part of the ritual. This whole problem of growth, accretion, and decay needs to be accounted for in any analysis of ritual.

The third problem which the philosophic analysis of ritual must deal with is the relation of ritual to symbolism. One of the most important characteristics of ritual is that its meaning cannot be exhausted by a statement of significance. A ritual is not a symbol. It doesn't point to anything else. Even symbols which are not capable of discursive analysis share with discursive symbols (or signs) the characteristic of reciprocal interchangeability with their meanings. That is, while certain components of experience normally refer to other components, the latter can on occasion be taken to refer to the former. Nondiscursive symbols embody meaning as well as refer to their meaning. But, unlike a symbol, a ritual doesn't refer to something else and it is not at all clear in what sense it embodies any meaning. Many rituals can be given explanations, but the explanation has a different character from that which might be given of a symbol. But on the other hand, a ritual is meaningful even if it does not have a meaning which can be expressed discursively. A ritual is an important and a significant action. This is true not only in the sense that much of the richness of existence comes from the sense of belonging which participation in ritual gives, so that the ritual is a meaningful part of personal existence, but also in the sense that ritual is often the vehicle of intense emotion. The range of the degree of intensity of emotion which a ritual embodies does not seem to correlate with the degree of discursive meaning which can be given the ritual. The meaning of a goodnight kiss can be expressed almost exhaustively in discursive analysis, yet the intensity of emotion accompanying it is far less than that accompanying some patriotic rituals which are far less capable of discursive statement. It seems to be the case that since all rituals are accompanied by a feeling of rightness, that is, since it is felt that they are the right things to be done on a particular occasion, there is a further attempt to clarify this feeling by giving a discursive explanation of the ritual. However, for a particular pattern of behavior to qualify as ritual under the given definition it must be distinguishable from symbol in that the explanation which might be given must not exhaust the total meaning of the action. A philosophy of ritual must explain why rituals seem to embody meaning, the manner in which they embody meaning, and why any meaning embodied cannot be expressed exhaustively apart from the ritual itself.

The fourth problem which an analysis of ritual needs to investigate is that of the value of ritual for society. Assuming that society should develop in the direction of more and more freedom for the expression of the individual, there is at least an apparent conflict between ritual and freedom, since the essence of ritual is the repetition of action which has been done before. But ritual has too great a signficance for the individual to be eliminated in the quest for freedom of expression, and is also too important as a force for the cohesiveness of society to be eradicated. Clearly a model for talk about ritual must provide some clue to evaluating the respective claims of self-realization in ritual and self-realization in freedom. But ritual is also curiously ambiguous in its own value as a cohesive force in society, since ritual may become so burdensome that it tends to harm the society by demanding too much energy for its performance. Also the value of ritual for self-realization is not simply positive. For example, a gift-giving ritual may be used to express hostility or it might become a guilt-caused substitute for a more positive expression of affection. The model for discussing ritual, needs to provide for this ambiguity.

II

Whitehead's discussion of ritual appears to be affected strongly by his evaluation of ritual in religion, an evaluation which is conditioned by the limited appreciation and understanding of the phenomenon of ritual which was prevalent in the early part of this century. However, Whitehead's definition of ritual as "the habitual performance of definite actions which have no direct relevance to the preservation of the physical organisms of the actors" [3] would encompass everything which has been discussed in this paper under the heading of ritual. But rather than try to develop what

[3] *Religion in the Making* (New York, 1957), p. 20.

Whitehead would probably have said about ritual it will be more to the point to see whether ritual can be successfully analyzed by a creative use of Whitehead's categories, a use that was never in Whitehead's mind. The primary problem is to give a metaphysical account of the ontological status of ritual.

The fact that most of the problems in the analysis of ritual are concerned with its interaction with the individuals participating in it, coupled with the fact that a ritual does not exist apart from some reference to the real world, provides a clue to what phases in the Whiteheadian system might provide a model for interpreting ritual. These facts rule out any possibility of analyzing ritual as an actual entity since the individual participants in the ritual are high-grade societies and since a society is a set of actual entities.[4] It also would appear that a ritual is not an eternal object by virtue of the two facts cited above. The pattern which the ritual might be thought of as exemplifying is, however, an eternal object, and the rules for the production of a ritual might be interpreted as a complex eternal object. Another fact which would also seem to tell against any attempt to view a ritual itself as an eternal object is the intimate connection between the action of a ritual and its meaning. As has been seen in the discussion of the problems which a philosophic analysis of ritual must solve, any attempt to separate radically action and meaning is fatal to the understanding of ritual. There may be confusion in ordinary usage as to just what kind of existence a ritual has but it is quite clear that the ritual is a thing which is both act and meaning of the act. And another point: A ritual may be a puzzling kind of thing but at least this much is clear, a ritual is not the same thing as the set of rules for its performance.

Now, there is one category in the Whiteheadian system which has precisely the in-between status that a ritual seems to possess. It shares with ritual a particular kind of combination of thinghood and meaning. The category is that of a proposition. In the Whiteheadian system, a proposition is, "a hybrid between pure potentialities and actualities." [5] There are three phases of Whitehead's theory of propositions which must be developed before an attempt is made to analyze ritual in terms of the Whiteheadian system. These are (1) a proposition as the possibility of a pattern in the real world; (2) a proposition as a "lure for feeling;" and (3) the distinction between a proposition and a propositional feeling.

First – a proposition as the possibility of a pattern in the real world. To embody a Whiteheadian proposition a statement must involve an expression

[4] A. N. Whitehead, *Process and Reality* (New York, 1929), pp. 51, 34.

[5] *Ibid.*, p. 282.

of possibilities in the real world. The statement may be about the present, the past, or the future, as they are or as they might have been, or as they could become, but the statement must include references to some actual occasions. Such a statement is further limited by the fact that the actual entities to which it refers (the logical subjects) must exist in the actual world of the actual entity for which the statement is meaningful. In other words, we can make statements of possibilities only about conceivable worlds.

While a proposition is far more particular than pure possibility (an eternal object) it still retains a degree of generalization. In the background of every statement of hypothetical or real possibility seems to be a generalization to the effect that certain entities are of such and such a kind and that kind of thing has this among its possibilities. In Whitehead's own precise formulation,

> A proposition ... is a manner of germaneness of a certain set of eternal objects to a set of actual entities. Every proposition presupposes those actual entities which are its logical subjects. It also presupposes certain definite actual entities, or a certain type of actual entities within a wide systematic nexus.[6]

Second – a proposition as a lure for feeling. In a very striking phrase Whitehead speaks of "a proposition seeking truth." [7] Whitehead develops a theory of the functioning of propositions which includes more than their manipulation in logic. He shows that the logical judgment, true or false, is only a rare concomitant of a proposition. Instead of being primarily subjects of logical judgments, propositions are, for Whitehead, primarily "lures for feeling." "A proposition is an element in the objective lure *proposed for feeling,* and when admitted into feeling it constitutes *what is felt.*" [8] Whitehead supports his account by examples from poetic and devotional language. If it were not for propositions functioning as "lures for feeling" we would not be able to entertain the possibility of alternatives to the world as given. In a more general sense propositions are the occasion for novelty in the universe. The actual entities which are the data are taken and part of their given characteristics are eliminated. Then forms of realization, other than that which the given data had, are visualized: the given actual entities become the logical subjects of a proposition. In this way propositions "constitute a source for the origination of feeling which is not tied down to mere datum." [9]

Third – the distinction between a proposition and a propositional feeling.

[6] *Ibid.,* p. 286.
[7] *Ibid.,* p. 342.
[8] *Ibid.,* pp. 284-285.
[9] *Ibid.,* p. 284.

It is often easy in explaining Whitehead's theory of propositions to talk about a proposition and a propositional feeling in the same way, but for clarity in the analysis of ritual it will be important to keep in mind the distinction between them. A proposition is a hybrid ontological category. It is a kind of object in the real world. It cannot be identified with its predicative pattern which is a complex eternal object. The proposition has both its predicative pattern and its logical subjects. Similarly, a proposition cannot be identified with its embodiment in the actual entity which entertains it. The entertaining of a proposition is the propositional feeling, not the proposition. A proposition may be considered as "the potentiality of the objectification of certain presupposed actual entities via certain qualities and relations," [10] while the propositional feeling is the actualization of this potentiality.

In every proposition, as such and without going beyond it, there is complete indeterminateness so far as concerns its own realization in a propositional feeling, and as regards its own truth. The logical subjects are, nevertheless, in fact actual entities which are definite in their realized mutual relatedness. Thus the proposition is in fact true, or false. But its own truth, or its own falsity, is no business of a proposition. That question concerns only a subject entertaining a propositional feeling with that proposition for its datum.[11]

The proposition in its own nature gives no suggestion as to how it should be felt.[12]

III

Given this account of Whitehead's theory of proposition, it is possible to see how interpreting a ritual as a Whiteheadian proposition answers the problems raised in the first section of this paper. If a ritual is to be analyzed as a proposition, it would seem that it is the individual performances of the ritual which are the propositions. The predicative pattern of the proposition is the total pattern of ritual acts, what is to be said and what is to be done, common to all performances of a ritual. This identification answers the question of the problem of a ritual's ontological status. A ritual in the primary sense is the performance, but in a secondary sense the ritual is the pattern embodied in the performance.

If a ritual is interpreted as a Whiteheadian proposition, the answer to the first problem – the relationship between personal identity and ritual – is readily clarified by the general features of Whitehead's system. Personal

[10] *Ibid.*, p. 299.
[11] *Ibid.*, pp. 394-395.
[12] *Ibid.*, p. 402.

identity in Whitehead's version of process philosophy does not derive from an underlying substance. Rather, it is the result of strands of inherited features contained in a four-dimensional nexus. Instead of atomic selves faced with the task of maintaining identity while at the same time exchanging personal identity for a ritual role, there is, on the Whiteheadian analysis, the realization of a ritual proposition in a section of the spatio-temporal continuum which contains, among other things, a number of high-grade societies which are human persons. Just as each person can react to the ritual proposition by prehending the logical subjects while not prehending them as embodying the predicative pattern of the ritual, *i.e.*, being so caught up in the ritual performance that only it exists, so the subnexus involved in the personal identity of the ritual actor can react differently to the ritual in which he is engaged. Prehensions of the ritual proposition become additional strands in the inheritance of the society which is the person acting out the ritual. This inheritance is subjected to continuing re-evaluation by each succeeding actual entity in the regnant nexus of the actor. This evaluation is the continuing integration of the ritual with all the other strands of inheritance which comprise the person's past. The varying degrees of intensity of apprehension of the potentialities of a proposition by the members of a society account for wandering attention and differing levels of involvement in the ritual by the same person. They also account for the fact that different performances of the same ritual "mean" different things to the same person; a fact which is not logically explicable if ritual is analyzed as either represented myth or as performative utterance.

In the discussion of the problem of spontaneity in ritual in the first section of this paper, we saw that the repetitive character of ritual was always qualified by two different kinds of spontaneity. These two types were the spontaneity which causes stylistic variation of a ritual and that which results in the evolution of a ritual into a more and more complex occurrence. The interpretation of ritual as a "lure for feeling" provides an answer to the problem of the relationship between spontaneity and repetitiveness in ritual as well as showing the essential relationship between the two kinds of spontaneity which have been distinguished. The embodiment of the ritual proposition provides the greatest satisfaction possible to those actual entities capable of being logical subjects. Since the function of a proposition is to aid in the greatest integration of the presented world accompanied by the highest intensity of feeling possible, similar possible occasions for ritual will lead to similar performances. But in the creation of intensity of feeling questions of order and harmony are important since order and harmony are themselves "lures for feeling." Aesthetic factors are used to heighten the intensity of feeling in the ritual proposition. However, if the aesthetic factors in a situation are such that greater intensity of feeling can be realized by embodying an aesthetic proposition than could be realized by embodying a ritual proposition, there will be a conflict which can only be resolved by the subordination or elimination of one of the propositions. This accounts for the importance of style in the performance of a ritual and for the constant tendency of ritual to become aesthetic performance instead of ritual performance.

The same wish that it intensify the "lure" that ritual provides is operative in the development of accretions to a ritual. Greater intensity of satisfaction is achieved by integrating a greater number of things, *i.e.*, by discovering a more complex proposition. So the more a ritual can integrate all of its surrounding events and things into its own performance, the greater the intensity of feeling which will be embodied in its performance. Unfortunately, the larger the number of actual entities necessary as logical subjects of a proposition, the more infrequent the occasions of its relevance. For this reason, some rituals become so developed that they become irrelevant, and if they cannot be simplified their performance lapses. It also may happen that some of the kinds of actual entities which are necessary subjects of the proposition cease to exist, and so the ritual proposition no longer can be germane. In either case, the ongoingness of the world demands some other proposition, one whose logical subjects occur, or at least occur more frequently.

In the statement of the third problem, *i.e.*, that of the relationship between ritual and symbolism, attention was drawn to the fact that sometimes we think of a ritual as having meaning, while at other times it seems that a ritual *is* its meaning. This ambiguity accounts for the partial success of interpreting a ritual as either a myth or a performative utterance. To the extent that a ritual symbolizes meaning it seems to be representing myth; while to the extent that the ritual is what it symbolizes it seems to be its own accomplishment. However, the Whiteheadian distinction between a proposition and a propositional feeling clarifies the relationship of ritual and meaning in terms of a unified account. Since it is a proposition, a ritual is a "lure for feeling." As such, its realization in a particular set of logical subjects is the most meaningful analysis of that particular set of logical subjects. In this sense then a ritual is its own meaning. However, the kind of feeling which a particular ritual proposition attracts is not the same as the proposition. This propositional feeling may be identical with the feeling generated by some other, nonritual proposition. This nonritual proposition may even share the same set of logical subjects with the ritual proposition.

In that case entertainment of either proposition will be quite similar and, to the degree that the two propositions are similar, in feeling as well as in logical subjects, the propositions may become symbols for each other. In this sense the ritual proposition can be said to have as its meaning the other proposition. When an explanation of a ritual which is felt to be satisfactory is given, what happens is that the "lures for feeling" given in the explanation are substantially similar to the "lure" of the ritual itself.

By now it should be quite evident that the ambiguous feelings about the value of ritual are well founded. Propositions are "lures for feeling" but the value of these lures in the total context of a culture cannot be determined *a priori*. The ongoingness of a culture depends upon a delicate balance of enduring elements which provide it with stability and novel elements which prevent stagnation. A ritual proposition has a twofold function. The proposition provides continuity since each performance involves reference to all its other instantiations. It also provides novelty since the performance requires that familiar objects be viewed under an unfamiliar, a ritual aspect. Under neither aspect, however, is the value of the proposition predetermined, for either the continuity or the novelty may be too extreme. But although the value of all rituals cannot be guaranteed, it is the case that any particular ritual must be valued positively to the extent that it is meaningful for its participants, *i.e.*, to the extent that it is a "lure for feeling" for the creative advance of the universe.

EXPLANATION AND LANGUAGE

BERKELEY AND RELIGIOUS LANGUAGE

by

JOHN A. MOURANT

Contemporary philosophy has recently shown an increasing interest in the problems of religious philosophy especially where such problems lend themselves to linguistic analysis. More often than not the consequence of such analysis has been a scepticism concerning the meaningfulness of religious language. Many philosophers regard theology as nonsense; religious belief is held to be unwarranted on any reasonable grounds. In his own time Berkeley contended against similar attitudes and attacks upon religious belief and religious language. For Berkeley the two great threats to Christianity and to religious belief in general were Materialism and Deism. These are historical issues of considerable interest but any concern we have with them will be only peripheral in character. My primary purpose will be to show that in his defense of religion Berkeley developed certain concepts of religious language that enabled him to establish the meaningfulness and the reasonableness of Christian belief. In contrast, then, to much of the contemporary effort, he provided for a justification of religious language and religious belief. More specifically, he contended that religious language, whether natural or theological, is both meaningful and true. (In the development of this thesis we have no intention of relating Berkeley's linguistic analysis to that of contemporary philosophy, nor shall we attempt to read the past in terms of the present. However, to a limited extent and wherever warranted we shall indicate Berkeley's anticipation of contemporary thought on the nature and function of language,[1] but avoid the contemporary controversies.) We shall endeavor to show that Berkeley's approach to the problem of religious language is essentially twofold and basically pragmatic rather than metaphysical. Religious language, he held, is exemplified in a natural language – the divine visual language – or in theological language which is extended to include the language of Scripture.

[1] It may be pointed out that Berkeley anticipated some developments in contemporary philosophy in such areas as sense data, causality, and scientific language.

Each of these concepts of language is pragmatic for they motivate our conduct, give us moral guidance, and conduce to our general welfare. The language of nature is both referential and pragmatic, that of theology is primarily pragmatic.

Before we consider in any detail these two basic approaches to religious language, it is necessary to note more precisely just what Berkeley means by language in general. In the *Theory of Vision Vindicated* he says: "A great number of arbitrary signs, various and apposite, do constitute a language. If such arbitrary connexion be instituted by men, it is an artificial language; if by the Author of nature, it is a natural language." [2]

The language of nature is essentially visual as he observes in the *Alciphron*:

> It is the articulation, combination, variety, copiousness, extensive and general use and easy application of signs (all of which are commonly found in vision) that constitute the true nature of language. Other senses may indeed furnish signs; and yet those signs have no more right than inarticulate sounds to be thought a language.[3]

The language of theology is primarily an artificial language created arbitrarily by man. However, with reference to Scripture such language would be considered by Berkeley as inspired by God.

The distinction between natural and artificial languages need not be taken too sharply. For although a natural language is considered to consist of signs reflecting God's immanence and omnipresence in the world it still must be articulated and created by man and in this respect may be regarded as artificial. Similarly the language of Scripture may be regarded as the Word of God but finds an inspired expression in the artificial language created by man. These distinctions will become more apparent when we consider in detail each of these types of religious language. Before doing so, however, some comments are necessary on what Berkeley considers to be the functions of language. One of his earliest and most explicit statements occurs in the introduction to the *Principles*:

> Besides, the communicating of ideas marked by words is not the chief and only end of language, as is commonly supposed. There are other ends, as the raising of some passion, the exciting to, or deterring from an action, the putting the mind in some particular disposition.... I entreat the reader to reflect within himself, and see if it doth not often happen either in hearing or reading a discourse, that the passions of fear, love, hatred, admiration, disdain, and the like

[2] *Works*, vol. I, p. 265. All references to Berkeley's works will be from the edition of A. A. Luce and T. E. Jessop.

[3] *Works*, vol. III, p. 157.

arise, immediately in his mind upon the perception of certain words without any ideas coming between them. . . .[4]

Putting Berkeley's views into contemporary terminology, it could be said that he looked upon language as cognitive, informative, emotive, pragmatic, and behavioristic. Speaking of the language of nature he will argue that not only does it provide us with scientific knowledge but it may "exalt the mind with a prospect of the beauty, order, and variety of natural things." [5] Or it may fulfill a pragmatic purpose "where we are instructed how to regulate our actions, in order to attain those things that are necessary to the preservation and well being of our bodies, as also to avoid whatever may be hurtful and destructive of them." [6] Similar functions as we shall see can also be shown for theological language.

Before raising any serious questions concerning Berkeley's account of the nature and functions of language, it is necessary to examine in greater depth the general features of the two forms of religious language: the language of nature or the Divine Visual Language, and theological language including the language of Scripture. Berkeley is also concerned with the language of science and mathematics in which he makes some noteworthy contributions, but these and other exemplifications of language are overshadowed by his more overriding concern with religious language in the two forms that it takes in his writings. Since he develops first the conception of nature as the language of God, we shall give it priority in our treatment.

The conception that nature somehow reveals the operations of the divine mind and will is not a novel contribution.[7] But the form that it takes in Berkeley's philosophy was clearly novel if not revolutionary and exemplifying his idealism it was one which astonished and dismayed his contemporaries. For Berkeley nature was not a congeries of material particles nor a complex of causally related physical forces. The context of nature was spiritual, known as a system of ideas which constituted the language of God and formed the means whereby He communicates with us, instructs us, and provides for our well-being. This language of nature is not easily read, but it is the true function of the philosopher to search after and to read the visible signs, the universal language instituted by the Author of Nature.[8] Such a divine visual language can be perceived by all but cannot be interpreted and understood by all. Just as an individual may see a word but

[4] *Works*, vol. II, p. 37.

[5] *Ibid.*, p. 89.

[6] *Works*, vol. I, p. 231.

[7] The Augustinian tradition always regarded nature as consisting of the "vestiges of God."

[8] *Works*, vol. II, pp. 69 70.

not comprehend its meaning, so he may also perceive the visible signs of the language of nature and yet fail to comprehend that language or even to acknowledge its author. Such a language, Berkeley tells us later in the *Siris*, forms "a sort of rational discourse and is studied with different attention, and interpreted with different degrees of skill." [9] Its immediacy and its referential character exclude any need for abstract ideas, which are wholly artificial, meaningless, completely without warrant, and conducive to error and confusion.

Although this language of nature is distinguished from the artificial language that man creates,[10] there are certain common aspects between the two languages. Fundamentally both are arbitrary in the sense that they are freely created by their authors. Each language possesses a certain order and uniformity, a syntactical character. And just as we may create new words for our language, so God is constantly creating new signs for us to read in the language of nature. For Berkeley the proper understanding of the language of nature avoids the notion of necessary connections because all that this language yields to our perception is order and uniformity. Just as there are no causes in nature, so there are no causes in language.[11]

The primary function of this divine visual language is informative. Obviously whatever we know of nature as a result of our scientific investigations constitutes a fulfillment of this function of language. But in addition to reading nature in this way, Berkeley is often concerned with the need to "read into" nature, that is in affirming that the divine visual language informs us and instructs us in the values conferred upon us by the divine Creator. As he puts it in the *Principles*:

> We should propose to ourselves nobler views, such as to re-create and exalt the mind with a prospect of the beauty, order, extent and variety of natural things: hence by proper inferences, to enlarge our notions of the grandeur, wisdom, and beneficence of the Creator: and lastly to make the several parts of the Creation so far as in us lies, subservient to the ends they were designed for, God's glory, and the sustentation and comfort of our selves and fellow-creatures.[12]

[9] *Works*, vol. V, p. 254.

[10] Obviously man creates the terminology which is applied to the particular ideas perceived in nature and which are designated by Berkeley as the divine natural language.

[11] For Berkeley all causal activity is limited to the activity of spirits. Hence, just as man may be said to cause a language so God causes or creates the visual language of nature, but the parts of each language have no causal or necessary relation with the other parts. Individuals may create different or new languages, and so God too is free to create different divine language.

[12] *Works*, vol. II, p. 109.

Thus the language of nature is not only a language of knowledge but also one of purpose. Berkeley shared the enthusiasm of many of the divines of the times for the teleological character of nature and a reliance on the teleological argument for God's existence. He felt strongly that in making nature a language of God and visual so that all might perceive it, he was not only making nature more meaningful but he was bringing God that much closer to man and making the evidences of God so much the more convincing to man. Like Alciphron he found the "thought of anarchy in nature" shocking and was convinced that the very uniformity and order of the divine visual language might perhaps provide a more positive verification for God's existence.

Berkeley believed that his conception of a divine visual language was preferable to the metaphysical hypothesis of Malebranche that we see all things in God or to any mechanistic hypothesis with implications of materialism and a *deus ex machina*. He feels that his own hypothesis best meets the requirements of his own empirical outlook as well as the requirements of Christian belief. For, as he points out in the *Alciphron*:

> But this Visual Language proves, not a Creator merely, but a provident Governor, actually and intimately present, and attentive to all our interests and motions, who watches over our conduct, and takes care of our minutest actions and designs throughout the whole course of our lives, informing, admonishing, and directing incessantly, in a most evident and sensible manner. This is truly wonderful.[13]

Berkeley's argument that this visual language "proves" a Creator and provident Governor actually relies more upon his own religious convictions and upon a rather radical form of empiricism. In his empirical approach he believes that not only does this language reveal to the beholder the wonders and order of nature betokening the presence of a deity, but that such a language is instructive and easily learned, for it provides "a more distinct knowledge of things than could be got by a discourse of several hours." [14]

Also this conception of nature as a divine language in which all things are merely signs by means of which God communicates to us not only brings God more immanently into the world but strengthens the empirical basis of Berkeley's position through the avoidance of all secondary causes and any apparent need of metaphysical hypotheses. Just as we perceive immediately the ideas without the interposition of any hypothesis of material objects, so we perceive immediately our ideas as signs in a divine language which does not require the interposition of secondary causes. This radically

[13] *Works*, vol. III, p. 160.
[14] *Idem*.

empirical stance of Berkeley also explains his rejection of any form of an ontological argument or of an argument for God's existence based upon the "absurdity of an infinite progression of causes." To Berkeley the most manifest way of establishing God's existence is the teleological, for it is based upon the evidence that the world about us is wondrous, instructive, and providential. This concern to establish the empirical character of our belief in God's existence is also evident in the *Principles* when he argues that:

> ... it is evident that God is known as certainly and immediately as any other mind or spirit whatsoever, distinct from ourselves. We may even assert that the existence of God is far more evidently perceived than the existence of men; because the effects of nature are infinitely more numerous and considerable than those ascribed to human agents.[15]

But all we perceive are ideas and to establish God as the author of these ideas and the creator of a divine visual language, requires an inference. There is no perceptual verification of the existence or nature of God. The divine language is still not God but merely a means by which God communicates to us. To identify the language of nature with God would entail a pantheism and the rejection of the Christian conception of God as a creator. This Berkeley cannot do. Furthermore, the experience of the language of God whether we see His word in nature or hear His word in Scripture, is still not the same as the actual experience of God Himself. A more complete empiricism that might have yielded an experiential verification of God's existence could have been found in some form of mysticism. A nature mysticism would have led Berkeley to some form of pantheism which he had to avoid. And the more traditional form of a Christian mysticism in which God is experienced in the personal life of the individual is not evident in Berkeley's writings. He is neither a mystic nor an ascetic. He not only shared Locke's distrust of the enthusiasts of the time, but his own religious development led him to the adoption of an attitude of moderation on religious issues. He consistently sought a *via media* between dissent and Rome. Undeniably there is a seeming tendency toward a mysticism of nature in his writing, but at best it is no more than a deep religious conviction that in nature we may see clearly the evidence of God in his divine language. Such an awareness of God does not, however, entail any personal unity with God which would be required for a Christian mystical experience. The conviction, however, that God reveals Himself in nature is evident also in Berkeley's treatment of miracles. Like Augustine he sees all nature as a miracle; he observes that it is the very frequency of the wondrous events

[15] *Works*, vol. II, p. 108.

in nature that leads us to overlook their miraculous character. He would be quite in accord with the remarks of Augustine:

> God's daily miracles were disesteemed, not for their easiness but their constant repetition.... Men wondered that our Lord God Jesus Christ filled so many thousands with five loaves; and yet they do not wonder that through a few grains the whole earth is filled with crops. When the water was made wine, men saw it and were amazed; what else takes place with the rain along the root of the vine? He did the one, He does the other; the one that thou mayest be fed, the other that thou mayest wonder....[16]

Yet no matter how impressive the wonders of nature may be, the identification of the language of nature with God lacks the experiential certitude of the more traditional forms of mysticism. To "see" God in nature or to discern nature itself as a constant miracle is not a direct perception of God but involves an inference, an intellectual "seeing" of God as the Author of Nature. His assertions to the contrary, therefore, Berkeley's empiricism and the claim of the immanence of God's presence in nature must be supplemented with a move toward rationalism. The logical demand made upon Berkeley's empiricism is well put by Alciphron when he states:

> ... surely, if there be such a thing as God, it is very strange that He should leave Himself without a witness; that men should still dispute His being; and that there should be no one evident, sensible plain proof of it, without recourse to philosophy or metaphysics. A matter of fact is not to be proved by notions, but by facts.[17]

Now Berkeley is well aware that he cannot meet this extreme requirement of Alciphron. He cannot establish God as a matter of fact. We cannot, Berkeley would contend, see the King of Kings as we might see the king of Great Britain. For only two kinds of knowledge can be apprehended as "matters of fact": the knowledge we have of ideas and the immediate awareness we have of the existence of the self, the former a passive and the latter an active reality. Even the existence of other minds or persons is not immediately perceived but requires an inference even though the inference be immediate. Berkeley feels that we are convinced beyond question of the existence of other minds, so much so that our certitude here is virtually equivalent to that of perception. Yet "A human spirit or person is not perceived by sense, as not being an idea; when therefore we see the color, size, figure, and motions of a man, we perceive only certain sensations or ideas excited in our own minds." [18] What is true here of the knowledge we

[16] Sermon 126.
[17] *Works*, vol. III, p. 144.
[18] *Works*, vol. II, p. 109.

have of another person is equally true of our knowledge of God. But if, Berkeley urges, we are certain of another person's existence, we should be even more certain of the existence of God. For just as certain ideas may be considered as signs manifesting the existence of other persons,

> ... so in the self-same manner, it seems to me that, though I cannot with the eyes of the flesh behold the invisible God, yet I do in the strictest sense behold and perceive by all my senses such signs and tokens, ... as suggest, indicate, and demonstrate an invisible God, as certainly, and with the same evidence, at least, as any other signs perceived by sense do suggest to me the existence of your soul, spirit, or thinking principle; which I am convinced of only by a few signs or effects, and the motions of one small organized body: whereas I do at all times and in all places perceive sensible signs which evince the being of God.[19]

Berkeley's argument is analogical and based upon the similarity between the language of nature whereby God is revealed to me and the language or the signs by which the mind of another person is revealed. His contention is that the language of nature is far more extensive and universal than the language of another person and that it can be read by all because nature with its innumerable signs is simply there for all to behold. Hence his conclusion that the language of nature testifies more obviously and strongly to its author than the language of another person enables me to infer the existence of the mind of that person. Now although this type of analogy has been generally recognized as the only way in which the existence of other minds may be established, it remains questionable whether this type of analogical inference renders God's existence as more certain than the existence of the mind of another person, as Berkeley contends. It might be urged against Berkeley's position that the signs by which I infer the existence of another person, either in his bodily or spiritual nature, are far more familiar to me than the signs, innumerable as they are, by which I infer the existence of a deity. Hence the strength of our conclusion would seem to depend more upon the nature of the language we read and not simply its extensiveness and abundance. The fact is that I can communicate with another but I can only commune with nature. Certainly an appeal to the experience of an individual would yield little doubt for another's existence as compared to the existence of God.

However this may be, the certitude Berkeley claims for his conclusion is not the certitude of the existence of ideas, for, as he always insists, God is not an idea and therefore can never be perceived. Actually the certitude Berkeley has of God's existence would appear to be more of a religious

[19] *Works*, vol. III, p. 147.

certitude based upon faith. Such certitude is brought to bear upon the reasoning here and leads him to the conviction that "nothing can be more evident to anyone that is capable of the least reflexion, than the existence of God, or a spirit who is intimately present to our minds,... *in whom we live, and move, and have our being.*" [20] However, unless this religious conviction is shared by others it is difficult to see how Berkeley's argument that nothing is so evident as the existence of God can be effectively persuasive.

The divine visual language has another appeal for Berkeley. He believes that the objectivity and universality of such a language obviates the need to resort to subjective criteria or some kind of misplaced religious enthusiasm. A statement by Alciphron may be said to reflect Berkeley's position:

> I am for admitting no inward speech, no holy instincts or suggestions of light or spirit. All that, you must know, passeth with men of sense for nothing. If you do not make it plain to me that God speaks to men by outward signs, of such and in such manner as I have defined, you do nothing.[21]

At best, however, Berkeley's empirically based arguments for God's existence fail to approximate the stipulation of Alciphron that God has to be shown to be a "matter of fact." Regardless of the emphasis placed upon the abundance of the signs of nature and their objectivity, the claim that such a language more evidently demonstrates the existence of God than the existence of other persons simply does not hold. The attempt to extend the empirical basis of the argument fails to overcome the need for certain very necessary and explicit inferences. God's existence cannot be accounted for by intuition or perception.

Finally, it may be asked to what extent can the language of nature convey to us any knowledge of the nature of God. That it does not prove his existence we have already maintained. But Berkeley constantly speaks of God as a provident Governor, concerned with our needs, and directing the ends of nature. He takes many of his descriptions of God from Scripture. His religious beliefs, in effect, are read into his interpretation of the divine visual language.[22] From a purely philosophical point of view it would also have been possible for Berkeley to say something of the nature of God. A doctrine like the *analogia entis* could have afforded Berkeley a limited description of the divine attributes. However, in order to effect this it would have been necessary for Berkeley to provide a metaphysics of being. And this he was

[20] *Works,* vol. II, p. 109.
[21] *Works,* vol. III, p. 149.
[22] The existence of evil in nature is recognized by Berkeley but is explained in accordance with the Christian tradition.

unwilling to do. Perhaps because in his later writings he experienced some difficulty with the doctrine of archetypes. Or perhaps because the requirements of his empirical epistemology would have made this a questionable venture at best. At any rate in his historical review of the doctrine of analogy in the *Alciphron* he seems willing to accept it in principle but does not actually embrace it or utilize it. He declares that it is "much misunderstood and misapplied by those who would infer from thence that we cannot frame any direct or proper notion, though never so inadequate of knowledge or wisdom as they are in the Deity; . . ." [23] I believe his hesitancy to accept a doctrine of analogy was also motivated by his conviction of the necessary immanence of God in the universe and the feeling that a doctrine of analogy might tend to minimize this immanence of God. Furthermore, Berkeley emphatically rejected abstract ideas and the "metaphysical jargon" that he was convinced would follow from their use. Again, he emphasized that ideas are passive whereas God is wholly active and thus there could be no proper analogy between the being of nature which was to be perceived, and the being of God. The problem is further complicated by the fact that other persons are merely ideas for me (although they may be active in their own right) and any analogy based upon active beings would have to be related solely to the being of one person and that of God.

It is time now to consider that second form of religious language: the language of theology in which we include the language of Scripture and such terminology as men have created that is relevant to their religious beliefs. At the outset we must not look to Berkeley's doctrine for any oversimplification of the kind of religious language described by some contemporary philosophers and theologians. Berkeley will not contend that religious language is wholly and essentially ethical, emotive, convictional, existential, obediential, etc., etc. What he says on theological language still falls within the confines that he already laid down in the introduction to the *Principles* concerning the functions of language and to which we have already alluded. The more distinctly original element in Berkeley's treatment of this kind of language is his concern to avoid religious disputations and to show that such language is or should be essentially pragmatic, functioning to motivate our conduct. Like metaphysical disputations, religious disputations are due fundamentally, Berkeley believed, to the employment of abstract ideas. His opposition to the use of such ideas is well known; he believed that they have caused only confusion and obfuscation for man, whether such ideas are found in religious language or in scientific language. Hence, the language of abstract ideas is to be avoided for it is deceptive.

[23] *Works*, vol. III, p. 170.

His particular concern, he says, is "to remove the mist or veils of words. This has occasion'd Ignorance and confusion. This has ruin'd the Schoolmen and Mathematicians, Lawyers and Divines." [24] And his essentially nominalistic and empirical position is revealed in the following remark: "I approve of this axiom of the Schoolmen, *nihil est in intellectu quod non prius fuit in sensu*. I wish they had stuck to it. It had never taught them the Doctrine of Abstract Ideas." [25]

Another motive for Berkeley's rejection of abstract ideas was the support they gave to materialism. In his eyes the greatest offender among abstract ideas was that of "matter;" although he also rejected the abstract ideas of "place," "time," "extension," "motion," "goodness," "virtue," "justice," etc.[26] Most metaphysical and religious disputes he was convinced could be removed once language was rid of abstract ideas.

Consistently Berkeley extends his rejection of abstract ideas equally to religion, materialism, metaphysics, and science. It was this that led him to develop a radically different theory of linguistic meaning for both religious language and scientific language. With respect to religious language, his position is projected upon certain contentions put forward by Alciphron who declares that religious words, such as "grace" and "faith," have no meaning because words are signs and have no meaning unless they refer to distinct ideas. As Berkeley puts it in the *De Motu*: "But to employ a term, and conceive nothing by it is quite unworthy of a philosopher." [27] Pursuing his attack Alciphron declares that the idea of force is clear and distinct, but the idea of a spiritual power of force like that of grace is not. "For, though the idea of corporeal force," he says, "be ever so clear and intelligible, it will not therefore follow that the idea of grace, a thing perfectly incorporeal, must be so too." [28] Alciphron contends that there is no referent, no clear idea for the word "grace" or others like it in religious language. And he concludes that this can only lead to the rejection of religious belief. "For there can be no assent where there are no ideas: and where there is no assent there can be no faith: and what cannot be, that no man is obliged to. This is as clear as anything in Euclid." [29]

Berkeley answers that by the same reasoning there can be no true assent to certain abstract ideas held by science. The term "force," for example, has no privileged position and analysis would reveal it to be as unclear and

[24] *Works,* vol. I, 642A, p. 78.
[25] *Ibid.,* p. 94.
[26] *Works,* vol. II, pp. 83-86.
[27] *Works,* vol. IV, p. 38.
[28] *Works,* vol. III, p. 290.
[29] *Idem.*

indistinct as the term "grace." Experience reveals no ideas corresponding to such names, we perceive neither "grace" nor "force." Also, ideas are essentially passive by nature and therefore the ideas of either physical force or spiritual power must be rejected because only spirits are active and possess causal power. To hold that God is an idea would be contradictory to his nature, for God is both a spiritual and an active being. So there must be another explanation, another theory of meaning, that can be applied to such religious terms as "grace" and "faith" and to such scientific terms as "force" and "gravity."

That words as signs may have another function than that of referring to distinct ideas is developed in some detail by Berkeley in the seventh dialogue of the *Alciphron*. Speaking through Euphranor Berkeley begins his analysis of the meaning of religious terms with the observation:

> Counters, for instance, at a card-table are used, not for their own sake but only as signs substituted to money as words are for ideas. Say, now Alciphron, is it necessary every time these counters are used throughout the progress of a game, to frame an idea of the distinct sum or value that each represents? [30]

This question leads Berkeley to the following conclusion:

> ... there may be another use of words besides that of marking and suggesting distinct ideas, to wit, the influencing our conduct and actions which may be done either by forming rules for us to act by, or by raising certain passions, dispositions, and emotions in our minds.[31]

Continuing along this line, Berkeley contends with consistency that certain scientific words like religious words are equally meaningless if they have no reference to particular ideas. Scientific language is just as likely to lead to meaningless nonsense as is religious language. As Popper observes,

> Berkeley's razor allows us *a priori* to eliminate from physical science all essentialistic explanations. If they have a mathematical and predictive content they may be admitted *qua* mathematical hypotheses.... If not, they may be ruled out altogether. This razor is sharper than Ockham's: *all* entities are ruled out except those which are perceived.[32]

Berkeley observes that it is equally difficult to form the idea of force as it is that of grace:

> That which we admit with regard to force, upon what pretence can we deny concerning grace? Ought we not by a parity of reason to conclude that there may be diverse true and useful propositions concerning the one as well as the

[30] *Ibid.*, p. 291.
[31] *Ibid.*, p. 292.
[32] Karl R. Popper, *Conjectures and Refutations* (London, 1963), p. 167.

other? And that grace may be an object of our faith and influence our life and acts ... although we cannot obtain a distinct idea of it, separate or abstracted for God the author, from man the subject, and from virtue and piety its effects? [33]

Just as the word "grace" may fulfill that function of language which Berkeley described in the *Principles* as "the raising of some passion, the exciting to, or deterring from an action, the putting the mind in some particular disposition," [34] so with other religious words, such as, "faith," "original sin," "Incarnation," and "Trinity." [35] Berkeley's comments on these religious words are worth noting. On the Trinity, he says

it seems to follow that a man may believe the doctrine of the Trinity, ... although he does not frame in his mind any abstract or distinct idea of trinity, substance, or personality; provided that this doctrine ... makes a proper impression on his mind, ... and becomes a lifely operative principle, influencing his life and actions, ...[36]

On faith he observes: "Faith is not an indolent perception, but an operative persuasion of mind, which ever worketh some suitable action, disposition or emotion in those who have it." [37]

Concerning the mystery of the Incarnation he questions why Christians should not believe in this doctrine when others cannot even explain the nature of personal identity in man.

On original sin he states:

man may find it impossible to form an idea of (it) in abstract, or the manner of its transmission; and yet the belief therefore may produce in his mind a salutary sense of his own unworthiness, and the goodness of His Redeemer: from whence may follow good habits, and from them good actions, the genuine effects of faith; ...[38]

The words comprising the language of theology have no causal power. As physical signs they are no more active than other ideas, for all active power is the sole prerogative of spirits. However, such words may suggest certain active principles, they may engender certain beliefs which in turn influence our behavior. Perhaps they may be regarded as occasions for God's actions

[33] *Works,* vol. III, p. 296.
[34] *Works,* vol. II, p. 37.
[35] Note how carefully Berkeley seems to have chosen certain key words in the language of Christianity. Each is not only highly significant for Christian faith but also each has led to more disputations among Christians than have any other words.
[36] *Works,* vol. III, p. 297.
[37] *Ibid.,* p. 301.
[38] *Idem.*

upon us, especially in the instances of "grace" and "faith."[39] Their meaningfulness lies in their pragmatic value, their utility, and in their motivation of our behavior. Placed as they are within the context of our dispositions and responses it might be contended that Berkeley in a way is anticipating a behavioristic theory of meaning.

To give added credence to his interpretation of theological language, Berkeley contends that what is true of a theological term like "grace" may also be said to be true of a comparable scientific term such as "force" and its equivalents, *i.e.*, "gravity," "reaction," "*vis inertia*," "impetus," "momentum," etc.[40] Terms like these do not designate distinct ideas, but they have utility and may lead to the development of scientific knowledge. But used in the abstract they have no meaning. As Berkeley says,

> Force, gravity, attraction, and terms of this sort are useful for reasonings and reckonings about motion and bodies in motion, but not for understanding the simple nature of motion itself or for indicating so many distinct qualities.[41]

They are occult qualities, the "mere shadows of scholastic things," and have no empirical meaning apart from their usefulness in explaining the world about us. As has been pointed out, Berkeley's attack on much of this scientific terminology and essentialistic explanations in science, represents an anticipation of Mach's criticism of the traditional principles of mechanics.[42]

In sum, then, Berkeley is telling us that there are some words which stand for ideas and are subject to verification in our experience. But there are other words, such as "force" and "grace" which have no descriptive function and no referential meaning. Words like these are meaningless and represent occult qualities or abstract ideas. Where such words are found in science they have meaning only in the pragmatic or instrumentalist sense. Their value is in their use as convenient symbolic summaries of that which we observe in nature. They may be said to be theoretical constructions of the world of physics and their real meaning lies in their practical value and the contribution they make to the progress of scientific knowledge. On the other hand, theological words like "grace" derive their meaning from another type of practical value – their effectiveness in influencing our moral behavior, thus contributing to our happiness. This type of theological lan-

[39] Precisely how such language operates upon us Berkeley does not explain. Perhaps we have here a kind of "linguistic occasionalism" in which the words of our religious language become the occasions for the causal activity of God.

[40] *Works*, vol. IV, p. 35.

[41] *Ibid.*, p. 33.

[42] Popper, *op. cit.*, p. 173.

guage is neither descriptive nor cognitive and its attempted use in this manner can lead only to religious disputations which have no value and little meaning. On the whole Berkeley pleads for a simple theology. He notes with approval the statement of St. Jerome: "Why after so many centuries do you pretend to teach us what was untaught before? Why explain what neither Peter nor Paul thought necessary to be explained?" [43] Thus Berkeley is convinced that religious disputations alienate the mind from the more practical value that religious beliefs should have. At best religious controversy has the negative function of excluding unwanted doctrines from Christianity. Berkeley here refers to the old debate of *homoousians* and *homoiousians,* and he contends that the mystery surrounding the Incarnation cannot be resolved dialectically. But through the controversy it engendered it did have the practical value of excluding polytheism and Sabellianism from Christianity.

Berkeley is really more the philosopher than the theologian as his writings and his analysis of language reveal. Such analysis not only possesses the functions already noted but in so far as it helps us to avoid confusion and error it leads to the clarification of our ideas and the attainment of truth. In this respect it may be said to possess also an argumentative or dialectical function. Such a function ought not to characterize theological language as Berkeley conceives it because it would lead only to religious controversy and divisiveness. Furthermore, religious truth has already been revealed to man in Scripture and stands in no need of dialectical demonstration.

Actually Berkeley was far more concerned with the menace of Deism and Materialism to Christianity than with the development of any systematic theology. To combat such enemies of Christianity he resorted to philosophical argumentation and the construction of a limited philosophical system. His philosophical defense of Christianity against Deism, which is the principal burden of the *Alciphron,* is not to explain Christian beliefs but to exhibit their reasonable character and the unreasonableness of those who attack Christianity.

In contrast to his analysis of certain theological terms Berkeley has very little to say concerning the functions of Scriptural language. However, by extrapolating certain observations and conclusions he has already made, it can be stated that most of the functions of language already noted can be applied to Scripture. Thus it is obvious that the language of the Psalmist as well as many other portions of Scripture is definitely expressive. Again much of Scripture is descriptive and informative, especially where it is

[43] *Works,* vol. III, p. 301.

concerned with the historical background and development of the truths of Judaism and Christianity. The ethical or pragmatic functions of language are very evident in the teachings and exhortations of the prophets and of Jesus. Berkeley does not develop any of these functions of language relative to Scripture, probably because he accepted Scripture as both meaningful and true. His sermons seem designed more to explain the ethical and practical values of the message of Scripture and to avoid religious disputation. It was said of his preaching that even the Quakers came to hear him knowing that the lessons of his sermons would be free of any intolerance born out of doctrinal disputation. Religion, our good Hanoverian Tory felt, must come from the heart; it "warms the affections and engages the will." For the challenge of theological issues, Berkeley was well content to substitute the care and administration of his diocese, to win the hearts of his parishioners, to experiment with tar water, and to indulge in philosophical discourse. Religious belief he was convinced would be far better served by the reading of the divine language whether that be in nature or in Scripture. Philosophically he was concerned that man might "see God and not merely hear His Word."

EMMANUEL LEVINAS' PHILOSOPHY OF LANGUAGE

by

HAROLD A. DURFEE

The renowned French philosopher Jean-Paul Sartre indicates that he came to phenomenology through Emmanuel Levinas.[1] In spite of such a distinguished recommendation, Levinas' thought has been little known, and his intriguing philosophy of language offers a major entrée to his position.[2] Language plays the central role in his philosophy, and in view of its centrality, as well, in a variety of contemporary philosophical traditions, it seems appropriate to concentrate on this aspect of his thought. Furthermore, analytic philosophy has concerned itself so intently with philosophy of language, and has been so separated from continental phenomenology, that to discover philosophy of language as a central factor in the position of a phenomenologist may serve to form a bridge, or at least enhance the dialogue, between analytic thought and phenomenological philosophy.[3]

Levinas has great independence of mind and thus his philosophy of language is a highly original contribution, serving also as the foundation for a new metaphysical position, a theory of epistemology and meaning, the basis for a creative ethics, the initiation of a philosophy of religion, and, strangely enough, a philosophy of war and peace. From within the phenomenological movement, his philosophy of language offers a major historical critique of classical philosophical positions. Furthermore, as a student of both Husserl and Heidegger, he clearly distinguishes himself from both of them, as well as from other significant phenomenologists. He offers an anti-

[1] Jean-Paul Sartre, *Situations* (London, 1965), p. 230. See also H. Spiegelberg, *The Phenomenological Movement*, Volume II (The Hague, 1969), pp. 751-752.

[2] This position is developed most completely in Emmanuel Levinas, *Totality and Infinity* (Pittsburgh, 1969). All page references within parentheses in the text will be to this volume.

[3] Other recent works enhancing this growing dialogue although not primarily concerned with the philosophy of Levinas include Richard Schmidt, *Heidegger on Being Human* (New York, 1969); Anthony Manser, *Sartre* (New York, 1966); Mikel Dufrenne, *Philosophy and Language* (Bloomington, Indiana, 1963); Frederick Olafson, *Principles and Persons* (Baltimore, 1967).

Platonic theory of dialogue, an anti-Hegelian philosophy of dialectic, a non-Husserlian phenomenology, an anti-Heideggerian ontology, and a non-Sartrian theory of freedom. In order to offer a rather complete interpretation of these complex relationships we shall analyze his thought in the following sections: (1) The Metaphysical Setting of the Phenomenon of Language, (2) Language and Exteriority, (3) Language, Significance, Meaning, and Reason, (4) The Ethics of Language, (5) From Plato to Heidegger, (6) Face-to-Face Dialogue.

I

THE METAPHYSICAL SETTING OF THE PHENOMENON OF LANGUAGE

Since Kierkegaard the question of system had offered a major problematic for modern philosophy. Existentialism itself, as a combination of Kierkegaardian and Husserlian foundations, offered at its very basis a mixture of incompatible motifs, for the antisystematic polemic of Kierkegaard's concern with the subject rested in uneasy tension with the Husserlian attempt to develop a "science of the sciences." Although various existential positions submerged this tension so that it has not broken out with violence, these positions always offered an uneasy peace.

Levinas is especially conscious of the problematic of systematization and offers a vigorous denial of such systematic possibility. Philosophical systems have continually attempted to achieve systematization by a theory of "totality" which would encompass all of reality. Usually the height of philosophical achievement has been to arrive at such a systematic totality. By some mode of insight or cognition it was proposed that all could be included within the totality of the system, and then the relationships internal to this system could be explored. Even perfection was frequently related to such totalization. Without exploring variations on this theme, it is sufficient to recognize that this motif has been central to widely diverse philosophical positions.

Kierkegaard's problem centered upon the difficulty of system ever properly encompassing the self, and thus the question was raised as to whether a "system of existence" was ever possible. Levinas, however, finds that the difficulty arises at another point, not with the self but with the presence of the "other." Systematization attempts to include everything within the system which the self develops, consequently encompassing all by thought, or intuition, or awareness. Everything would be placed upon the level of the subject producing the system, and thereby would be reduced to the "same." This does not mean that everything would be understood as of the same kind or nature as the subject, for the system might well include nonpersonal entities. Nevertheless, everything was encompassed by the thought of the subject, reduced to the "same" and put on the level of the subject inasmuch as it was within the cognition of the subject encompassing everything else. The phenomenon which breaks such totalization, and disrupts such systematization, is the presence of the "other." The "other" if it is to be a genuine "other" can never be included in such a totality and reduced to the "same." The "other" is always the one to whom a system is presented, always before one, not as the "same" but as "other," and thus constantly breaking out of any totalization which tries to include it. The "other" as a genuine "other" is never to be grasped within a system or within any totality, and any such attempt will in effect lose the real presence of the "other."

It is the "other" therefore which defies and negates all totalization and thereby opens philosophical thought to another concept, that of "infinity." Infinity is set over against totality as the arena of the "other." The other as never to be included in any system, however complex and encompassing, ultimately denies the possibility of totalization and necessitates an openness which can only be conceptualized as infinity. The infinite is the other which can never be reduced to the same, or any system of the same. The other always transcends the totality, breaks the threat of being rationally included, and remains forever beyond one's grasp. Our knowledge, our thought, our system, and our awareness are thus transcended by this transcendence which is infinity, as primordial a part of the situation as is the subject with his thoughtful system.(23)

Obviously it is difficult to discuss the relationship with infinity just because it cannot be included within any system. It is not to be analyzed in terms of an experience, however objective, for in experience one sums up the intake from an experience in a conceptual scheme that can be totalized, but the infinite and the other constantly overflows any such conceptualization. It is not an experience which overflows the thought that tries to think it.(25) Furthermore the infinite so conceived, has broken with the entire philosophical history which would develop its analysis in terms of immanence. When the other escapes any attempt to be thought, any doctrine in which the other becomes a concept of the same and thus immanent has been broken irreparably.

The relationship which we must consider, and in which language is to be understood is not a relationship of knowledge. Although knowledge has been the constant goal of the philosophical enterprise, nevertheless philosophy has thereby lost the fundamental relationship, which is not cognitive and upon which even knowledge is founded. This emphasis is so central to Levinas' position, and stands in such opposition to the central thread in the history of philosophy that he should be quoted.

For the sense of our whole effort is to contest the ineradicable conviction of every philosophy that objective knowledge is the ultimate relation of transcendence, that the other (though he be different from the things) must be known objectively, even if his freedom should deceive this nostalgia for knowledge. The sense of our whole effort lies in affirming not that the other forever escapes knowledge, but that there is no meaning in speaking here of knowledge or ignorance, for justice, the preeminent transcendence and the condition for knowing, is nowise, as one would like, a noesis correlative of a noema.(89-90)

In discussing the other we must recognize that there are various kinds of intentionality at work. Intentionality in the realm of thought is appropriately enough the adequation of the mind or the concept to the data before it, but the relation to the other is not to be analyzed in terms of adequation which is a cognitive intentionality. If the idea of infinity could be considered a representation of infinity, adequation would be appropriate, but we must speak, rather, of a concept that overflows thought and thus is not confined to the intentionality of adequation but is, rather, its very foundation.(27)

Levinas' position, therefore, is seen to rest between antithetical poles neither of which he finds satisfactory. One pole is that of a philosophy of transcendence which would situate one's real existence on another plane. Such a philosophy of mysticism, which may also be achieved by dying, is far from satisfactory. The other pole is a philosophy of immanence and totalization where the other is encompassed by the same, and thus known, and thereby included in a system. In place of either of these positions we need to develop a philosophy of relationships where the other remains truly other, is not encompassed, and where the real existence of man may be found without leaving existence.(52)

Although the infinite overflows thought, this is not the fault of the self or thought. It is not because the self is inadequate but because the infinity of the infinite resists any such encompassing. Hence the very infinity of the other prevents such totalization, (80) and it is this relationship with the other which we must analyze. "Such a relationship is metaphysics itself."(52) In spite of the fact that it is not a cognitive relationship, and cannot be totalized into some whole, this relationship is the "ultimate structure." We have a subject whose thought is not adequate for its other, and which other constantly transcends capture; a relationship of true exteriority, a reality that by its very nature remains exterior to the self, never to be encompassed. We have a relationship between entities which by their very nature remain exterior to one another, and yet are in a unique relationship with one another, a philosophy which intends to be one of genuine exteriority. It is in this setting that language must be analyzed and understood. As yet nothing has been mentioned about the phenomenon of language, but if the setting within which it has its place had not been noted first, the very phenomenon and its analysis which follows would have been misinterpreted.

In spite of the fact that analytic philosophy has concentrated much effort upon philosophy of language, one of its limitations has been that it seldom clarified the setting within which language occurred. One is often uncertain just what the entities are which are communicating via the language being analyzed. The somewhat ambiguous attitude toward metaphysics by philosophers of language has no doubt contributed to the difficulty, but at this very point Levinas offers a helpful supplement. Regardless of the validity of his analysis, it is at least quite clear how we are to understand the entities between which language is to pass. Although all of the metaphysical questions about persons have not been clarified, nor was that the intent, it is fairly evident where communication occurs. Compared with other philosophies of language, something rather definite is proposed concerning the status of the relationship between persons across which opening language must flow and be effective, thereby establishing the fundamental setting within which linguistic occurrence is to be understood.

II

LANGUAGE AND EXTERIORITY

The metaphysical setting of language suggested above emphasized that the other is thoroughly exterior to the self and not encompassed in any theory or conceptual structure which the self might develop. Such complete exteriority, regardless of how unlike previous philosophical positions, is the reason why language is so central in Levinas' philosophy, for language, and only language, not thought, nor conceptualization, nor awareness of any kind, can form a connecting link between the self and any other which is so completely exterior. If the other were not so exterior some totality or whole might encompass all, allowing exteriority to vanish in totality, but the complete exteriority of the other not only denies the possibility of totalization and systematization, but necessitates the centrality of language as that which relates the plurality of selves. The other as exterior is not included in the metaphysician's knowledge or vision. "To die for the invisible – this is metaphysics."(35) The metaphysician's totalities never suffice. "The metaphysician is absolutely separated."(35) It must even be recognized that the same and the other can not be correlated into a system where the relationship is a reversible correlation, which would suggest that the correlation could be apprehended from the outside, and which would simply be a last effort at totalization attempting to deny exteriority. There is no standpoint outside of this irreversible correlation from which to gaze at the correlation, for such is simply to try to capture both the same and the other under one vision and eliminate the differences between them.

With such uncompromising insistence upon the complete otherness of the other the setting is established for the centrality of language. "We shall try to show that the *relation* between the same and the other – upon which we seem to impose such extraordinary conditions – is language."(39) The relationship is "conversation" in which relationship the other remains truly other, and in which the self or subject "leaves itself" and moves toward the other. Conversation never negates the distance between the self and the other, but it does allow for a communication between them without absorbing the other into one's thought or cognition, and without losing one's own being in the discussion. Language so understood is not simply some cognitive theme expressed vocally, but such a theme "turning into conversation,"(51) nor is the relationship to "the idea of the other in me,"(50) but is a relationship to the truly other. Genuine conversation is to receive and welcome the expression of the other, which is not to receive an idea, for conversation overflows ideas to a relationship of the same to that which really transcends it.

We have posited the fundamental opposition of the same and the other in genuine exteriority. These are not only opposites of one another, but also "call for one another."(53) Exteriority provides even a unique relationship to history, for regardless of one's historicity, the other is "a point that is absolute with regard to history." History is not a totality of the same and the other, for their separation remains in the very midst of history. "When man truly approaches the other he is uprooted from history."(52) The epistemological difference in the approach to the self and to the other suggests that one does not see one's self externally as one does the other, and thus cannot speak of the self and the other in the same sense, which is a further obstacle in the way of any attempted totalization.

At this point Levinas begins to introduce ethical features in his analysis, but for now it will suffice to note that the relationship of conversation is the relationship of being taught, at least when the conversation is welcomed.(51) In speaking, as the relationship of the same and the other, the other, as the realm of infinity defying totalization, is revealed, not as a cognitive relationship open to one's gaze or contemplation, for the other is not the object of a look. The relationship to the other in conversation is the abode of truth.(62) Truth is more intimately related to speech than historical theories of truth have recognized, and than recent philosophy of language has analyzed. Truth, pursued through conversation, and reaching the other without encompassing him, is established by language in the metaphysical setting of exteriority.

> Truth is sought in the other, but by him who lacks nothing. The distance is untraversable, and at the same time traversed. The separated being is satisfied, autonomous, and nonetheless searches after the other with a search that is not incited by the lack proper to need nor by the memory of a lost good. Such a situation is language. Truth arises where a being separated from the other is not engulfed in him, but speaks to him. Language, which does not touch the other, even tangentially, reaches the other by calling upon him or by commanding him or by obeying him, with all the straightforwardness of these relations. Separation and interiority, truth and language constitute the categories of the idea of infinity or metaphysics.(62)

Language is the occasion for the revelation of the other, but more subtly than is usually recognized, for when the other expresses himself and thus reveals himself there is a unique intimacy of the person with his expression or his language. Here are intimacies of biological, formal, and linguistic aspects untouched by modern philosophy of language. The other presents himself in a certain form, let us state it precisely, in a certain *face*. When the person speaks, however, the form is undone, or overcome, or exceeded. "The face speaks."(66) The nature of language is such that the form is surmounted, providing the entrance to the problem of signification, to which we shall return. In speaking the other presents, and thereby reveals himself, the presentation of the exterior to the same in conversation, a uniquely linguistic occurrence. Such discourse is "an original relation with exterior being."(66)

Language is not simply to be understood as act or a mode of behavior, (67) for so to conceive of it is to miss the intimacy of revelation, the affinity of the self and his expression, which is teaching. The heart of such teaching is the "vocative."(69) In conversation the other is sustained as other, and yet the distance is traversed.

> The other is maintained and confirmed in his heterogeneity as soon as one calls upon him, be it only to say to him that one can not speak to him, to classify him as sick, to announce to him his death sentence.(269)

When one calls upon the other invoking his presence, one does not place him under a category, but calls upon him to speak and thus present himself, thereby assisting his language. This "actualization of the actual,"(69) this "struggle against the past," is speech. "Speech consists in explaining oneself with respect to speech; it is a teaching."(98) It is even crucial in the apprehension of objects, for they too need to be presented, which occurs when we "welcome an interlocutor."(69) In fact, "the objective exteriority of works is already situated in the world established by language."(70)

Conversation is not, as often philosophically conceived, the elaboration of thought existing prior to language which unites us all in reflection. Such an interpretation would turn the ability of language to reveal into its coherence as it approached the coherence of thought, and would also lead to language as the "suppressing" of the other by forcing him to abide by the coherence of thought. The function of language is not to suppress but to free. The other is allowed to disrupt the coherence of thought, and it is the function of language to sustain the other in the very initiative of expression in revelation. Consequently the linguistic relationship, conversation, can not be adequately analyzed in subject-object terms, nor does one call upon the other as an idea to be represented, or as a given or a particular to be cognized. One asks, rather, that he reveal himself in his own expression and conversation. "Language presupposes interlocutors, a plurality.... Discourse is thus the experience of something absolutely foreign, a *pure* 'knowledge' or 'experience,' a *traumatism of astonishment*."(73)

Conversation is teaching, but only that which is so separated, so transcendent, so infinite, so foreign, so other, so exterior, can teach. Furthermore, "it is only man who can be absolutely foreign to me;" only he has the freedom and the uniqueness to defy every classification, revealing himself by his expression and conversation. Separation relates one to one who is truly a stranger, and who needs to teach if one is to know. Language occurs where there is no community, so that his freedom which only he can express, the stranger teaches one and gives one a knowledge which is not reducible to, or analogous to, the knowledge of objects. Our freedom separates us and does not allow us to place him under categories and classifications. In fact, the relationship of conversation is to one who "is wholly by relation to himself."(74) One meets him in his pure presence as he reveals himself linguistically, and overcomes the gap of exteriority. Knowing in this context is not a subject-object relationship, but is a welcoming of the other's revelation. The metaphysical setting which we analyzed in the previous section, and this analysis of distance, knowledge, revelation, teaching, and exteriority is the very "condition for language."(88) Apart from these conditions, language, even philosophical language, would be an illusion and a pretext.

Teaching occurs in conversation overcoming the distance. Such revelation of the other is truly teaching, for otherwise one merely discovers what he has within himself, or can achieve by his own efforts. Genuine teaching occurs from the height of that which transcends, from the other who, in his freedom, is alone in a position to make himself known by conversation. We must not misinterpret this situation. "And the whole infinity of exteriority is not first produced, to then teach. Teaching is its very production. The first teaching teaches this very height, tantamount to its exteriority. . . ."(171) Teaching, out of the other's freedom, breaks all rational structures and all totalizations, teaching its own exteriority, and doing so by the mystery of language. The ethical implications of such a proposal will be considered in Section IV.

The uniqueness of teaching, this conversation across a void, transcends even the classifications of formal logic. It allows the other to appear in the "said," but the conditions of language disrupt all formal logic which can not conceive of absolute difference. Such a distance "is established only by language."(195) Where the infinity of the other has violated all unity, language restores a relationship. "Language is perhaps to be defined as the very power to break the continuity of being or of history."(195) In breaking such continuity teaching allows truth to appear, not as derived from me, but as a relation of language. Intentionality is no longer the noesis-noema structure of objective knowledge or of vision, nor does revelation of the other present an object to be judged as to its adequacy by one's interiority. Levinas insists that the other always remain exterior, thereby not open to the judgment of one's interior being. It is not even a relation which is open to totalization by the philosopher, nor is it an idea to be thought, which would make it simply another concept rather than a relation of genuine exteriority. Too readily the philosopher would wish to conceptualize it, totalize it, and thereby destroy it, attempting to convey this systematization to someone, which would be the greatest violation of genuine conversation. Language, most expecially for philosophy, remains a conversation with one who is really exterior. "Exteriority is signifyingness itself."(262)

III

LANGUAGE, SIGNIFICANCE, MEANING, AND REASON

The way in which language signifies and conveys meaning has been a classical theme in historical philosophical reflection and receives concentrated attention in contemporary philosophy. To these problems Levinas brings his own suggestions uniquely grounded in the interpretation of language already before us. Although he does not deal with some of the technical questions currently under discussion, he does attempt to make clear how language signifies, has meaning, and is related to the function of reason.

It is the relation of exteriority that institutes language, for the relation to the other as the "ultimate relation in being,"(48) "precedes all ontology." As we have seen, this is not a cognitive relation of representation but the establishment of conversation which is the primordial relationship and the very nature of philosophy itself. To think the other as other is not to relate to an object, and to relate to what is not truly an object is not simply to think.(49) To be separated from the other is to stand in a quite different relationship than that of a thought and its object which it tries to represent. In representation one tries to possess the object and thus "suspend" its independent being, but the relationship of transcendence is to maintain the exterior in its being. Cognitive objectivity is a different kind of intentionality than the intentionality of "expression" conversing with the other, the latter being not to cognize some theme, but any theme becomes conversation. Consequently the relationship of objectivity and representation in thought differing fundamentally from the relationship of transcendence, exteriority and conversation, is basic to all of Levinas' reflection. The intentionality of conversation is the "condition for theoretical truth and error."(51) It is the *expression* of the other which is foundational for truth. Truth is not some rational totality in which both the same and the other participate, but they relate to one another through conversation in the "risk of the quest for truth." Truth would not have appeared without such distance and transcendence, nor does the quest for truth undo transcendence and establish a totality. Conversation toward truth is not unity of being, but is a linguistic communication between entities which would otherwise be totally separated.(60)

In the first instance what expression expresses is the expression. One is to receive the other as he presents himself in his expression, which is to be taught, and which is not simply the conveying of an idea which one could abstract from the expression and take away with him. Here is the entrance for Levinas' analysis of meaning. It is the other, the infinite, the transcendent, who speaks, but the biophysiology of language has been neglected in contemporary philosophy of language. Consequently, we must recognize more directly the nature of speech, and the implication of this act. "The face speaks."(66) Levinas makes much of the presence of the face and its speech, for it has immediate relevance to the problem of significance and meaning. In view of the fact that it is the other who speaks one is confronted by a meaning independent of one's self which one is asked to welcome. In expression one's speech "undoes the form he presents,"(66) and this change of the form in expression "is to signify or to have a meaning." Speaking is presenting oneself by signifying, the other is presented, but the presentation is the said. Signifying is not a giving, nor is it an intuitive relationship. Rather than being primarily and fundamentally a cognitive relationship, speech itself is a fundamental relationship to exteriority. Speech is the "production of meaning."(66)

> Meaning is not produced as an ideal essence; it is said and taught by presence, and teaching is not reducible to sensible or intellectual intuition, which is the thought of the same. To give meaning to one's presence is an event irreducible to evidence. It does not enter into an intuition; it is a presence more direct than visible manifestation, and at the same time a remote presence – that of the other.(66)

The other is called upon to speak, and in speaking presents himself as well as or with his expression. Speech is the "actualization of the actual," for the mastery and majesty of speech through which conversation and teaching can occur first teaches about itself.

We suggested earlier that the very presence of the world or of objects is a function of speech. An object as presented is not simply a given of perception but is rather presented "when we have welcomed an interlocutor."(69) The world is presented to me by speech. "The world is offered in the language of the other; it is borne by propositions."(92) This centrality of the other's speech, presenting not only himself but the objects of the world, thereby focuses upon the act of signifying. When one finds speech as signifying, one is not merely noting relationships within the given, for the given is presented as taught. "The other is the principle of phenomena."(92) The appearance of things does not somehow lead back from the things or the signs to the presenter. Things do not lead to a community of selves. The other is not deduced, but is rather "presupposed by every proof,"(92) for the given functions as a sign signifying a speaker.

> He who signals himself by a sign qua signifying that sign is not the signified of the sign – but delivers the sign and gives it. The given refers to the giver, but this reference is not causality, as it is not the relation of a sign to its signification.(92)

The intimacy of signifying is still more subtle. The very "objectivity of the object," as well as its significance is due to language. It is the signifier who proposes a world by suggesting an object as a theme. This is not simply the referring of the subject, for the world is a world proposed, a world expressed, and because it is so expressed it has a meaning not to be discovered otherwise. A significance is not simply given nor is it merely a reference to some reality. "The meaningful refers to a signifier,"(96) but it does not thereby intend the signifier as its object or content. The signifier rather shows himself indirectly by proposing the world or an object as a theme, and so proposing, the subject or signifier is still presented, for in presenting a theme in a proposition he proposes the opportunity for conversation. The other is presented in the theme as one who may question or respond. In receiving the proposition from the other one receives the other by accepting "the possibility of questioning."(96) To receive the theme or the sign from the other is to accept one who can "come to the assistance of his discourse" and thereby teach. Significance does not lie in an identity of meaning due to the identity of an object, nor does it arise from the identity of the signifier who remains complete and self-contained while proposing the object. Significance is not the filling of an emptiness by which one gives anything that may fill such a void a meaning but rather arises out of a plentifulness of the signifier or the receiver of the proposition, who welcomes the expression and thus the proposed theme of the world, and where the signifier is conveyed in this plenitude along with the object or theme.

> Significance arises from the other stating or understanding the world, which precisely is thematized in his language or his understanding. Signification starts with the speech in which the world is at the same time thematized and interpreted, in which the signifier never separates himself from the sign he delivers, but takes it up again always while he exposes. For this assistance always given to the word which posits the things is the unique essence of language.(97)

Thus, the significance of things is not given in a kind of finality established by the referent, but in language. It should be noted that there is no totalization in this relationship of terms. Conversation, constantly teaching, defies any such totalization for it promises the "taking up again of what was a simple sign cast forth by it." To have meaning is to be related to such a surplus and not simply to the self-identity of some referent. "To have meaning is to teach or to be taught, to speak or to be able to be stated."(97) For those philosophers who have been especially concerned with language as the achievement of clarity this surplus in the realm of meaning and signification is a necessary affirmation to meet the demand for clarity. "Language is exceptional in that it attends to its own manifestation. Speech consists in explaining oneself with respect to speech; it is a teaching.... The world is said."(98) This event where objects become themes of speech, and beings enter into propositions, is the origin of their *"taking on signification,"* and is the clue to referring in all significance, while speech becomes the foundation of all signifying. Consequently language is not simply one kind of symbolism among many but is the fountainhead of all symbolism. As the theme is given in speech, the object stands out from what is otherwise a vast realm of ambiguity or a world of silence. Speech defines, mystery is penetrated and confusion is modified. Speech teaches and I have objects. The signifier, never to be neglected, "dispels the anarchic sorcery of the facts," by presenting objects. Things are thus fixed by the speech which presents them, and being so fixed, their representation and their acceptance as objects are functions of communication between men. It is in a world of conversation that there are objects or themes. One speaks the world to the other,(173) and thereby puts the world in common between us, enabling language to establish the universality of the thing. The object is abstracted by language from the mystery in which it was set. "The generality of the word institutes a common world."(173) We have already seen that language is not simply the elaboration of a prior thought, nor is it the elaboration of a "representation preexisting in me."(174) Language makes things enter a common world whereby they "receive a name and become concepts;" even evidence is so established. In view of the fact that it is language that offers a world, language is not simply one meaningful action among many actions, but the very offering which is the initial presentation of any meaning.

We have noted that the speaker attends his speech and the signs he gives, but the signifier is not signified. Furthermore one must be in the community or society of signifiers for the sign to occur as a sign, suggesting an obvious connection between language and community, whose ethical aspects will be considered later. In view of the primacy of the signifier, he must appear before the sign, by himself, as a face. The signifier attends his speech, but this attendance is especially the case in the spoken language, distinguishing it from written language. "Signs are a mute language," apart from this attendance. Language is not a mere grouping of symbols, but rather and primarily a "deciphering" of symbols. With such attendance not merely verbal signs but all signs can function as language, for other things than merely words can express. Communication or expression with the exterior uproots me from my interiority, thus offering the unique possibility for conversation, but only with speech does one transcend both one's own interiority as well as one's words and actions.

Let us now turn more directly to the discussion of reason and its role in conversation. When the presence of the face initiates speech and thereby discourse or conversation one is solicited to respond, even if one tries to avoid the solicitation by retreating to his own interiority. This presentation of the face and thereby speech is the foundation of the "true universality of reason."(201) The relation to the one that expresses himself is the basis of all knowing, and prior to any "disclosure of being" or any revealing of the "meaning of being."

As we have noticed, language is not the incarnation of prior thought, nor is it the representation or actualization of intelligible form where terms are connected with terms into an intelligible totality of meaning. Any such co-ordination is preceded by expression, where one is "bearing witness to one-self and guaranteeing this witness."(201) The manifestation of the self is possible only as speech. "It produces the commencement of intelligibility, initiality itself, principality, royal sovereignty, which commands unconditionally. The principle is possible only as commanded." This solicitation "founds Reason."(204) "Language thus conditions the functioning of rational thought; it gives it a commencement in being. . . ."(204) Language functions as an "attitude" of the self, but in language the self constantly "undoes" the elaboration of himself in his signs. Language constantly transcends consciousness, for the other is never contained in consciousness, and always puts one's conversation in question. Such a proposal destroys any theory of immanence and any reduction of language to activity. Levinas joins those recent philosophers who have noted the intimacy of thought and speech. "Already thought consists in foraging in the system of signs . . . and receiving signification from this very operation."(206) Thought does not begin with prior representation, or with significations. "Signification surprises the very thought that thought it."(206) We have already seen that the world of objects is a function of language. It would almost seem that an object needs a name in order to become a signification. The sign does not simply represent but signification makes the sign function as a sign. The heart of the linguistic situation is not the presentation of words which thus establish thought, but rather the presentation of meaning. Signification is not presented to a consciousness but *"the being of signification consists in putting into question in an ethical relation constitutive freedom itself."*(206) Such meaning lies in the face, and the life of words takes place within this context. "Signification is the Infinite," and as we have seen this infinite does not present itself simply to thought but to the other. Signification is correlated with language "because the essence of language is the relation with the other."(207) Face-to-face relationship within the context of exteriority founds language, introduces signification, and the language thus founded is reason itself. Any impersonal reason prior to language would encompass the same and the other, present a totalization, and destroy the distinct speakers. Language is not simply signs passing from one consciousness to another and initiating similar ideas, but "reason lives in language" and is "defined by significance." "A meaningful world is a world in which there is the other through whom the world of my enjoyment becomes a theme having a signification."(209) In this way things have a rational significance, and not simply a significance in terms of their use. One points out a thing to an other which takes it out of one's own possession and presents it to the other's view. This use of a designation is not putting the thing into direct contact with the other, but makes the thing exterior and offerable. The word that presents, points not only to the object but also to the relationship between the same and the other. This objectivity of the object puts into question one's possession and allows the object to enter the world of the other. "To thematize is to offer the world to the other in speech."(209) Objectification is a function of language. In this way language conditions thought, "for the first intelligible is not a concept, but an intelligence. . . ." (216) Language is an interchange between intelligences face-to-face, and not merely the attempt to find some universal. Such universalism would be but to found impersonal reason and negate the individuality of both the same and the other. In such a philosophical interpretation of language discourse would be eliminated and the metaphysics of exteriority would be destroyed. It is the other that is intelligible and whom one solicits, for one does not merely await the appearance of meaning.(293)

The work of reason thus begins with speech. It is not the awakening of common ideas, but is rather the introduction of the new, it is teaching. When one gives the object, the world, and thereby expresses himself, a common order between the same and the other is established. One may also justify one's self before the other by apology, thereby never reducing the same and the other to mere concepts. Reason presupposes their individuality. In the acceptance and welcoming of the other, the face, "the will opens to reason" and conversation can begin. "Thought consists in speaking."(40) This establishment and founding of reason is not an abdication of one's individuality, but is a presentation of one's world, or an apology for one's stance and an invitation to conversation. Obviously only a personal response is sufficient to this invitation, and it is equally obvious that at this point we are deeply involved in an ethical situation. The personal response which is invited and which would be sufficient is an ethical act. "The essence of discourse is ethical."(216)

IV

THE ETHICS OF LANGUAGE

One of the unique and most creative aspects of Levinas' thought is his elaboration of the ethics of language. In the twentieth century there has been major discussion of the language of ethics, but recently as well as historically, little attention has been given to the ethics of the linguistic situation itself. Even contemporary philosophy of language has neglected this interesting arena.[4] However neglected, the linguistic situation itself functions in or as an ethical context, and has its own moral dimensions of which Levinas is keenly aware. The point is not simply that language can be used for moral and immoral purposes, but rather that the philosophy of language itself, the theory of the linguistic situation, the understanding of what language is all about has its own profound ethical dimensions, constantly neglected, but highly significant. If "the essence of discourse is ethical" these dimensions of the linguistic situation must be explored, and the subtlety of these aspects of language furnishes one of the most creative achievements of Levinas' philosophy. In many ways his entire philosophy of language serves an ethical intention. Our task here is not to develop all of Levinas' ethical position but to concentrate upon that aspect of his ethics which is intimately related to language.

In the relationship of exteriority, where the same and the other converse, either party to the dialogue is called forth from history to responsibility. These individuals are both in history, in being, and yet personal. These existents are not simply manifestations of history "lending their lips to an anonymous utterance of history,"(23) but can speak for themselves. There is present here a complex doctrine of eschatology, which sets aside the cultural history of wars and empires "in which one does not speak." "Peace is produced as this aptitude for speech."(23) By so isolating and identifying the individual the reign of totality has been broken, and we have introduced "the possibility of *a signification without a context.*"(23) Ethics offers fulfillment for this vision of eschatology. "Ethics is optics."(23) The eschatology here envisioned is once again not a system of totalization with its accompanying objectification for it does not involve an intentionality of a totalizing vision, but is an ethical eschatology corresponding to a completely different intentionality.

[4] The late J. L. Austin approached this concern more directly than most philosophers. For the relationship of his analysis to Levinas see Harold A. Durfee, "Austin and Phenomenology," *Journal of the British Society for Phenomenology,* October 1971.

The intentionality of the ethics of language is intimately related to the analysis of desire. The concept of desire has a long and noble history in philosophy, at least since Plato. For Levinas desire plays a central role, but it is desire of the "absolutely other," not grounded upon some earlier association or participation. Metaphysical desire transcends desire simply for that which is its fulfillment or completion. In metaphysical desire for the other, which transcends mere cognitive fulfillment, "the desired does not fulfill it, but deepens it."(34) It is desire for the other, the new, desire for the infinite which never totalizes and thereby completes. The infinite and the other appears in the same and the finite as desire, not merely for the fulfillment of a lack or a need. The desirable will not be possessed, and does not so much fulfill a need as arouse desire for the infinite and the other – and thereby disinterested – "goodness."(50) Society where the same and the other converse is the immediate sphere of the separation demanded by exteriority. One might be tempted to think that if infinity demands such separation, then to analyze reality in terms of such exteriority would be to interpret it as in some fallen state, whereas such an interpretation would simply betray the prejudice of totalization, and would also interpret separation and exteriority simply in terms of need. For Levinas separation is built into the very nature of things and is not a distortion or fall from some original totalization, for the nature of desire is more related to the depth of goodness than to the fulfillment of need. The dichotomy of need and desire is basic to the ethics of language. In need the same can encompass the other and fulfill itself, but in desire there is no satisfaction, only the openness appropriate to being taught, to one truly exterior, to the open future of conversation. In fact the very ontology of the ethics of need rests upon a prior ethics of desire, for it is by labor, and thereby with time that the other may be encompassed by the same when reinterpreted as need.(117) This would be a distortion of the fundamental ethical situation, but it also provides Levinas with a philosophy of work and economy transcending the limits of this essay.

Conversation between the same and the other maintains the distance and the separation between them. In conversation neither loses its individuality, but the individuality is modified by the fact of conversation. To enter into such a relationship is to try to justify oneself, to offer an apology and hence a recognition of a right on the part of the other over the self. Apology is an intimate aspect of conversation in which one asserts the self and yet bows before the request for justification made by the other. Goodness may come forth from conversation, but never in such a way as to eliminate the demand for apology. Obviously there is a fundamental moral and ethical feature at the very heart of the linguistic situation.

Apology is a feature of the lack of totalization and a continual resistance against impersonal developments of history and universal principle, while reliance upon impersonal principles is a renunciation of the singularity of direct speech. On the other hand direct conversation always adds its unique and irreducible feature to what is otherwise merely the objective cognition of judgments. The words of judgment which accompany such conversation differ significantly from the words of other types of judgments. "It presents the will at its trial; it is produced as its defence."(242) The subject present in conversation, and open to the judgment of the other is not simply presence but is itself apology, where one justifies oneself in one's freedom. Apology is not simply an assertion of the same, but also an appeal to the other.(252) "It is the primordial phenomenon of reason, in its insurmountable bipolarity."(252) The participants in conversation are not simply the concepts they project in speech, for they manage the conversation. Reason assumes this presence, of the same and the other, as faces who can justify and offer apology. The other is the one who has to justify my freedom; he does not obtain from me a mere meaning, but an apology, to which he has to respond. In conversation there is not simply the single subject, nor the object fitting into the world, but there is the discourse of apology and justification before the only one who can offer the reply of justification. To converse is to offer a "moral summons," a solicitation. Once again let us note how morally laden is the linguistic situation. When so summoned by discourse one's freedom is promoted and in view of its call for justification the summons arouses one's goodness.(200) There is, thereby, an intimate bond between language and responsibility, and this ethical dimension is the essence of language. Language is not simply the elaboration of prior thought, but is the word which is obligation, from which one can not hide by receding into one's interiority. The initial word is a word of obligation, summoning me to enter into conversation and thus found reason. The very face of the other obliges one and this ethical moment founds society. Furthermore the ethical dimensions here are not merely the ethical seriousness and responsibility of a given consciousness, for in conversation consciousness is taken from its center and presented to the other as no longer the ethics of a solitary consciousness.(207) Separation is maintained but the gap is overcome. In the unpredictable reaction of the other's freedom one meets an ethical resistance which summons one to justification. Through speech one does not disappear in his own discourse, but offers an apology. In founding reason by speech, individuality is not destroyed but a moral summons is offered which can be properly responded to by an ethical act. (219) The summons, calling and questioning, which speech initiates and which questions the very freedom of the other, is ethics.

Early in this essay we noted that Levinas offered, among other things, a philosophy of war and peace which is intimately related to the ethical aspects of language and should be introduced at this time. In the first instance this has to do with reality and language. It is the warfare of the real and words, for the real constantly wars against the words which try to focus it and disrupts their expression. "In war reality rends the words and images that dissimulated it, to obtrude in its nudity and in its harshness."(21) Nevertheless without such expression no world would be presented to us. A silent world, without speech, would be a world "anarchic, without principle."(90) It would be a world with no beginning, no real object for thought, and thus with no knowledge. Even in this state it is incipient with language, for "its presence to consciousness lies in its expectation for a word."(93) The world as a world arrives as a function of expression. "The world is said."(98) Expression is a giving which gives the world, or gives a theme to the other, as over against the silent world the word defines, and thus the ambiguity and mystery of the silence is overcome by a gift. One has been taught by the other who thematizes in speech, and by this "I am not the plaything of a mystification, but consider objects."(99) As reality wars against words, reason, society, and the world are founded in conversation.

A further aspect of the ethics of war lies in totalization. Any totalizing theory which neglects exteriority, or which presents itself through institutionalized society thereby forming a social totality, may find war in the oppression by the totality. Power elaborated in such a philosophical theory is murder, properly responded to by the ethics of desire for the infinite, true exteriority, apology and justification, consideration for the other, Justice.(47) Conversation is thereby the arena of justice. The nontotalized community of conversation of the same and the other is thereby the intimacy of language and goodness. It is the presence of the very essence of nonviolence, for it calls one's freedom to be responsible and justify itself. "It is peace" (203) because it does not violate the integrity of either the same or the other. "The I is conserved then in goodness."(305) This is to suggest that goodness lies at the heart of the linguistic situation, and that conversation, when truly conversation, is "friendship and hospitality."(305) In such hospitality one enters through language into conversation with a "nudity," an entity with a meaning to teach, not constricted by some prior form, presenting itself as value. "Such a nudity is the face."(74)

The peace which is inherent in and encouraged in or essential to conversation may, of course, be seriously distorted. Desire and discourse go together, but by this same token language which does not accept the invitation of conversation may distort language so as to dominate, to kill, to murder.

Freedom can find itself violent with morality beginning when one finds this possibility within one's speech. Violence is possible because language itself may be distorted so that it is not a real call to, or relationship with, what is exterior. In rhetoric, as distinct from discourse, it may oppose discourse, or it may lead to discourse, but as rhetoric it is a distortion of the primary linguistic situation. Philosophical discourse constantly tries to overcome such rhetoric, which presents itself to the other but not to meet in face-to-face conversation. Rhetoric distorts one's freedom and, because it rejects true conversation, is thereby violence and injustice.

Conversation is to hold the world in common. Speech is not a way of obtaining mutual concepts but rather a way of obtaining a common world. By this commonality the world is changed, as it is no longer the world one enjoys by himself, but rather the world one communicates and gives. In conversation the same and the other do not separate themselves from the world and from other selves, but converse in their presence. "Discourse is not love."(76) In such giving of the world to the other community is grounded.

We have seen that a fundamental ethical character pervades the speech situation. Language, signifying, teaching, and justice go hand in hand and can not be put asunder, and are a foundation upon which all other structures, even ontological structures, are grounded. Through the labor of speech the world is offered as moral giving, and in this offering meaning can appear. "Transcendence is not an optics, but the first ethical gesture." Uprooted from interiority, one offers the world and with it himself. "The ground of expression is goodness."(183) The significance one presents is not offered to some transcendental consciousness, but asks for the apology of any such consciousness, thus putting it into question ethically. Language presupposes this basic character of significance, so that conversation is not simply "consciousness of," but is obligation and community.(206) "To be for the other is to be good."(261) Ethics itself is built into the linguistic fact that in existing before the face of the other I exist completely differently than in simple interiority. Although the ethical dimension of language now before us completes the analysis of exteriority, and the theory of meaning which we have developed, this entire philosophy of language, including the ethical dimension, exists in profound dialogue with the entire history of Western philosophy.

V

FROM PLATO TO HEIDEGGER

Implicit and sometimes explicit in Levinas' analysis of language is profound comment upon the history of Western philosophy. He is well aware that his position stands in a unique relationship to, and as a corrective of, the thought of many significant philosophers. In making this dialogue more explicit, it bears special note that his entire philosophy including his analysis of language stands in immediate conversation with major figures of recent phenomenological and existential philosophy. His critique of his phenomenological colleagues furnishes a major dialogue regarding the epistemological and metaphysical themes in that movement.

The heart of Levinas' historical commentary is directed against or in contrast to the rationalism which has dominated Western philosophy. Rationalism constantly developed systems of totalization, proposing to conceptualize all relationships and then develop a total conceptual system to become the object of cognition. Such conceptualization and cognition is of course contrary to all that Levinas intends by the exterior, and the infinite. Furthermore, it should be clearly noted that such totalization was itself the seed of numerous moves toward mysticism as the attempted mode of cognition of the totality. The logic that "totalizes the multiple" interprets multiplicity as a fall, but the logic of exteriority is set against such a logic of totalization.

The combination of rationalism, conceptualization, totalization, cognition, and mysticism was especially evident in Plato. In spite of his concern with dialogue he nevertheless failed to develop the metaphysical condition for real dialogue which rests on exteriority. For Plato the foundation of metaphysical desire rests on a prior intimacy of the self and the intelligible world, but for Levinas no such prior intimacy is necessary. True desire, rather, is for that which is totally other and with which there is no intimacy.

A further unfortunate aspect of Plato's thought is that Platonic dialogue was primarily a way to get in touch with the concepts and ideas. Dialogue itself occurred with the presentation of the ideas, which led ultimately to impersonal and solitary discourse as the self conversed with itself in the realm of reason, turning conversation into a relationship with objects rather than with selves.(71) It was but a way of indicating that being was open and manifest to thought and was built upon factors common to men as men.

A still further unfortunate aspect of Platonic dialectic is that in the last analysis dialogue was not among equals. When truth was reached, it was by the intervention of the gods. Consequently there was privileged status in the dialogue, thereby negating the possibility of its being dialogue among equals.(72) Furthermore, he made a fundamental distinction between an objective realm of truth which was to be discovered, and a realm of opinion. Truth, therefore, was not arrived at in the lived discourse between the same and the other, but resided in a much more impersonal realm where living discourse was less essential to its being.(73)

The realm of truth was ultimately discoverable because of the intimacy of one's interiority and the realm of truth and reason itself. Teaching in such a situation was to recollect what was deep within. The Socratic-Platonic interpretation provided for the "primacy of the same," where one possessed all that one needed and was free because one needed nothing.(43) True teaching, however, is for the infinite and other to introduce into the same that which it does not know. One's own interiority is not the abode of truth and is not the realm of being itself. One can learn and thereby contain more than he is.(180) Truth is not arrived at without violence by awakening what is already within the self, but arrives from the other, for there is true teaching only in the realm of the infinite and serious conversation. To think is not to be reminded but to be taught.

One major element of Platonic philosophy, however, is not to be neglected, for not only did it point in the right direction, but it proposed a central and profound philosophical truth. The separation and transcendence of the Good from or over the essences was not a doctrine of fall or diminution, nor a philosophy of need, but rather a genuine separation, not due to theological necessity but to genuine philosophical insight. In this matter Plato is to be honored and developed.(103)

Levinas finds seeds of this Socratic theory in Descartes, in spite of Descartes' objections to Platonism. He sees also in Descartes suggestions of the appropriate idea of infinity. The Cartesian idea of infinity introduced into the self by the infinite held the clue, however undeveloped, of true exteriority. One must remember that Husserl had considered his own position as radical Cartesianism. Even though Levinas has his serious objections to Husserl, to which we shall turn, nevertheless he is himself a phenomenologist and it is not strange that he finds in Descartes hints in the right direction, sometimes even, as opposed to Husserl. Levinas is not prepared to begin philosophy with the transcendental subjectivity of Husserlian phenomenology, and he finds in Descartes a proper corrective. Philosophy does not start with an independent *cogito,* as the transcendental ego of Husserl. As in Descartes, the ego is supported on the ground of the infinite, and it is in this relation that the ego is grounded. "Descartes, better than an idealist or a realist, discovers a relation with a total alterity irreducible to interiority, which nevertheless does not do violence to interiority – a receptivity without passivity, a relation between freedoms."(211) This in itself is an anti-Husserlian proposal, and as a true philosopher in the French tradition, Descartes is seen as pointing in the proper direction.

It is not strange that Levinas also offers critical reaction to Hegel for obviously Hegelian monism is a paradigm case of totalization. The unity which is at the heart of the Hegelian synthesis is the very opposite of the exteriority to which Levinas' thought is dedicated. The separation of things or subjects in the Hegelian analysis is but a fall from such unity. True separation of the same and the other, however, is no fall, and to interpret it in this way is to analyze separation as a need rather than the very nature of the metaphysical situation. Hegel, by making divisions among what is not really divided establishes the primacy of the same finding itself in the opposition of objects cognized.

The impersonal character of reason in Hegel is also a difficulty, for within this impersonality dialectic may elaborate the movement of ideas, but this is to announce the end of philosophy, "for they exalt the obedience that no face commands."(298) It is an old complaint that such Hegelian idealism absorbs and thereby destroys the subject. There are important matters which Hegel could not and did not explain including the need to clarify how it was possible to have a rational being, how the sheer universality of reason can affect the particular individual, and how a particular ego can abandon its subjectivity and particularity.(208)

The relationship of will and reason in Hegelianism is also of importance, for to maintain real conversation and dialogue one must do more than simply distinguish these. Frequently, when they have been distinguished, the good and proper will has been the one which followed clear and distinct ideas, or in some other way made itself subservient to reason. Levinas, however, argues that such subservience is negated by human history, and Hegelianism turns real history into mere subjectivity.

We must now turn to Levinas' reaction to more phenomenological philosophers thereby placing his thought in proper relationship to existentialism and the phenomenological movement. Levinas is devoted to what he considers a phenomenological method, which, nevertheless, is significantly distinguished from Husserlian analysis.[5] The fundamental difficulty with

[5] Space obviously does not allow us to elaborate the complete exposition of Levinas' interpretation of Husserl to which he has devoted a complete book. We confine ourselves to a few central points crucial to Levinas' interpretation of language. See Emmanuel Levinas, *Théorie de l'intuition dans la Phénoménologie de Husserl* (Paris, 1963). A translation of an excerpt from this is published in Joseph J. Kockelmans, *Phenomenology* (Garden City, 1967).

Husserl's analysis was that it was carried on too strictly and too completely within the cognitive arena as consciousness or thought related to its object. (28) Levinas, as well as Husserl, is devoted to intentionality, but as we have already seen, there are varying types of intentionality, and cognitive intentionality is not the fullness of concrete phenomenology. The intentionality of exteriority underlies thought and cognitive intentionality, but nevertheless it was the development of Husserlian phenomenology that made such intentionality of exteriority possible. Intentionality is not confined to the Husserlian noesis-noema structure nor is that structure primary.

At this point a further superiority of Descartes over Husserl appears. Whereas Husserl set no limits to "noematization," Descartes recognized that sense data were not simply clear and distinct ideas. For Husserl noematic content was constituted by thought, but Levinas is aware that the conditions for such constitution are established when the other is freely welcomed or denied. This movement itself is not constituted by thought and is not a simple instance of cognitive representation. In such an anticipation Descartes was obviously pointing in the proper direction.(130)

The Platonic relation of language and reason has played a major role in Western philosophy. Words were subordinated to reason and reflected thought. Husserl continued this Platonic initiative making words so subordinate to thought that if they did not reveal they must be changed. Such a proposal, of course, did not allow for the initiative of speech to which Levinas is committed. We have already seen how language founds reason rather than being dependent upon it, and that such a thesis is necessary to maintain genuine exteriority. If reason were primary and language subordinate, speech would be but the internal relationships within reason somehow awakened by the linguistic sign.

The other with whom speech is possible was constituted for Husserl by thought, and thus the objectivity which was the ground of conversation was grounded in subjectivity. Husserl's "ontological imperialism" is evident especially in his doctrine of horizon, which has been so much a part of phenomenology. The particular existent is discovered against this horizon, which horizon provides the foundation for any cognition of the existent. Such a position may offer the basis of an ontology, but does not offer the primacy of the world of justice. For Levinas no such subjectivism is sufficient, and objectivity itself is built on much more dialogical foundations.

A comparable critique applies to Levinas' interpretation of Heidegger.[6] To the extent that Heidegger continues the cognitive interpretation of in-

[6] See also Luk Bouckaert, "Ontology and Ethics: Reflections on Levinas' Critique of Heidegger," *International Philosophical Quarterly,* X (1970), 402-419.

tentionality he too is open to the same objections, but with Heidegger this matter takes on unique formulation. The heart of the Heideggerian development is the employment of the phenomenological method for the investigation of being. This obviously is merely a further attempt, not only at cognitive intentionality, but at the development of totality. One must also object to the entire concept of "disclosing" which dominates Heidegger's philosophy. When one responds to the invitation to speech, and thus to justify oneself, the concept of disclosure is not adequate, and, as we have seen, it is this invitation which stands at the initiation of truth. Conversation is not the knowledge of the other by the same, nor is it the revelation of the exterior to the self, though even the latter would not be disclosure.

Levinas suggests that the early Heidegger emphasized one main theme to the effect that "Being is inseparable from the comprehension of Being which unfolds as time."(45) This he suggests is itself an appeal to subjectivity.

> But it is also to emphasize the primacy of Being over the existence. This in itself sets philosophy upon a particular course. It is to interpret the relation of the same and the other (which as we have seen is an ethical relation) to a relation with the "*Being of the existent.*"(45)

It is to make the relationship impersonal, to transform what might be real conversation into a cognitive relationship, and "subordinate justice to freedom."(45) The relation which could be conversation is turned by Heidegger into a relationship with Being, thereby giving freedom dominance over ethics. The primacy of the same is in fundamental continuity with the history of Western philosophy, in spite of Heidegger's attempt to move in a uniquely existential direction. "Absolute experience is not disclosure."(67) Such subjective disclosure is to miss the truly other. Although Heidegger attempts to avoid reducing disclosure to cognition, ultimately it is grounded in a relationship to "*being in general.*"(67) Existence appears on the horizon of Being, which suggests that we never are directly related to the other, for direct relationship requires not the horizon, but the language which passes between the same and the other. Furthermore, upon this same horizon he speaks of intersubjectivity and analyzes this in terms of a "we" which precedes the same and the other. This is coexistence, and "neutral intersubjectivity." Simple disclosure is not sufficient for the presentation of the other, for in order for the same to "let the other be" it is necessary to employ discourse, not just disclosure. Disclosure suggests the reflection of vision, but truth, as we have seen, has its origin in discourse.

Even the context of objects differs from Heidegger's proposals. Objects furnish, for him, the field of our activities, in which being is revealed. What needs to be emphasized, however, is that the relationship of exteriority is primary and that things are given to the other in conversation. The problem with Heidegger is that he subordinates conversation to ontology rather than allowing the ethical relationship with the other to serve beyond all ontological systems of Being. In conversation one is in the world, but not fundamentally with the care of being, for one is there to converse with the truly other. The enjoyment of living is not such a care of being, but is genuine enjoyment. It is conversation, and not "letting be" which properly appeals to the other. Heidegger's approach to language makes an advance over Husserl in being closer to historical reality, but nevertheless it is still viewed primarily within the context of understanding rather than conversation.(205)

Heidegger's return to the pre-Socratics is not only a return to being, but also a turn to a theory of possession. Man is to be the possessor and builder, although possession is but another way for the same to encompass the other. Although Heidegger objects to the dominance of technological power he turns to a more primitive form of possession as the self relates itself to an impersonal being without a face.(46)

Levinas's critique is still more devastating, for it is an objection to the philosophy of the neuter. Heidegger's analysis of being is an impersonal neuter being which presents no face and which is the speech of no one. This is the death of philosophy. We are to be obedient, with no one offering the summons for apology. Desire for such a neuter being initiated in pre-Socratic metaphysics culminates in art, which is but to encompass the self with totality in a way analogous to Hegelian totalization. This is materialism, which essentially is not the concern with the sensible but the fundamental character of the neuter. To put neuter being above selves which these selves are then to reveal is materialism, precisely where Heidegger locates "Dasein" in his attempt to found the human. "The Being of the existent is a *Logos* that is the word of no one."(299) Surely this is not conversation with the face.

Let us turn now to a few comments upon other existential and phenomenological philosophers, even though Levinas directs his main criticism toward Heidegger. Although he does not dwell directly upon his thought, he is especially conscious of his affinity with the thought of Franz Rosenzweig. He finds in Rosenzweig a comparable resistance to the idea of totality, and recognizes his constant influence throughout his writing.

He also distinguishes himself from the metaphysics of Sartre. Recognizing that time is sufficiently present in the self to make it a "not yet" nevertheless he suggests that this is not a nothing, but simply maintains the self as "at a distance from itself."(54) "It is not all at once," which is quite different from being nothing. We have already seen that desire is not in correlation with a need, and thus the self in its deficiency is not a lack or a need as in Sartre. In conversation one is in relation but because "one lacks nothing," existence is not "condemned to freedom, but is *invested* as freedom."(84) It is the other who invests my freedom, and thus is not in conflict with it, but its ground. Metaphysics is not the analysis of the "for itself" in order to approach being. Such an I, such a "for itself" is arbitrary and unjustified, it is egoism. Sartre of course gives up the theory of participation in some totalizing reason, and to this extent anticipates the road to justification. As described, however, the for-itself never arrives at justification and genuine conversation. To be the origin is not to be a for-itself which refers simply to itself, and any such for-itself would lose significance and be unapproachable. Speech is an explaining of one's self, speech teaches.(98) Bare existence, as one finds it in the for-itself "dissolves into a shadow." (112) Life does not precede existence. "Its essence makes up its worth [*prix*]; and here value [*valeur*] constitutes being."(112) Once again we reach a point at which life reaches beyond ontology. Situated in this world life or existence does not find it absurd as certain existentialists have proposed, but rather a world which "contents me," where there is enjoyment and the ethics of labor.

Finally we should mention Levinas' evaluation of the philosophy of Martin Buber.[7] In view of the fact that Buber developed a careful and persuasive philosophy of dialogue it is obvious that Levinas' thought stands in a special relationship to his. A major development of contemporary metaphysics is the abandonment of fulfilled being as the object of philosophical analysis. Philosophy had turned instead to the betweenness of personal relations as the locus for meeting, and to this extent Buber's analysis moves in the right direction. Philosophy is not simply to concern itself with the self as a more complex being than had been proposed earlier, but must rather turn to the meeting which is the act of being. Buber (and also Marcel) had recognized that the presence of the other could not be turned into objective knowledge, and that truth is not a cognitive content but a meeting. Levinas' entire position is a development of this theme which has by now become a major factor in recent philosophy, but he is doubtful that Buber's analysis establishes the primary status of this relationship. Furthermore it remains "formal" inasmuch as it can apply to things as well as to man. The develop-

[7] See also Emmanuel Levinas, "Martin Buber and the Theory of Knowledge," in *The Philosophy of Martin Buber,* ed. Paul A. Schilpp (La Salle, Illinois, 1967); Sydney and Beatrice Rome, *Philosophical Interrogations* (New York, 1964).

ment of Buber's position arrives at friendship where the I and the thou "remain, in a sort of disdainful spiritualism, unexplored and unexplained." (69) Levinas, on the other hand, has a quite different starting point, for he begins with the other, exteriority, the infinite, and develops the theory of speech and conversation from there. "The interlocutor is not a thou, he is a you."(101) To explicate the relation with a "you" is the burden of Levinas' position, the fullness of which is realized only in conversation with the face.

While these historical comments have been all too sketchy, they nevertheless may help to establish the contemporary setting for his innovations and also serve to show how his position differs fundamentally from the core of Western philosophy since Plato. We have not yet, however, analyzed the fulfillment of this goal and the culmination of this analysis in the description of true conversation, real exteriority, which appears in the meeting "face-to-face."

VI

FACE-TO-FACE DIALOGUE

In view of the interest of analytic philosophers in language it is strange that they have devoted so little analysis to the real meeting in the linguistic encounter of the self with the other. This occurs face-to-face, which is, of course, the proper human relationship beyond its possible distortions. It is also the point where the metaphysical analysis of exteriority finds its fulfillment, where meaning can truly be conveyed, as well as the very presence of the other who attends his speech. It sets the boundaries within which linguistic occurrence operates, and is the arena for apology and justification.

We have already seen that the face speaks. When we do not have totality but nevertheless a relationship by way of language, we have the face-to-face. There is distance here, due to genuine exteriority, but not the type of distance appropriate to understanding. In this unique distance the noumena are really present. It is here that real frankness may appear, but in this intimacy also one may transcend his interiority and exist beyond himself, reaching a type of experience fundamentally different from all sensible experience.(182)

We have seen that such an encounter is ethical in its very depth. It is to meet a resistance, not of power but a moral resistance that asks for justification. We have already noted that language is not love but justice. Justice is not simply a concern of one who happens to speak. "The epiphany of the face qua face opens humanity."(213)

In face-to-face relationship one is not simply defined as subject, nor a thing with its locus in some totalization. The relationship is apology where one's freedom is justified; not a self waiting for a meaning, but a self in conversation offering itself, its presence, its freedom, its apology, its justification, and the world – all to the other. Here truth is grounded, but not from my interiority.

The entire philosophical proposal at this point offers its own interpretation of philosophy itself. Philosophy is such a teaching, such a face-to-face, such an exteriority, such a same and other, such a speaking, such a language. To have recognized that philosophy is precisely this discourse was a discovery of the Greek philosophers, for they knew philosophy was not simply the community of a species, nor the anarchy and chaos of pure division, but that communication was discourse, even though they may not have developed the philosophy appropriate to such an insight. The philosopher is not merely to introduce the other into his system, or the relation of the same and the other into a theme of reflection, as though they could be captured, for the relation can not be totalized or encompassed. If, as philosopher, one should try to think this relationship into some conceptual scheme, one would but establish a new exteriority in being, for he would relate this system of totalization and conceptualization to some other. Even philosophical discourse is addressed to some other, to some student. Philosophy therefore is not conceptualized wisdom, for the other is always present to justify even the philosopher's freedom. Philosophy is not the relation of a subject to an object, but by its very nature involves exteriority, unconceptualized. Philosophy is face-to-face.

CONCLUSION

After such a lengthy excursion this is not the time for some summary statement of Levinas' position, nor is it the place for any lengthy proposals as to how differently to analyze language. My own sympathy for the creativity of Levinas must have been evident throughout the essay. Neither do we need to emphasize again the creative role which his analysis plays when placed within the setting of analytic philosophy of language. I would be prepared to defend the thesis that this analysis of language offers suggestions regarding its metaphysical setting, proposals about the poles between which language passes, suggestions about significant meaning, the foundation of reason, and most especially an analysis of the ethical dimensions of language which supplement in a most fruitful way anything which has been proposed from analytic philosophy of language. In the face speaking and offering its apology, thereby founding reason, dimensions of the linguistic situation have been brought to our attention which fruitfully supplement what has been significantly developed by the theory of language in the much more abstract and formal terms current in analytic thought. One can hardly help feeling that Levinas is talking about language, whether properly or not, just where language is spoken and welcomed. It is indeed strange that in the concern for ordinary language in its ordinary setting, these dimensions of the speech act have not been more fully explored.

Furthermore, Levinas has offered a theory of language which properly places it in its historical context. He carefully notes the dichotomy between his position and a more rationalistic and intellectualistic theory of the speech act. He thereby confronts contemporary philosophy with a decision as to the validity of the tradition of rationalism which has dominated it and continues even today, and which in both analytic and phenomenological circles still interprets the linguistic situation within the context of the cognitive interpretation of meaning, significance, and understanding.

Levinas makes a noble effort, to say the least, to escape the difficulties of self-reference. The problem as to whether a theory is applicable to itself has been a constant source of philosophical difficulty. It might too quickly be challenged that Levinas has urged exteriority and then included the exterior, the other, the infinite, within his system and thus offered the very totalization which the system was designed to deny. But this is not quite the case, for he explicitly recognizes that the other has not been included within any conceptual totalization and that the other, as other, ourselves if you will, is the very one or the very other to whom the analysis is addressed. There are however at least three points at which one might be somewhat critical. These are not merely matters of disagreement, as requests for an apology, for a justification by the interlocutor, the reader, the student to whom the philosophy is addressed – the other. These are requests for elaboration.

1. The first point concerns his implicit philosophy of religion. Although we have not dwelt explicitly with his philosophy of religion, and this is not the time to start, there are however implications and overtones regarding philosophy of religion throughout the essay, and sometimes explicit comment. The point we need to make however does not depend entirely on explicit statements about religion but upon his philosophy of language. One senses in his use of the term "infinite" that this term hides some ambiguity, perhaps symbolically, and perhaps intentionally. One senses that he is using the term to speak of the other, another self, another finite being such as I am but not me. But these are also hints, suspicions, and suggestions

that the other and the infinite may also refer not simply to other finite selves, but to some transcendent infinite as well with whom we may also converse. I suggest that at the very least this matter deserves further clarification. To what extent are we just talking about other finite selves, and to what extent does he intend to mean some transcendent other? To the extent that there are implications for a transcendent other, the problematic of language raises innumerable difficulties. We have here a problem similar to the ambiguous status of the ego in Fichte. One is frequently unclear as to what extent the Fichtean ego that sets itself problems and then tries to solve them is simply the finite ego, or some infinite or absolute ego. I would suggest that similar ambiguity is present in Levinas' explication of the other.

2. A second ambiguity needing clarification lies in the very concept of exteriority. It is clear what Levinas intends regarding the other, but the other is a unique kind of being, who is absolutely foreign, totally other, exterior, infinite, transcending myself and yet is most like me in that he too is a man with language. It is at this point that we need some metaphysical clarification, not contrary to Levinas' central concern but consistent with this concern. If metaphysics is language, conversation with exteriority, we need to know how it is that one can be so other, so totally independent, so nontotalizable, and at the same time so much like me in my fundamental nature. In fact, the other is so much like me that he too can converse, apologize, and justify. We have here a prime example of the metaphysical problem of the same and the other, the problem of identity and difference, the problem of individuation. Even assuming that the other is as infinite as Levinas proposes, how he is so individuated and thereby separated and yet so alike in respects which are fundamental to Levinas' own position remains unexplored metaphysical territory. Having clarified the complete exteriority of the other, we now need metaphysical clarification of his similarity and continuity with me which allows for conversation.

3. A further difficulty occurs more directly in the linguistic situation as Levinas analyzes it. Assuming all that he says regarding how language overcomes the gap between the same and the other, of how conversation is what unites, in a certain sense, what would otherwise be plural interiorities, there is nevertheless a strange silence at a central point. By what means language makes contact, on either side of the conversation remains largely a mystery. That it does, and thereby relates what would otherwise be quite separated may well be a major philosophical contribution, but how my speech reaches him and is received, or how his conversation impinges upon me so as to ask for an apology and justification remains shrouded in mystery. I am not trying to suggest that no answer would be possible consistent with the thesis,

but only that the position itself stands seriously in need of some philosophical psychology regarding the receptivity of the speech act by the interlocutors. Understanding would be encouraged if it were clarified how in the face-to-face it is possible for the face not just to speak, but to hear, understand, and be morally impressed by the request for justification. When the request arrives from an other only by way of language one is somehow able to receive the question and respond, but precisely how this contact is made remains something of a mystery. We have here a theory of interaction between essentially separated entities with language furnishing the point of contact. But in what way it does this remains ambiguous.

I do not wish these difficulties to detract from the creativity of Levinas' proposals. They are offered rather as internal questions after a sympathetic reception. Such serious questions are not only what one would expect from the other to whom the proposals are made, but are inevitable in a philosophy of language where it is abundantly clear that philosophy itself is such conversation.

THE PHYSICAL-TAINT OBJECTION

by

BARRY L. BLOSE

I

Phenomenalism today gets a very bad press, thanks in large part, though just in large part, to the influence of what might be named The Physical-Taint Objection. The argument behind this objection is, roughly, that (a) a minimum condition for any statement to be a translation of some other is that the other statement *entail* it; but (b) no ordinary synthetic statement purely in the physical-thing idiom ever entails a synthetic statement purely in the sense-datum idiom; hence (c) no synthetic statement purely in the sense-datum idiom is ever a translation of an ordinary synthetic statement purely in the physical-thing idiom. The argument is that in any effort to frame a synthetic pure sense-datum statement (hereafter called just a sense-datum statement) so as to follow from an ordinary synthetic pure physical-thing statement (hereafter, physical-thing statement), the sense-datum statement will lose its purity: the achievement of an entailment relationship will inevitably introduce physical-thing nomenclature into the sense-datum statement. Thus, it is held that the only sort of translation of physical-thing statements into sense-datum terms will be into a sense-datum idiom that is physically tainted. And translation into a physically tainted sense-datum idiom will be of no use to the phenomenalist who wishes to show that physical-thing talk is just, as it were, a shorthand for sense-datum talk. If physical-thing talk were such a shorthand, there would have to be an autonomous, untainted sense-datum idiom equivalent to the physical-thing.

Roderick Chisholm has probably been the most steady sponsor of The Physical-Taint Objection, though he does not call it this. His article "The Problem of Empiricism" [1] and his appendix on "Phenomenalism" in *Per-*

[1] *Journal of Philosophy,* XLV (1948). Reprinted in *Perceiving, Sensing, and Knowing,* ed. Robert J. Swartz (Garden City, N. Y., 1965).

ceiving[2] are especially clear presentations, but the objection has also received some development from A. J. Ayer, J. O. Urmson, R. J. Hirst, J. J. C. Smart, Don Locke, and others,[3] becoming in the last years – now decades – an impressively powerful force in the diminution and indeed the mortification of phenomenalistic enthusiasms.

Nevertheless, despite the broad following that the objection has won, a few among both phenomenalistic partisans and critics profess to be uncowed by it. Their opinion, apparently, is that phenomenalism is not necessarily a translation doctrine – that, indeed, once the nature of the phenomenalistic position becomes clear, it can be seen that the impossibility of translation from physical terms into sense-datum is utterly irrelevant to the defense of phenomenalism's main ground. Phenomenalism, as they see it, is a co-topicity thesis rather than an insistence on translatability or on the short-hand status of physical-thing talk. The phenomenalist wants, they think, only to maintain that physical-thing talk is wholly *about* sense data, that the topics of physical-thing statements are intensionally one and the same with the topics of certain sets of sense-datum statements. Statements entirely about physical things are intensionally *also* entirely about sense data; that is, physical things and some sets of (possible) sense data are in some more than extensional sense the same things. The intensional co-topicity of two sorts of statements, they think, may very well be maintained independently of the translatability of one sort into the other.

It is true that neither the partisans nor the critics who impute to the phenomenalist only a co-topicity thesis and not also a doctrine about translatability, speak in so many words about *intensional* co-topicity. In general, they content themselves merely with attributing to phenomenalism the view that physical-thing talk "refers to" nothing except what is referred to by some sense-datum talk or other. But it is plain that the mode of referring they have in mind cannot be simply extensional: it cannot be simply that, according to phenomenalism, physical-thing expressions denote, as a matter of fact, only the same things as are denoted in sense-datum talk. For this would be to forget the chief motive of the phenomenalist in promulgating a co-topicity thesis. The phenomenalist wants to show how we can make physical-thing claims with a good intellectual conscience; to this end, he

[2] *Perceiving: A Philosophical Study* (Ithaca, N. Y., 1957).

[3] See A. J. Ayer, *Language, Truth and Logic,* rev. ed. (London, 1946), pp. 12, 13, and 24; *The Foundations of Empirical Knowledge* (London, 1940), p. 240; J. O. Urmson, *Philosophical Analysis* (Oxford, 1956), chapter 10; R. J. Hirst, *The Problems of Perception* (London, 1959), p. 84; J. J. C. Smart, *Philosophy and Scientific Realism* (London, 1963), p. 20; Don Locke, *Perception and Our Knowledge of the External World* (London, 1967), p. 52.

desires to prove that physical-thing claims entail nothing except what in principle can be confirmed by appeal to sense data. And his co-topicity thesis is designed to demonstrate that physical-thing entailments (statements entailed by physical-thing statements) require for confirmation nothing beyond such an appeal. But if the co-topicity thesis is just a thesis about what physical-thing talk *denotes,* it says nothing about the *entailments* of physical-thing talk. Hence, it would be compatible with the co-topicity thesis, as a thesis about denotations, that physical-thing talk have all kinds of entailments about the transsensible. And hence it would also be possible that we could not adequately confirm physical-thing talk by appeal simply to sense data even if the co-topicity thesis were correct. For the co-topicity thesis to do the job that the phenomenalist wants, it has to follow from the co-topicity of physical-thing and sense-datum statements that physical-thing statements entail nothing that an examination of sense data cannot in principle confirm. But the co-extensionality of two kinds of expressions never has the effect of proving co-topicity in this sense. Witness

(a) the co-extensionality of "birds of the kind mentioned in Mill's chapters on induction" with "swans," where there is patently information conveyed in a statement employing the former phrase that cannot be confirmed through a simple examination of swans;

or

(b) the co-extensionality of "the office held at present by the best-known man ever to have had a temper tantrum upon losing a gubernatorial election in California" with "the Presidency," where a similar point can be made.

For the sake of philosophical interest, physical/sense-datum co-topicity, if the whole of the phenomenalist's thesis, must be more than extensional. But it takes some pains to see what might be meant by a more than extensional, an intensional, co-topicity. While a full analysis of the notion of intensional co-topicity cannot be attempted, a few remarks can be made. Though those who interpret the phenomenalists as exponents of translationless co-topicity want to say that two statements are about the same things in the relevant sense of "about" only if there is some intension equivalence, they evidently do not want to insist on there being complete intension equivalence; for by so insisting, they would be requiring translatability, after all, for co-topicity. For the time being, perhaps it is enough as an approximation to say that for two statements to be wholly about the same things, the noun expressions, including direct modifiers (subject adjectives when the noun is a subject; predicate when a predicate; etc.), must be synonymous in the two statements, though the verb expressions and indirect modifiers need not be. A colloquial way of expressing this is to say that the statements must be about the same things but need not say the same things about these same things. But this is only an approximation, since the phenomenalist has to leave it open for two statements to be wholly about the same things even if one of the two contains no *single* noun expression corresponding to a noun expression in the other. Here matters will have to be left at an intuitive level; in such a case there must be complete statement translatability *or somehow else* (how may become clear later) the two statements must succeed in making intensionally equivalent object references.[4]

The endeavor to liberate the phenomenalist from the translation doctrine can be seen very nicely in the writings of David Armstrong. Armstrong, a critic of phenomenalism who believes that there is abundant metaphysical evidence against any reduction of the physical world to the sense-datum, nonetheless in *Perception and the Physical World* spurns The Physical-Taint Objection as an antiphenomenalistic weapon:

> Phenomenalism is not fundamentally a doctrine of the translatability of certain sorts of statement into certain others, but is a doctrine of the nature of the physical world. For the Phenomenalist, the physical world is nothing more than sense-impressions, actual and possible. In talking of physical objects and in talking of our sense-impressions "of" them, we are not referring to two distinct sets of entities. But this need not imply any possibility of finding an exact equivalence between physical-object statements and sets of sense-impression statements. The "fit" between physical-object language and sense-impression language (insofar as the latter exists at all) may be extremely loose. Yet the Phenomenalist contention that we can give an account of the concept of a physical object or event purely in terms of sense-impressions may still be true. The doctrine of "translatability" is simply a misleading way of putting the point, based on a quite over-simple view of what it is to assert the existence of logical relations between certain sorts of things.[5]

Armstrong recommends us to use the model of a nation and its nationals to understand how intensional co-topicity (let us call it just co-topicity) is possible in the absence of translatability. No one, he believes, takes the nation to be something over and above some very complex sets of relations holding among certain persons, yet no translation is possible from the

[4] To be noted is that this account of intensional co-topicity renders the same statement to be about different things depending upon with what other statements it is compared. Thus "Cats prowl," when compared with "Cats purr," is about only cats, and, hence, is entirely about the same things as the second statement; but "Cats prowl," when compared with "Cats are prowlers," is about both cats and prowlers, and therefore is entirely about the same things as this statement too – despite the fact that "Cats purr" and "Cats are prowlers" are *not* entirely about the same things. That what a statement is correctly to be described as being about is context-dependent is not, however, excessively paradoxical.

[5] *Perception and the Physical World* (London, 1961), p. 48.

nation idiom into the citizen. Armstrong does not offer any formal account of what exactly the character of the relationship is between co-topical but mutually nontranslating forms of discourse, but he does in a later book supply a metaphorical description of the relation. Armstrong is in this book speaking directly about analytic behaviorism rather than phenomenalism, but what he says might, *mutatis mutandis,* be appropriated by the phenomenalist:

If we demand *translations* then Behaviorism seems enormously implausible. It proves quite impossible to get rid of all mental expressions. But why should we demand translation? We will do better if we think of mental language, on the one hand, and language about bodily behavior, on the other, as two separate and differently constructed grids drawn upon, or throwing their shadows upon, one and the same surface. Transformation from one grid to another, that is to say, from one way of speaking to another, might be impossible in any but a rough way. But this is not to say that the two grids are projected upon different surfaces.[6]

For the phenomenalist the two grids would be physical-thing language and sense-datum language.

Still, this figurative description is not altogether satisfactory, since it is not plain how it is to be converted into literal coin. In particular, we should like to know what precisely Armstrong thinks it is that makes different modes of discourse incommensurable in the way that physical grids sometimes are. Here, however, we find in both of Armstrong's books only a retreat into silence. One can only conjecture that maybe Armstrong's thought is that when one sort of talk is *indefinitely* about what another sort of talk is about, there will be co-topicity even though the very indefiniteness of the first sort of talk rules out as a translation any statement in the second mode of speaking. Anyway, such an idea would echo an earlier treatment of the same issue by Ayer, who was at the time a defender of phenomenalism:

But if one infers . . . that sentences referring to material things cannot be translated, without alteration of meaning, into sentences referring to sense-data, one must not then conclude that to speak about a material thing is to speak about something altogether different from sense-data, or that it is to speak about sense-data but about something else besides. For that would be a mistake analogous to that of supposing that because sentences referring indefinitely to what is red cannot be translated into a finite number of sentences referring to particular red things, therefore "redness" is the name of an object with a distinct existence of its own. . . .[7]

[6] *A Materialist Theory of the Mind* (London, 1968), p. 67.
[7] *Foundations of Empirical Knowledge,* p. 241.

The relationship between physical-thing and sense-datum statements is likened to the relationships between "vague" [8] statements about red things and presumably more precise statements about particular red things.

But this raises the question whether indefiniteness in a mode of discourse really implies the impossibility of translation into a co-topical mode of discourse the indefiniteness of which is less, or at least different. The vagueness or indefiniteness of the statement about what is red is apparently taken by Ayer to be an indefiniteness of empirical reference. And surely it is true that the empirical reference of a sentence beginning "Red things..." is indefinite. If "Red things..." is read "Some red things..." there is an indefiniteness owing to the absence of any indication whether a given red thing is among those being spoken of or not. And if "Red things..." is read "All red things..." there is still an indefiniteness of reference since (tritely) it is not discoverable from the sentence itself where the boundary between red and its neighbors is to be drawn. Ayer may think that the indefiniteness of empirical reference found on either reading is the source of an impossibility of translation. For if translation is to be made into explicitly individual-referring terms, the series of referring expressions will have explicitly to cover, say, the reddish but not quite red pomegranate in the basket or not; but either way the resulting enumerative statement will commit itself to being about or not about the pomegranate, and thus it will diverge necessarily from the original statement, which was not definitely either about or not about the pomegranate.

This example, however, invites comment on two points. In the first place, it is not clear just what is signified by the contention that statements beginning "Some red things..." or "All red things..." are not definitely either about or not about the pomegranate, if it is not just that they are perhaps about the pomegranate and perhaps not. But if this is so, then, assuming a universe of finite duration, it would seem as if a finite, but very long, conjunction of references explicitly to particular things, named, could refer to the same things that "Red things..." indefinitely refers to, for this conjunction might include as one of its conjunctive members the phrase "and perhaps the pomegranate in the basket," thus building into itself the vagueness of the original sentence explicitly about "red things."

In the second place, though, and less trivially, only a fundamental confusion could nourish the belief that if statements explicitly about "red things" are translatable into statements explicitly about individual red things, as against being about an "object with a distinct existence of its own" that is named by the term "redness," these latter statements must be

[8] Ayer speaks of physical-thing statements as vague, on p. 242.

explicitly about particular pomegranates *named or marked by a name surrogate,* particular gobs of ketchup named or marked, particular spurts of blood named or marked, particular scarlet tanagers named or marked, etc. To think this is to forget that the co-topicity of statements explicitly about "red things" and those explicitly about individual red things must be an intensional co-topicity if the analogy with physical-thing/sense-datum co-topicity is not to be lost. But then when it is said that statements explicitly about "red things" are co-topical with statements explicitly about individual red things, it cannot be intended that they are co-topical with statements explicitly about individual red things named or marked, since it is preposterous to suppose that "Red things..." intensionally refers to any pomegranates, ketchup, blood, or scarlet tanagers at all, much less to individually *named or marked* pomegranates, ketchup gobs, blood spurts, etc. To say that "Red things..." does intensionally refer in this way would be to say that ketchup and scarlet tanagers might explicitly be mentioned in a *meaning* analysis of "Red things...." But it is certain that this is not so: the meaning of "Red things..." can be seen not to involve the notions of ketchup or scarlet tanagers, since the meaning would not be changed in the slightest if, contrary to fact, no one had ever conceived of either. Moreover, if we are asked for the meaning of the phrase "Red things...," we do not, as we should if the meaning involved *named or marked* tanagers, consider it necessary first to determine whether there are such birds, nor on the other hand, do we believe that such birds' existence can be learnt *a priori* by reflecting on the meaning of the phrase: no one would attempt an *a priori* proof for a truth of ornithology by concentrating on the phrase. But if statements explicitly about "red things" are not co-topical, in the relevant sense, that is, intensionally, with statements explicitly about individual red things named or marked, there is no reason to believe that if statements explicitly about "red things" are to be translated into statements explicitly about the individual red things that the original statements are intensionally about, as against being statements about "an object with a distinct existence of its own," the translating statements should be explicitly about individual pomegranates, tanagers, and suchlike. Since the statements explicitly about "red things" are intensionally about individual red things only under the description of "individual red things" and not under a description including names and marks, all that is needed is that the statements be translatable into predications with the phrase "individual red things" as grammatical subject. And about this possibility there can be little question. Of course, it might be felt that one is cheating, if, when asked for a translation of a sentence beginning "Red things..." in terms of individual red things, one offered "All *individual* red things..." as one's translation. Generally, to ask for a translation in terms of individual red things would be construed as a request for a translation including a series of proper names of surrogates therefor. But if the goal in seeking a translation is only to avoid an "object with a distinct existence," the "unsatisfying" translation will suffice.

Thus, Ayer's example of "Red things..." does not illustrate, after all, the possibility of co-topicity in company with nontranslatability, since in the only sense in which translation might be needed it is with this example also possible. But this may be assessed as just a debater's point. It may be said that though Ayer's example of translationless co-topicity has been subverted, there remains a valuable insight in his suggestion that the reason why translation is sometimes impossible between co-topical modes of discourse is to be found in the indefiniteness of the mode of discourse for which translation is sought. Ayer's mistake was in thinking that this indefiniteness is an indefiniteness of empirical reference. In fact, it may be suggested, it is one of meaning. Two forms of discourse may be about the same things even though there is no translatability between them, so long as the nontranslatability is because of the meaning vagueness of the form of discourse for which translation is sought. And it may seem likely that physical-thing talk is co-topical with, but nontranslatable into, sense-datum talk because of the meaning vagueness or potential meaning vagueness – as Waismann would call it, the "open texture" – of such physical expressions as, say, "cat." The translation seems impossible owing to our uncertainty about the class of sense data that should be mentioned in translations of cat statements: it is uncertain, for instance, whether sense data as of five-legged creatures or creatures revivable from death should be included.

But, alas, it can *never* be argued that translation is impossible between co-topical modes of speech because of a vagueness or open texture that attaches to the meaning of the statement for which translation is sought. For no matter what set of things, each a τ, a statement is entirely and explicitly about, if the statement is also wholly about a set of things, each describable as a ϑ, the original statement's meaning vagueness, to the degree that it is due to the meaning vagueness of the substantive "τ," can be incorporated into statements entirely and explicitly about ϑs – simply by introducing the adjective "τ-like" into the language used in talking explicitly of ϑs. And no matter what predicate "ϱ" is applicable to a τ, the meaning vagueness of "ϱ" can be duplicated in the ϑ language simply by introducing the adjective "ϱ-like." Thus even if physical-thing statements are, as may responsibly be doubted, universally vague and open-textured in virtue of the *meaning* of particular physical-thing expressions, there will be no reason to think that this explains why translation is impossible into a mode of speech explicitly about sense data. Vagueness will not be the explanation, since one can introduce terms like "catlike" into the sense-datum language, avoiding any decision whether sense data as of five-legged or revivable creatures are catlike or not.

Still, there may appear to be room for dissent from this conclusion. For it may seem to be the case that there are exceptions where "τ-like" and "ϱ-like" expressions cannot be introduced into a τ-co-topical language explicitly about ϑs. And, correspondingly, it may seem that the claim that translation is *never* impossible because of meaning vagueness is incautiously general; translation is impossible precisely in those cases where some "τ-like" or "ϱ-like" expressions are not introducible into one's ϑ language. Moreover, it may seem as if sense-datum language itself is a perfect example of a ϑ language for which there are some inadmissible "τ-like" or "ϱ-like" expressions, and that expressions like "catlike" are examples of such inadmissible predicates. Traditionally, anyhow, it has not been the case that just any "τ-like" or "ϱ-like" could be imported into the sense-datum idiom. Traditionally, that is, certain sense-datum descriptions have been considered alone apt for recording one's experiences. For instance, descriptions like those that the painter might give have seemed to many philosophers, particularly in the seventeenth and eighteenth centuries, to be somehow uniquely suitable for logging one's visual experiences. These philosophers apparently believed that nonpainterly descriptions in some manner go beyond what is actually "given" in a visual sense datum, while a description in terms of color expanses confines itself to the immediate content of the experience.[9] The reason for this belief is not counterintuitive; if, for all we can tell from a single experience, what we have before our eyes in looking at a book may be two-dimensional rather than three-, it may seem indeed as if we shall remain nearer to what is given in the experience proper if we elect to describe the experience in a two-dimensional vocabulary.

What a descriptive purism of this sort neglects to observe, however, is that an entirely comparable line of thought would lead to the conclusion that we ought not even to use a *two*-dimensional vocabulary to describe our visual sense data. For the ground for refusing to use a three-dimensional vocabulary is that, for all we know, what we have before our eyes may not

[9] See Hume's *Treatise*, ed. L. A. Selby-Bigge (Oxford, 1888), p. 56: "'Tis commonly allow'd by philosophers, that all bodies, which discover themselves to the eye, appear as if painted on a plain surface, and that their different degrees of remoteness from ourselves are discover'd more by reason than by the senses."

be three-dimensional at all. But for all we know, what we have before our eyes may not be two-dimensional either; it may not be an objective color expanse. Hence, by parity of reasoning, we ought to refrain from describing our experience as being as of a two-dimensional surface. Nor is it any defense to say that in the example of illusion, there is *something* two-dimensional present, namely an image, for an image, if present, must be mental rather than retinal to appear immediately, and, of mental images, there seems no psychological foundation for insisting that they must, in their own mental space, be two-dimensional instead of three-.

This is a *reductio ad absurdum* of the refusal to describe visual sense data three-dimensionally. Once we see that the same argument that might justify this refusal could equally be used to reinforce a refusal to describe visual sense data two-dimensionally, we are much less likely to persist in the original refusal. We shall realize that the words "sense datum" and "appears" are enough hedge words in themselves: if we use them, we can describe visual sense data using any vocabulary we desire – two-dimensional painterly, three-dimensional geometric, minimal product-descriptive ("... appears booklike"), fuller product-descriptive ("... appears like an English book"; "... like a Basil Blackwell book") – fearless of committing ourselves to the position either that we do or that we do not know anything about what *really* is before our eyes – whether it is, really, two-dimensional, three-dimensional, booklike, or what have you. A description of a sense datum as booklike or like a Basil Blackwell book can be a perfectly correct description of the sense datum even if what we have before our eyes is, really or for all we know, two-, or even non-, dimensional. The crux is that there is no reason for thinking that only what we know cannot be otherwise than τ or ϱ should be described as appearing τ-like or ϱ-like. Any descriptive word that has a role in thing statements, has a legitimate counterpart in sense-datum terminology: any descriptive words "τ" and "ϱ" that are applicable to physical things can be transferred to the sense-datum language by suffixing "-like." [10]

[10] To be noticed is that the employment of product descriptions of sense data does not of itself result in a physical taint in sense-datum statements: "τ-like" in a sense-datum statement is a sense-datum, not physical-thing, locution, despite its homonymy with a physical-thing expression. For we can employ, say the predicate "heaplike" in the description of sense data without a comparison with physical heaps being logically implied. We simply use the word "heaplike" to refer to the contents of experiences – to pigeonhole the not sharply circumscribed sense data that *happen* to be associated under normal conditions with those physical things denominated by the meaning-vague term "heap." This would be like Chisholm's "noncomparative" sense of "appears" (*Perceiving,* p. 51). No doubt, in any actual language, the sense-datum term "heaplike," when first introduced, has a comparative (and thus physically tainted) sense. But once the usage of the term is established, the comparative sense can be superseded entirely by the noncomparative.

Painterly descriptions of sense data differ markedly from product descriptions in at least one respect: It is exceedingly difficult for a person who is not artistically trained, to give painterly descriptions of what appears to him, while there is ordinarily no impediment to his drafting full and minute product descriptions. It is much easier, in looking across the room at a book on the table, to report that we are experiencing a booklike sense datum than to attempt an account in the terminology of plane geometry. It is only with conscious practice that we become proficient at deciding what the plane-geometrical shapes of sense data are. Our embarrassments when we come to recreate appearances on canvas are partially (*partially*) a token of the difficulty of attempts to furnish painterly descriptions. It is acutely ironic that philosophers of the seventeenth and eighteenth centuries chose to describe sense data in this discouragingly difficult terminology; for one of their principal reasons for trying to describe all experience in terms of sense data (or "impressions" or "ideas") pivoted on their desire to describe experience purely as it comes to us, prior to any *inferences* on our part. But if there are any experiential descriptions that require us to make inferences, surely they are these; before we can describe in plane-geometric terms how the book across the room appears, we must infer the shapes that the book would project on a vertical backdrop at right angles to our line of vision. The mediation of relatively difficult inferences about projections is required before we can describe sense data, unless we consent to avail ourselves of a product vocabulary.[11]

The conclusion must be that the relationship between physical-thing statements and statements about sense data will not be one where statements of the first kind are wholly about what statements of the second are explicitly about but where the first are untranslatable into the second *because* of a vagueness of some order belonging to the first, since, we have seen, there is no case where vagueness of itself makes translation between co-topical languages impossible: either the vagueness involves merely the empirical reference of the original statements, in which case the vagueness is entirely irrelevant to the question of translatability; or it also involves the meaning of the original statements, in which case it can be embodied in the translations of these statements by introducing an appropriate set of descriptive predicates (*e.g.*, "τ-like").

I conclude, therefore, that the easy dismissal of The Physical-Taint Objection, by Armstrong and Ayer, is much *too* easy, and that the objection

[11] G. J. Warnock, in *Berkeley* (London, 1953), p. 172, asserts that painterly description "is comparatively simple and involves less risk of error." It is this very popular claim that we are at pains to upset.

deserves a new and thorough study. Any hope for breathing new life into phenomenalism lies, I think, either in showing that The Physical-Taint Objection cannot be sustained – showing, in short, that something is wrong with the objection and that translation from physical discourse to sense-datum may yet be possible – or in showing that a better account than that of Ayer and Armstrong can be given of the connection between physical and sense-datum languages though an account that still allows co-topicity without translatability. In what follows, I shall argue that such an account is available *and* that its availability implies, if a certain assumption is made, the failure of The Physical-Taint Objection as an objection against translatability. I shall not argue that translation is possible. Such a claim would go beyond that concerning the untenability of The Physical-Taint Objection in two different ways.

First, in order for translatability to be defended, it would have to be shown not only that physical-thing statements entail sense-datum statements but also that some sets of sense-datum statements entail physical-thing statements. And about this latter entailment relationship there can also be questions. Reciprocal to The Physical-Taint Objection, which contests the existence of entailments from the physical to the sense-datum, there is what we can call The Infinity Objection, which denies that any set of sense-datum statements ever entails a statement about physical things. What this objection is premissed on is the conviction that no matter how much sense-datum evidence one amasses, it never logically follows that a physical thing exists: there always remains the possibility of deception. Only if one had an infinite aggregation of sense-datum evidence could one be absolutely sure of the physical thing. What would be needed for decisive evidence in favor of a physical-thing statement is an infinite series of sense-datum tests. Hence, any sense-datum statement that entails a physical-thing statement will require a conjunction of an infinite series of descriptions of sense-datum tests. The sense-datum translation of a physical-thing statement will thus be infinitely long; and this is as much as to say that one will never get such a translation. It is agreed that at a certain point in the infinite expansion of one's translation, it might be appropriate merely to add "... and so on." But an "... and so on" can be countenanced only if a rule for the generation of what it replaces can be stated. And it is widely denied that such rules are statable.[12]

[12] The Infinity Objection can be found in John Wisdom, "Metaphysics and Verification," *Mind*, XLVII (1938), 478; Ayer, *The Foundations of Empirical Knowledge*, p. 239; Warnock, *op. cit.*, pp. 181-182; Hirst, *op. cit.*, p. 84; Urmson, *op. cit.*, p. 157; D. G. C. Macnabb, "Phenomenalism," *Proceedings of the Aristotelian Society*, XLI

Insofar, then, as translatability means mutual entailment and insofar as the claim to mutual entailment must face The Infinity Objection beyond The Physical-Taint Objection, the claim of translatability exceeds that concerning just the failings of The Physical-Taint Objection as an objection against translatability. Second, however, even if the mutual entailment of physical-thing and sense-datum statements can be exhibited, there is some doubt about whether this is enough for showing translatability. Translatability means synonymy and not everyone is convinced that synonymy and mutual entailment are the same. Armstrong's metaphysical antiphenomenalistic arguments, as well as the celebrated arguments of Sir Isaiah Berlin,[13] might continue to be pressed against the phenomenalist even if the mutual entailment of physical-thing and sense-datum statements were firmly established. The arguments would, in effect, then be denying that mutual entailment makes synonymy.

My own belief is that it is hopeless to try to sunder synonymy from mutual entailment.[14] There shall, however, be no argument to this effect in the sequel. I shall content myself with showing the failings of The Physical-Taint Objection. In showing this, however, I shall also show, incidentally, the defects in The Infinity Objection. Thus, the upshot of the discussion will be the discovery that, one supposition being granted, the mutual entailment of physical-thing and sense-datum statements can be demonstrated. My dialectic is designed, however, so that those unwilling to grant the supposition may still come to a sympathetic understanding of phenomenalism by realizing how even without either translatability or mutual entailment, the co-topicity thesis might be supported.

II

Chisholm presents his argument as one enforcing the conclusion that ordinary physical-thing statements never individually entail sense-datum statements. He imagines a phenomenalist holding that "There is really a door in front of me" entails "If such-and-such visual appearances should be sensed (namely, those associated with reaching), then such-and-such tactual appearances would be sensed." But if this is an entailment, there logically cannot be a physical-thing statement consistent with "There is really a door in front of me" such that the two physical-thing statements together entail

(1941); Charles A. Fritz, Jr., "Sense Perception and Material Objects," *Philosophy and Phenomenological Research*, XVI (1955-56); Paul Marhenke, "Phenomenalism," in *Philosophical Analysis*, ed. Max Black (Ithaca, N. Y., 1950).

[13] In "Empirical Propositions and Hypothetical Statements," *Mind*, LIX (1950).

[14] See my "Synonymy," *The Philosophical Quarterly*, XV (1965).

the negative of the sense-datum statement. Yet, as Chisholm remarks, there are many such statements, among them "The object seen is really behind me and I am viewing it in a mirror." Chisholm concludes

> By similar reasoning it would seem possible to formulate for any complex appearance statement R' that might be thought to be an analytic consequence of [any standard physical-thing statement] P, some statement S' consistent with P and such that P and S' entail not-R'.
>
> I believe we may say, therefore, that no synthetic thing statement P entails any appearance statement unless P is taken in conjunction with some *other* thing statement referring to observation conditions.[15]

In fact, Chisholm sometimes says that a physical-thing statement entails a sense-datum statement only if the physical-thing statement is taken together with *two* other statements, one purely physical and about observation conditions (for example, "This is observed under normal conditions") and the other psychophysical and about sense data that obtain understated physical conditions (for example, "If this is ϑ and is observed under normal conditions, ϑ ness, will appear").[16] He admits, however, that the second of these appended statements is perhaps analytic and, therefore, may be dispensable. But it remains, he thinks, that the purely physical observation-condition statement cannot be avoided.

Now, it is the claim about the indispensability of this observation-condition statement that permits us to take Chisholm as promoting The Physical-Taint Objection. To say that the original physical-thing statement a translation for which is being sought must be supplemented with his observation-condition physical-thing statement before a sense-datum statement will be entailed, is the same as saying that the original physical-thing statement will entail only a mixed physical/sense-datum statement: to say that two physical-thing statements p_1 and p_2 entail when conjoined a sense-datum statement s, is the same as saying that p_1 by itself will entail the mixed statement that if p_2, then s.

Perhaps Chisholm's argument deserves one more illustration. Take, for instance, "A pair of skis is in the closet." Chisholm's objection to any attempted sense-datum translation of this will be that no matter how much in sense-datum terms we build into the translation we shall not have built in enough: there will remain imaginable occasions when the ski statement is true though the sense-datum statement is not. Now, it is usually believed that if translations of physical-thing statements into sense-datum statements were possible, the sense-datum translations would take the form of con-

[15] *Perceiving,* pp. 193-194.

[16] "The Problem of Empiricism," p. 352 in Swartz.

junctions of conditionals. Thus, the statement "A pair of skis is in the closet" would, in translation, become "If p, then q; and if r, then s; and if t, then u; and . . ." where p, q, r, s, t, u, and all other variables would be replaced by expressions in the sense-datum idiom. For a sense-datum translation to be true whenever the ski statement is true, then, every conjunct of the translation would have to be true, since a conjunction as a whole is false if one or more of its conjuncts is false. Suppose that we attempt to formulate just one of the conjuncts of a translation of the ski statement. Let us try to express it so that it will be true on all occasions when the ski statement is true. What we are doing, that is to say, is attempting to delineate a necessary condition, in terms of sense data, for the ski statement's truth. We are trying to secure the entailment of a sense-datum statement by the one about skis.

We shall essay as our first approximation toward a translational conjunct "If an observer experienced closetish sense data, he would experience skiish sense data." Now, it is evident that this first attempt is, as it stands, inadequate: the new statement may be false in many imaginable cases where the original statement is true. Jones, an observer, may go blind and suffer closet images without ski images; or he may, though remaining sighted, overlook the skis despite their being in plain view when he opens the closet; the skis may be hidden behind the rhinoceros heads; or for any number of other reasons he just may not see the two skis that are nevertheless very much in the closet. If the sorts of possible frustrations of an observation of skis were enumerable, this obstacle to finding a necessary condition in sense-datum terms would be merely practical. We should need patience and perseverance to determine exactly what the possible frustrations were, so that we might incorporate riders about them into our conjunct; we should not, however, be prevented, in principle, from succeeding with our conjunct. Unhappily, though, it would seem as if an *infinite* number of things might keep Jones from seeing the skis. An infinity of riders would therefore apparently have to be added to our conjunct in order to guarantee that it be true whenever the ski statement is true. The conjunct would read "If an observer experienced closetish sense data, if he did not become blind, and if he were attentive, and if . . . , then he would experience skiish sense data." But, of course, to say that an infinity of riders is needed, is to concede that no adequate conjunct can be contrived.

Another way of putting the same thing is to say that the conjunct sought must point to some regularity or pattern in the succession of sense data: if such-and-such a configuration of sense data occurs, then so-and-so in the way of sense data will also occur. But sense data simply do not follow each other with such regularity of pattern. There are, to be sure, some regular successions of sense data (for example, skiish sense data may regularly attend rhinoceros-head sense data if our skis and rhinoceros heads are stored side-by-side in the closet), but these are only rough-and-ready regularities; they are insufficient for abstracting universal generalizations – conclusions about successions that would *always* (under all conditions unexcluded by the antecedent clause of such generalizations, and within a set temporal span; for instance, so long as skis and rhinoceros heads are in the closet) obtain. But only if there were these universal regularities, could conjuncts be fashioned to express necessary conditions for the truth of ski statements.[17]

But this is just the beginning of difficulties for the attempt to formulate a necessary condition. We have said that the conditional conjunct seems to require an antecedent clause of infinite length if the conjunct is to be true whenever the ski statement is true. Now, the example of an antecedent clause that we gave was "If an observer experienced closetish sense data, and if he did not become blind, and if he were attentive, and if. . . ." But surely this clause is not entirely in the sense-datum idiom. The criterion for visual acuity is physical; the criterion for attentiveness is physical behavior; and so for every addition one might make to the clause. If one is to procure a necessary condition for the truth of "A pair of skis is in the closet" that is entirely in sense-datum terminology, it looks as if one will first have to cast "The observer did not become blind" into the terminology, since "The observer did not become blind" is part of the statement of the necessary condition for the truth of "A pair of skis is in the closet." One must, apparently, in other words, produce a sense-datum translation for "The observer did not become blind" – in terms of how the observer would

[17] This argument is based on one by Wilfrid Sellars, in *Science, Perception and Reality* (London, 1963), pp. 79-83. The same argument is summarized by Smart, *op. cit.*, pp. 23-24. But where Sellars speaks of "essentially autobiographical generalizations" I speak of "rough-and-ready regularities." I do so because I refuse to concede that the mere fact that a regularity is peculiar to one's own situation renders it incapable of being a necessary condition of the truth of a physical-thing description, for very often what a condition in sense-datum terms is meant to be *of* is the truth of a description of one's own situation, a situation as marked by the indexical expressions in the description. All that is necessary is that others too be able to place themselves in one's situation. Sellars, in insisting that universal generalizations are required for sense-datum conditions, places too stringent requirements on such generalizations. What are needed are not pure universal generalizations but universal generalizations temporally and topically limited. Thus as a necessary condition for the truth of "A pair of skis is in the closet" we do not need a generalization relating *all* closet sense data under certain conditions to ski sense data; we instead have need only of a generalization relating all sense data topically demarcated by the person who says "in the closet" – meaning perhaps the closet in the next room – under certain conditions and for a certain duration, to ski sense data. My claim is that we do not have even these.

appear to examiners. As in any sense-datum translation of a physical-thing statement, a necessary condition for the physical-thing statement's truth must be formulated; and this formulation will require an antecedent clause of infinite length. But of course the examiners may not be blind either; and so apparently a translation for "The observer's examiners are not blind" enters ultimately into the translation of "A pair of skis is in the closet." Similarly, it would seem as though a translation for "The observer's examiners' examiners are not blind" must appear in the translation; and *ad infinitum*. The result is that not only does the translational conjunct seem to require an antecedent clause that is an infinite series of "if..." conditions, but that each of the "if..." conditions must itself be unpacked into a conjunction, each conjunct of which involves an infinite series of "if..." conditions, some conjuncts of which in turn must be unpacked into an infinite series of "if..." conditions, and so on indefinitely, multiplying infinities many times over.

It may be that The Physical-Taint Objection is undergirded entirely by considerations similar to these. But the assertion about the need for entailed sense-datum statements to have a physical taint might also be taken as more than a conclusion drawn from the infinite-series difficulties. As these difficulties were told, it seemed to be allowed that if the proper infinitude of conditions were, it would be said *per impossibile*, formulated, no additional physical condition would require mention. The Physical-Taint Objection, on the other hand, might, as developed by Chisholm, be unwilling to concede this. Though a study of the text is not particularly helpful in deciding this, Chisholm might be interpreted as saying that even if, *per impossibile*, statements covering infinitudes of conditions could be given, this would be to no avail. There is no "proper" infinitude such that the necessity for explicit reference to a physical condition in the antecedent is averted. Even if infinite sense-datum clauses were securable, one would still become involved in a regress in any attempt at expressing entailed sense-datum statements, since any such statement would have to include at least one physical-thing clause, which, itself to be translated, would require another, and so back without limit.

Now it is evident that this construction of The Physical-Taint Objection is, potentially, gravely injurious to the translation thesis: an analysis may not contain mention of the very sort of thing that the analysis is designed to eliminate mention of. At the same time, however, this reading of the objection, in comparison with the earlier infinite-series reading, is a more dubiously grounded objection against translation. It can be seen intuitively that reference to infinitudes of sense-datum conditions is necessary for translation, at any rate if translation is to take the conjunctive hypothetical form we have been supposing; but it is an open question whether one can show that besides this reference there is always necessary an explicit physical-condition reference too. An appeal to intuition and to one's sense of reality is not enough for establishing any need for explicit physical-condition reference beyond the need for a reference to infinitudes of sense-datum conditions. For to become aware intuitively of such a need would involve acquaintance with examples of physical-thing statements and candidate sense-datum translations where the sensed inadequacy of the translations were sufficient for indicating the need. But in point of fact whatever examples are attended to, the sensed inadequacy of the sense-datum translations will be insufficient for this. If the attempts at sense-datum translations fail to refer to an infinitude of sense-datum conditions, there will always remain viable the rival hypothesis that, *could* infinite sense-datum references be achieved, there would no longer be a sensed inadequacy in the translations, and so, no longer a need for explicit physical-condition reference either. And if, somehow or other, the attempts at translation might – as we yet have no grounds to hope – be made finitely to refer to an infinitude of sense data and if, at the same time, their sensed inadequacy persisted, there would remain viable the hypothesis that this inadequacy is born entirely of a simple failure to find the *right* infinite constellation of sense-datum references. Either way, whether the candidate sense-datum translations incorporate infinite sense-datum references or not, felt inadequacies do not demonstrate the wanted diagnosis of the inadequacy. It would seem, therefore, that the Physical-Taint Objection would on this reading have to be premissed on the acceptance of some independent argument. The Physical-Taint Objection would not be a self-sufficient objection against translation. It would rather, if true, be symptomatic of some other objection. It is an objection standing in need of defense; if the defense can be given, the defense by itself will serve as a demonstration of the impossibility of translation; if it cannot be given, the objection is without any effect against the translation thesis. Worse, the needed defense must be of a particular kind. Unless it independently overturns the cotopicity thesis, it will not be able to support The Physical-Taint Objection when the objection goes beyond the infinite-series objections. For a sense-datum statement with the equivalent of an infinite antecedent clause that made mention of *every* possible type of relevant sense-datum condition – made mention as the infinite series objections say it must – could not, if cotopicity were the case, be condemned as unentailed by a physical-thing statement on the grounds that its antecedent clause failed to refer to some relevant physical-thing condition, since the statement as it stood, and without supplement by further physical-thing condition reference, would already, by virtue of referring to every possible type of relevant sense-datum condition – giving a yes-or-no answer to every possible yes-or-no question about relevant sense data – also refer – in the same yes-or-no way – to every possible type of relevant physical condition. But plainly Chisholm does not believe that an independent argument against co-topicity is to be had. If he did believe this, he would have argued against phenomenalism directly, without introducing The Physical-Taint Objection at all. Chisholm, therefore, would be well advised to represent his objection as but a formulation of the infinite-series difficulties. As maintaining that there would still be a physical taint even if infinite sense-datum references could be made, the objection becomes nothing but a front behind which are hidden the facts that independent arguments against co-topicity are needed and that they are by no means at hand.

III

If then the more promising form of The Physical-Taint Objection trades entirely on the need for an infinite expansion of the antecedent clause of each conjunct in a sense-datum translation, the objection is patently very much akin to The Infinity Objection. The Physical-Taint Objection is as much an infinity objection as The Infinity Objection itself. In both cases, what is urged against the phenomenalist is the necessity of a translation's explicitly reckoning with an infinitude of possible sense-datum configurations, configurations that must be mentioned within any single antecedent clause (according to The Physical-Taint Objection) and collectively in all of the antecedent clauses in the conjunctive description of all possible test situations (according to The Infinity Objection). It is obvious from this that the configurations that pose infinity problems for the phenomenalist according to The Physical-Taint Objection are exactly the same as those posing problems according to The Infinity Objection. For every configuration that must be mentioned in *some* individual antecedent clause must *a fortiori* be mentioned in the conjunction of *all* of the antecedent test descriptions. And since any configuration that must be recognized in the totality of all antecedent clauses would, by an intrusion into a test situation in the positive description of which its occurrence is not included, be a potential hitch, capable of preventing the sense-datum test from yielding a positive result, every such possibly intrusive sense-datum configuration must be mentioned in each antecedent clause containing riders about what might go wrong in a given testing.

It appears, hence, that any successful rejoinder to either Objection – The Physical-Taint or The Infinity – will be a successful rejoinder to the other. If the infinite sense-datum configurations focused by either objection can be codified to show that the configurational infinitude is an infinitude of variations on a finite though large number of configurational themes, this will indicate that "... and so on" phrases can be used to cover the infinities. The existence of infinities will be no obstacle to the translation enterprise, since all that will have to be included in sense-datum translations will be descriptions of certain paradigmatic configurations with "... and so on" phrases annexed, phrases that are admissible to the translations since there will be rules explaining the generation of the infinitude of descriptions of nonparadigmatic configurations from the paradigmatic.

In the literature, one not infrequently sees efforts bent toward displaying how configurational infinitude is largely just variational. Hirst, in particular, though hostile to phenomenalism, has done work in this direction.[18] He has, for instance, proposed listing in phenomenalistic translations only extreme tests, adding that for intermediate tests there will be sense data proportionally intermediate.

Now, in the painterly mode of sense-datum descriptions, this may be possible. In the product mode, however, it is evident that there are *not* gradations in sense data corresponding to gradations between extreme tests. In poor light without my eyeglasses the rock looks like a kitten. In better light or with my eyeglasses, the rock is clearly a rock. With intermediate light or with eyeglasses of intermediate power, there is *not* an intermediate appearance. The rock does not look less like a kitten and more like a rock than in poor light and without the eyeglasses, nor yet more like a kitten and less like a rock than in good light or with my powerful eyeglasses. Nor does it look like perhaps a kitten, perhaps a rock. Rather, there is a range of lights and powers where the rock clearly looks like a rock, but no more or less for the different lights and powers, and there is a range where the rock looks very much like a kitten but no more or less for the different lights or powers. There is no range where the rock looks a little bit like a rock and a little bit like a kitten, though conceivably there is a range where the rock does not look like anything definite at all.

But if this is the reason why we cannot use extreme tests as effective paradigms, we are in possession of a hint as to what our paradigms might better be. Instead of extreme tests and a rule for gradations between them, we might use threshold tests and a rule for tests on the far sides of the thresholds. Thus, in the kitten example, instead of taking, as our paradigms,

[18] *Op. cit.*, pp. 83-84.

tests in very full light and very poor light and with very strong eyeglasses and with no eyeglasses at all, we might take tests in just full enough light to see the rock as a rock and in just poor enough light to see it as a kitten, and so forth, adding the rule that for tests in still better light and still poorer light (up to a point) the results should be like in the threshold tests.

But while something is to be achieved along this path, it can be seen, I think, that success cannot be complete. For even if it could be shown that the threshold tests are not themselves infinite in kind, it must be recognized that sense-datum statements about all the various threshold tests *will never be entailed by "A pair of skis is in the closet."* This can be proved, I believe, by means of an argument that removes the need for examining individually *many* of the more customary efforts at securing finite sense-datum translations.

All along, the discussion, including the reconstruction of Chisholm's challenge, the statement of The Infinity Objection, and attempts at retort, has been conducted on the supposition that mutual entailment between sense-datum and physical-thing statements requires formulating an all-condition-covering sense-datum conjunction. I wish to argue that this supposition is mistaken. Just as we saw that names and marks of particular scarlet tanagers do not enter into an analysis of the *meaning* of the phrase "Red things . . ." so we must realize now that not every condition or every type of condition must figure explicitly in a mutual-entailment counterpart of "A pair of skis is in the closet." Indeed, if every type of condition did figure in any sentence, we could on that very basis be sure that the sentence was *not* entailed by "A pair of skis is in the closet." While the existence of skis in my closet may portend results for what would happen if there were a fire there hot enough to melt steel, certainly predictions about what would happen are not part of the *meaning*, and so not part of the entailment, of the ski sentence. If every type of condition figured in the entailed counterpart, all natural science would be redundant; anyone really knowledgeable of the meanings in our language would be able deductively to elicit all scientific truths. After all, all that should be required of a sense-datum counterpart of a physical-thing statement is that sense data figure in the counterpart under the descriptions under which the physical-thing statement is intensionally about them, not under the descriptions under which the physical-thing statement is extensionally about them. It is surpassingly curious that for so long, so many philosophers have believed that entailed sense-datum counterparts to physical-thing statements must take a form which would itself entail that the counterparts are *not* entailed. Even those who have been uneasy about all-condition-covering conjunctions have drawn surpassingly curious morals from their disquietude. For example, Macnabb, in "Phenomenalism," mentions that he finds it inconceivable that anything so complicated as such a conjunct series could be what we actually mean in ordinary life by our physical-thing statements. But along with Don Locke,[19] he takes this to suggest that entailment counterparts are impossible, since what are proposed as counterparts are clearly not entailed, while I am about to suggest that entailment counterparts are possible, since what are found to be impossible by defenders of The Physical-Taint Objection are not entailment counterparts at all.

IV

But this still leaves us with the question of what form the counterparts are to take. Let us begin to seek our answer by trying once more to discern, through analogy, the relationship between physical-thing statements on the one hand and sense-datum statements on the other. Our inquiry here will be like that of Ayer and Armstrong, differing only, I hope, in its circumspection.

One suggestion about the relationship takes as the analogue the relationship between theories and their evidence. The relationship, it is suggested is like that between theoretical statements and the nontheoretical observation reports that support them. But even before a careful examination of this suggestion, it is clear that problems beset it, since physical-thing statements are manifestly dissimilar from ordinary scientific theoretical statements when these statements are interpreted instrumentally, as a phenomenalist would want to interpret them. Theoretical statements are, on an instrumentalist interpretation, possible only in a context that allows the co-ordination of statements in the theory with universal or statistical generalizations in the observation framework.[20] We have seen, however, that whatever regularities there are in the realm of sense data are merely rough-and-ready regularities. Now, of course, these rough-and-ready regularities might lend themselves to *statistical* formulation. But physical-thing statements are to all present appearances not of the nature of substitutes for, or even idealizations of, *statistical* laws.

Apparently, then, if physical-thing statements are to be compared to theoretical statements, the theoretical-statement analogues cannot be

[19] *Op. cit.*, p. 64.

[20] The point is Sellars', in *op. cit.*, pp. 84-87. I should like despite Sellars) to read "universal statements" and "universal generalizations" as "universal statements (or generalizations) whether or not temporally or topically limited." See footnote 17.

ordinary scientific theoretical statements instrumentally interpreted. There must be some other kind of theoretical statements. That there is, is intimated by the fact that a number of commentators, all of whom are well aware of the logic of ordinary scientific theoretical statements, persist in drawing the analogy.[21]

What they seem to mean by theoretical statements might better be called "elastic summarizing statements." Now, scientific theoretical statements interpreted instrumentally would be summarizing statements too. Their job would be just to organize instrumentally our knowledge about observables. They would at any rate not, however, be elastic. Theoretical statements that are co-ordinated with universal inductive generalizations in the observation framework have for the instrumentalist, without exception, the truth values of their co-ordinate generalizations. Elastic summarizing statements, on the other hand, are co-ordinated only loosely with generalizations in the observation framework. That is, their truth values are not entirely determined by their co-ordinates'. In fact, the chief virtue of elastic summarizing statements is their relative independence of the truth value of the inductive generalizations in the observation framework. One can abandon an inductive generalization as universally or even largely true, even within a temporally and topically demarcated field, without relinquishing the elastic summarizing statement that is co-ordinated with it, and one can retain an inductive generalization unviolated at the same time that one relinquishes on a given occasion though not in a wholesale way its co-ordinate elastic summarizing statement; provided in both cases that two conditions are satisfied. The first condition is that the inductive generalization continues to be held universally true of the *central* cases of the elastic statement's truth. By the central cases are not necessarily meant the preponderant cases: central cases may be in a decided minority. Instead, central cases are those that are conventionally taken by users of the elastic summarizing statement *as not requiring any description beyond* the assertion of that statement. The second condition is that plausible explanations, in terms of the given elastic summarizing statement in association with other elastic summarizing statements of higher orders, be possible for exceptions to the universal generalization where the elastic summarizing statement is not relinquished; and also that plausible explanations, in terms of higher-order elastic summarizing statements alone, be available for inductive regularities, of the kind spoken of by the generalization, where the given elastic summarizing statement is surrendered. Elastic summarizing statements, in other words, comprise a hierarchy such that phenomena that are construed as

[21] See *e.g.*, Ayer, *The Problem of Knowledge* (Harmondsworth, 1956), p. 132.

central cases of the truth of statements in the upper reaches of the hierarchy are often also construed as noncentral cases of either the truth or falsity of statements in the lower reaches. This hierarchy has the structure of descriptive science.[22]

Thus, the interpretation of physical-thing statements as elastically summarizing of sense data would co-ordinate "A pair of skis is in the closet" with an inductive generalization, for instance, "If there were closetish sense data (where 'closetish sense data' is as specifically about a certain kind of closetish sense data as 'closet' in the physical-thing statement is specifically about a certain closet), then there would be skiish sense data." But it would not insist that the inductive generalization be held universally true even within a temporal and topical field. All that is necessary is, first, that in those cases where "A pair of skis is in the closet" is taken as a complete account of what appears to one, the inductive generalization is universally true; and, second, that in those cases where the ski statement is held true but where there are exceptions to the sense-datum generalization, and where the ski statement is held false but where the sense-datum generalization is unviolated, the most plausible explanations [23] of the actual course of sense data can be given respectively in terms of higher-order elastic summarizing statements plus the elastic summarizing statement in question or in terms of higher-order elastic summarizing statements alone. As examples of higher-order statements that might figure in plausible explanations one might cite (a) "The viewer was bludgeoned after opening the closet door and before he could discover the skis;" or (b) "You are known to suffer frequent ski hallucinations;" or (c) (perhaps) "But now they are talking – and about Hegel's *Phenomenology*." With the first of the three statements we could explain a phenomenon (closet sense data but no ski sense data) that, as a central example of a higher-order statement's truth, becomes a noncentral example of the ski statement's truth. With the latter two statements, we

[22] There is no begging of any question about physical determinism here, since there is no desire to exclude *ab initio* high-order summarizing statements of the sort "Things are chancy today."

Nor is this description of physical-thing statements one that represents them as indefinitely (vaguely) about sense data. If it were, it would follow from our account that the introduction of "τ-like" predicates would be enough to permit translation. Rather, physical-thing statements are, on the present picturing, about sense data in a specifiably rule-governed way.

[23] *Most* plausible explanations. Physical-thing statements are not tendered as noncompetitive. Contradictory physical-thing statements are not both true even if both plausibly in their own ways summarize sense data. In deciding between contradictories, *degree* of plausibility must be measured. One might say that physical-thing statements are tendered not as just elastic summaries but as the *best* elastic summaries possible.

could explain phenomena (closet sense data and ski sense data) that as central examples of higher-order statements' truth, become noncentral examples of the ski statement's falsity.

If this is a correct portrayal of the relationship between physical-thing and sense-datum statements, *i.e.*, if physical-thing statements are "theoretical" in the sense of being elastic summarizing statements, then the co-topicity thesis can be sustained without translatability or mutual entailment. But, more significantly, even the aim of showing a mutual entailment relationship between physical-thing and sense-datum statements will possibly be achieved; from the "theoretical" account it will follow that there is perhaps no need (other than heuristic) of the account, since mutual entailment will, with a single "provided that . . . ," be possible. Mutual entailment will be possible because it will be as easy a matter to build the account of when identical truth value is to be expected, into the sense-datum counterpart of each physical-thing statement individually, as into the general description of the relationship between physical-thing and sense-datum statements.

A mutual-entailment counterpart of "A pair of skis is in the closet" will include as a main clause "If there were closetish sense data (again with the proviso about 'closetish'), then there would be skiish sense data" but will have to subjoin to this a clause indicating that the main clause covers only the central cases of the truth of the elastic summarizing statement undergoing translation. It will have, in other words, to convey that if there were no skiish sense data, the most plausible explanation why there were not would contain "A pair of skis is in the closet" or an equivalent statement, sense-datum or not, as one constituent, where the most plausible explanation is the one that would be accepted if there were an unimpetuously full acquaintance with the sense data associated with all those logically possible past and future testings for sense data a mere description of which does not commit one to the inclusion or noninclusion of "A pair of skis is in the closet" in the explanation.[24]

The big question, of course, is whether this can be conveyed entirely in sense-datum terms or whether any clause about all this will perforce contain a non-sense-datum surd. The question is whether the information can be

[24] In defining maximum plausibility in this way, we connect it with a family of concepts apart from the family that includes "truth," "correctness," etc. If "plausibility" were defined in terms of truth, it would follow that "A pair of skis is in the closet," in being analyzed in terms of the plausibility of the statement "A pair of skis is in the closet," would be analyzed in terms of the truth of "A pair of skis is in the closet." But to offer for any sentence "s," a counterpart that includes " 's' is true" is to offer, it might be objected, a useless counterpart.

inoffensively put, by factoring it into sense-datum terms.[25] This, however, brings us to the "provided that..." in the pitch about the possibility of finding a counterpart. Counterparts for physical-thing statements will be possible *only provided that* a naturalistic analysis of explanation is also possible; such a naturalistic analysis must be attained before the clause about the most plausible explanation can be cast into the sense-datum idiom. For the only predicates eligible for sense-datum descriptions are predicates that are compatible with the logical possibility of the sense datum's being "of" a physical thing or physical things. Thus if there are to be sense-datum predicates suitable for transmitting information about explanations, explanations will have to be nonresidually resoluble into naturalistic, or physical-thing, elements – elements like scratches on paper, sounds, and human behavior.

But, even supposing a naturalistic account possible, this will make the explanation clause just another physical-thing clause, and accordingly, a clause to be analyzed in the same fashion as the original ski statement. But to include within a counterpart of "A pair of skis is in the closet" a clause that must itself be unpacked in the same way as the original statement may seem an unacceptable move. The difficulty, obviously, is that an infinite regress is spawned. Schematically, the phenomenalist begins with "A_1 or E_1" as the consequent clause of his counterpart (where "A_n" is an explicitly sense-datum disjunct of the clause – *i.e.*, in the present case, "there would be skiish sense data" – and "E_n" is a naturalistically phrased disjunct about the most plausible explanations). He sees that "E_1," being naturalistic and physical, is translatable as something containing as its own consequent clause "A_2 or E_2;" thus that the original consequent clause ("A_1 or E_1") goes over into "A_1 or if . . . ,[26] then A_2 or E_2" and subsequently into "A_1 or if . . . , then A_2 or if . . . , then A_3 or if . . . , then A_4 or E_4" and so on. The problem, depressingly, is that no matter how far the phenomenalist takes the expansion, there remains an "E_n," a clause employing physical-thing locutions. Hence, a translation entirely in terms of sense data is not achieved.

[25] Someone might say, however, that, even if communicable in sense-datum terms, the information about explanations no more enters into translations of ski statements than does the notion of, say, melting at a certain temperature. That an explanation is possible under certain conditions is, in short, someone might say, *shown* but not *stated* by physical-thing statements. But this is an objection to translation, not to entailment counterparts. Whether shown or stated, the information is communicated through the logic of the ski statement. Hence, there is a difference between the information about explanations and that about melting.

[26] The "if . . ." clause is not given since its shape depends on the naturalistic analysis of explanation. In any case, the clause must be in sense-datum terms.

Agreeably, however, this regress can, assuming that sense-datum predicates are available for communicating about explanation plausibility, be replaced by a clause that recurs explicitly only to sense-datum references and not to physical-thing. The situation is one where the phenomenalist finds an infinite regress of explicit physical references in his first attempt at a counterpart, but an infinite regress that dissolves into an infinite collection of explicit sense-datum references. The equivalence with an infinite collection of sense-datum references is evident upon remembering that the phenomenalist is now assuming the correctness of the account of physical-thing statements as elastic summarizing. It is plain that it follows from this assumption that whenever a physical-thing statement is properly held to be true despite there being in some test cases no sense data of the sort centrally associated with the truth of the physical-thing statement, it will be found if one goes far enough that, *inasmuch as the physical-thing statement is elastically summarizing only of actual or possible sense data,* there is in every such case something among possible sense data capable of indicating the maximal plausibility of an explanation that contains the physical-thing statement in question. The maximal plausibility of the explanation sooner or infinitely later is mirrored in sense data or the physical-thing statement is not elastically summarizing only of actual or possible sense data. But then there need be included no regressive "E_n" after all in the counterparts of physical-thing statements. The job of every explanation clause ("E_n") is now seen to be to summarize the fact that if the central sense data associated with a certain explanation's being the most plausible would not turn up, then sooner or infinitely later, sense data associated centrally or noncentrally with a maximally plausible explanation of the noneventuation, an explanation containing the statement that the original explanation is maximally plausible, would themselves, conditions being right, turn up. Because the existence of an explanation regress does not refute the co-topicity thesis, a thesis implied by the conception that physical-thing statements are elastically summarizing only of sense data, but instead arises as a harmonious consequence of the thesis (since of the conception), the regress does not constitute the independent argument in favor of The Physical-Taint Objection – when the objection goes further than the infinite-series troubles – that it would have to if it were to be prejudicial to the effort to transform a physical-thing statement into one making no physical-thing reference but an infinity of references to sense data. A disjunctive listing of sense-datum clauses can accomplish the same as any "E_n" provided the listing is endlessly about sense data associated centrally with "E_n" and centrally or noncentrally with a maximally plausible explanation for its not appearing as if E_n. A collection of clauses after the fashion of "A_n of if . . . , than A_{n+1} (*i.e.*, there would be sense data as of [27] 'E_n' 's being true) or if . . ., then A_{n+2} (*i.e.*, there would be sense data – call them a_{n+2} – as of 'E_n' 's being included in the most plausible explanation for 'A_{n+1}' 's falsity) or if . . ., then A_{n+3} (*i.e.*, there would be sense data – call them a_{n+3} – as of the truth of 'The most plausible explanation for the absence of a_{n+2} contains the statement that 'E_n' is included in the most plausible explanation for 'A_{n+1}' 's falsity') or if . . . , then A_{n+4} (*i.e.*, there would be sense data – call them a_{n+4} – as of the truth of 'The most plausible explanation for the absence of a_{n+3} contains the statement that the most plausible explanation for the absence of a_{n+2} contains the statement that 'E_n' is included in the most plausible explanation for 'A_{n+1}' 's falsity') . . . etc.," would, could it be articulated, convey the same as any "A_n or E_n" disjunction. But if this is so, the defender of mutual entailment has reached his goal. For the infinite series that the disjunctive listing would comprise is an infinite series with an inherent pattern. This means that the infinite series is replaceable by an ". . . and so on" after the point where the rule for this ". . . and so on" becomes apparent.

It is true that a sense-datum counterpart of this rule will set one upon the same kind of regress with which the phenomenalist has just wrestled. The sense-datum counterpart of the rule will have to replace its own "A_n or E_n" regress with an infinite collection, and then that with an ". . . and so on." But there is no reason to agonize over this. Nor are difficulties like this peculiar to the statement of this rule. If ever an adequate naturalistic analysis of the subjunctive conditional is effected, it will almost certainly not be in sense-datum terms; to get a counterpart in sense-datum terms, subjunctive conditionals will have to be employed. The analysis of subjunctive conditionals will require, at the sense-datum level, the employment of subjunctive conditionals. But no one takes this as disqualifying subjunctive conditionals from utilization in sense-datum counterparts. Therefore, to disqualify the utilization of ". . . and so on" on the grounds that the rule for the ". . . and so on" needs, at the sense-datum level, the use of the same expression suggests partiality. The important thing is that the rule can be learnt; having been learnt, it can be summarized by an ". . . and so on."

But now it may look as if the counterpart, even if it is immune to The Physical-Taint Objection, fails *vis-à-vis* The Infinity Objection: it may look as if the offered counterpart can be true while the ski statement of which it is to be the equivalent is false. It may look, in short, as if the sense-datum statement does not entail the statement about skis. Surely

[27] Sense data "as of" refer only to central sense data in the same way that "xish" sense data refer only to central x sense data.

there are cases where, if there were closetish sense data, there would be skiish sense data, but where there are not skis in the closet but only, for example, a *trompe-l'oeil* painting of skis. If it is true that if there were closetish sense data there would be skiish sense data, then clearly it will also be true that if there were closetish sense data there would be skiish sense data or else p, where "p" is any subjunctive-mood clause at all. But then it will be true that if there were closetish sense data there would be skiish sense data or else the most plausible explanation why there are not skiish sense data would contain "A pair of skis is in the closet" or an equivalent as one constituent. And, as we see, this will be true at the same time that "A pair of skis is in the closet" is false, showing, it is claimed, that the attempt at a counterpart for the latter statement has not triumphed anyway.

This objection, however, misreads the counterpart. It takes a single instance of closetish sense data accompanied by skiish sense data as verifying the statement that if there were closetish sense data there would be skiish sense data, and consequently, as verifying the counterpart statement as a whole. But the counterpart statement is intended as a general statement – a statement about what *always* happens when there are closetish (remember the proviso) sense data – and, hence, no experience of a single conjunction of sense data can possibly verify it completely. Only a very large number of ski-in-closet appearances, mediated by a number of senses, or a large number of maximally plausible explanations of the required kind, can approach to this effect. The *trompe-l'oeil* painting, thus, does not present a counterexample to the counterpart's claim to be true always and only when the ski statement is true. For the case of the painting to serve as a counterexample, the painting would have to mislead consistently under all logically possible observation conditions and when perceived by no matter what sense, but this it cannot do if there is to be any significance to calling it a painting and to the resistance against taking it to be a presentation of real skis. Either the painting will not mislead under all logically possible observation conditions, in which case the actual misleading conjunctions of skiish and closetish sense data produced by the painting will verify the counterpart statement only tentatively and only to the same degree that they will verify the ski statement; or else the painting will mislead under all logically possible observation conditions, in which case, however, the painting ceases effectively to be a painting and becomes indistinguishable from real skis.

V

The method of achieving an entailment counterpart for "A pair of skis is in the closet" has a certain instructiveness for other forms of reductionism too. The unreconstructed reductionist may be able to find here a way to reconstruct, so to say, his reductionism. Specifically, the analytic behaviorist may find it useful to explore whether phychological statements are elastically summarizing of what physical-thing statements say and whether physical-thing counterparts may be found. Offhand, one would expect that it would, if anything, be easier for the behaviorist to frame counterparts than for the phenomenalist, since the behaviorist, if he assumes naturalism, is not under the phenomenalist's constraint to banish explicit references to explanations from his counterparts. But, then, even if things are constructions out of appearances, this is not to say that things will always turn out to be as they casually seem.

EXPLANATION AND PHILOSOPHICAL SYSTEMS

THE CERTAINTY OF THE *COGITO* AND THE EXISTENCE OF GOD

by

WILLIAM WIEBENGA

I

The problem which I wish to discuss in this paper can be presented in the first instance as a problem concerning the structure of the *Meditations*. The *Meditations* begin with a discussion of what can be brought within the sphere of the doubtful. In this discussion Descartes notes that a vast portion of his beliefs rest on his senses. He then turns his attention to the senses as a basis of belief and observes that his senses sometimes deceive him. Having observed this, his problem becomes that of arguing from this sometime fact to the general proposition that in all of his beliefs he is being deceived. This he finds is no small feat. After all, he is very mindful that there is a big difference between himself and those who have fallen prey to the black bile – the most violent of vapors. Here he sits in his dressing gown while such as these fancy themselves clad in the robes of kings.

To assist himself in the project of generalizing the possibility of deceit, he turns away from his waking life to his dream life. Here he finds ready assistance. In his dream life he has almost been able to match the feats of those who are victims of the black bile and to turn his dressing gown into a robe of kings. But even his heady dreams succumb to the penetrations of reason. Dreams after all are not so different from the stuff that paintings are made of. Just as in paintings there have to be colors and lines, pigment and canvas, so in dreams there have to be qualities and properties that are configured together according to the dictates of fantasy. As he begins to think about the basic stuff from which things are made, it becomes less important that he cannot distinguish between dreams and waking life. For whether asleep or awake, it is quite difficult to argue with properties about basic or simple things and with propositions – propositions like "2 + 3 = 5," and "A square can never have more than four sides."

But even as he here approaches some apparently constant and reliable beliefs he is overcome by an overwhelming bit of fantasy. He runs head on into the possibility of an all-powerful deity who instead of being good is of ill disposition and engages in deceit. And with this possibility nothing seems to be such that it cannot be brought into the sphere of the doubtful.

Before going on it is important to pause and take note of something that may prove relevant at a later point. To give even the status of possibility to an all-powerful being requires a rather large capacity for fantasy. Thus, Descartes does give pause to consider the position of those who would deny the existence of an all-powerful God. To such as these he gives little comfort. He reminds them of their imperfection – the imperfection of error and deceit – and notes that in the absence of a perfect being, or all-powerful being, there is nothing but a progression in imperfection. Such a progression increases the possibility of constant deceit. With this observation, his doubt becomes complete. Apparently for Descartes the possibility of being deceived *sometimes* is such as to make it impossible to rule out the possibility of his being deceived *all the time* and as such carries with it the possibility of a general doubt.

As Descartes continues to reflect on his doubt, he finds that he must place some limits on his doubt after all. Grant the possibility of an arch-deceiver, he says, there is still something that cannot be doubted:

> But there is some deceiver or other, very powerful and very cunning, who ever employs his ingenuity in deceiving me. Then without doubt I exist also if he deceives me, and let him deceive me, as much as he will he can never cause me to be nothing so long as I think that I am something. So that after having reflected well and carefully examined all things, we must come to the definite conclusion that this proposition: I am, I exist, is necessarily true each time that I pronounce it, or that I mentally conceive it (*The Philosophical Meditations,* II, in E. Haldane and G. Ross, *Works of Descartes,* vol. I, Dover Edition, p. 150).

Having arrived at this proposition, a proposition necessarily true each time it is pronounced or thought, Descartes probes in earnest to discover just what it is that he is certain about when he thinks this proposition. He quickly finds that he must rule out any propositions relating to or depending upon his body – for his body is known to him through his senses, and thus, subject to doubt. Thus, all that is left as a matter of certainty is the activity of thinking, and that activity is left only as an activity distinct from sensation (here sensation is not be identified with perception). His existence, *i.e.,* the existence of which he is certain, is restricted to his engaging in the activity of thinking.

Descartes' treatment of this small gem of certainty is definitely marked by two sides. On the one hand, in his certainty about the activity of thinking, Descartes is not at all in a position to claim certainty about any other information with which he is provided through his senses. He considers a particular piece of wax and finds that his senses are not able to provide him with such information as leads him to judge that it is the same whether it is a cool lump or a hot liquid. This judgment is the work of the mind alone. On the other hand, in that the only reliable knowledge which he has of the wax depends on the mind alone, *i.e.*, on thinking, he is quite confident that in being certain about the mind, there is much that he is certain about.

As a first step in expanding and explicating his knowledge of himself, Descartes asks himself what it is that makes it possible for him to be certain of the truth that he exists. His answer is as follows: "Certainly in this first knowledge there is nothing that assures me of its truth, excepting the clear and distinct perception of that which I state, . . ." (Haldane and Ross, *op. cit.*, vol. I, p. 158). And he immediately proceeds to generalize this point: ". . . which would not indeed suffice to assure me that what I say is true, if it could ever happen that a thing which I conceived so clearly and distinctly could be false; and accordingly it seems to me that already I can establish as a general rule that all things which I perceive very clearly and very distinctly are true" (Haldane and Ross, *op. cit.*, vol. I, p. 158). With the establishment of this general rule, the discussion of the certainty of the *Cogito* is for the present brought to completion by Descartes. His *Meditations* turn to quite another topic, or seemingly so: *the existence of God.*

This fact about the structure of his *Meditations* provides us with an initial formulation of the problem of this paper. Once having established as a starting point for knowledge the certainty of the *Cogito,* and having found in this knowledge of the *Cogito* a criterion of certainty and truth, namely, the clarity and distinctness with which he conceived the existence of the *Cogito,* why does Descartes find it necessary to go on to concern himself with the existence of God? A solution to this problem can be readily suggested. It can be suggested that the existence of God had to be demonstrated to eliminate the possibility of his being deceived. Descartes himself begins his discussion of the existence of God with a reminder that even in matters in which he believes himself to have the best evidence, it is possible for an all-powerful God to cause him to err. He goes on to say that in order altogether to remove his doubt he must inquire "whether there is a God as soon as the occasion presents itself; and [he says] if I find that there is a God, I must also inquire whether he may be a deceiver; for without a knowledge of these two truths I do not see that I can ever be certain of anything" (*Ibid.*, p. 159). This last statement suggests that the general rule, established only two paragraphs back, has been set forth too hastily. Before anything can be known with certainty the evil genius must be dispensed with once and for all. The existence of God, the guileless one, must be established before anything else can be known with certainty.

This solution is, however, not without problems:

(1) This point does not seem to extend to the certainty of the *Cogito*. Descartes reaffirms in this very paragraph his conviction concerning the existence of the *Cogito*.

(2) Descartes further explicates his criterion of truth by making reference to the principle of contradiction and urges that such propositions as " '3 + 2 = 5' depend upon it for their truth" (*Ibid.*, p. 159).

(3) The proof for the existence of God is itself a venture of the *Cogito* which on the surface at least only leads to certainty about the existence of God if it is possible for us to think without being deceived.

We are, thus, left with a problem: Given the certainty of the *Cogito*, why does the existence of God need to be proved? If the *Cogito* is not certain, can the existence of God be proved?

II

This problem is not by any means a new problem in the study of Descartes. This problem appears already in the objections to the *Meditations* presented to Descartes by his contemporaries. In the second set of objections collected by Father Mersenne, the problem is formulated as follows:

> Since you are not yet certain of the aforesaid existence of God, and yet according to your statement, cannot be certain of anything or know anything clearly and distinctly unless previously you know certainly and clearly that God exists, it follows that you cannot clearly and distinctly know that you are a thinking thing, since, according to you, that knowledge depends on the clear knowledge of the existence of God, the proof of which you have not yet reached at that point where you draw the conclusion that you have a clear knowledge of what your are (*Objections*, II, Haldane and Ross, *op. cit.*, vol. II, p. 26).

This presents the problem in what might be called a converse form: If the certainty of the *Cogito* does depend upon certainty with respect to the existence of God, how can one be certain as to the *Cogito* before achieving certainty with respect to the existence of God?

In the fourth set of objections, those of Father Arnauld, the problem is also discussed:

> The only remaining scruple I have is an uncertainty as to how a circular reasoning is to be avoided in saying: The only secure reason we have for believing

that what we clearly and distinctly perceive is true, is the fact that God exists.

But we can be sure that God exists, only because we clearly and evidently perceive that; therefore prior to being certain that God exists, we should be certain that whatever we clearly and evidently perceive is true (*Objections*, IV, *ibid.*, p. 92).

In this objection, the problem is presented as a problem in circular reasoning. We can only believe that what we clearly and distinctly perceive is certain because God exists, but God's existence is certain only because we clearly and distinctly perceive that he exists. With reference to the *Cogito*, it can thus be said that either the fact that I know that I exist is sufficient to establish the principle that what we clearly and distinctly perceive exists or there will be no way in the absence of this principle to prove the existence of God.

This same formulation of the problem is made by Gassendi and is referred to in Descartes' letter to Clerselier (*Ibid.*, pp. 130-31). In the fifth set of objections Gassendi also suggests that the proof of the existence of God is somewhat irrelevant to the issue of whether anyone would regard as certain the propositions of geometry and the conclusions of mathematical demonstrations. In emphasizing this point he says:

So true is this [that the demonstrations of geometry have a certainty about them without reference to God] that the mind will as likely as not bid that the evil genius go to perdition; just as you might have done when you (although the existence of God was not yet known) asserted with much emphasis that you could not be imposed on about that proposition and inference: I think, hence, I exist (*Objections*, V, *ibid.*, p. 189).

This point also occurs in the sixth set of objections where it is observed that the atheist cannot even frame statements such as those of mathematics and geometry mentally without believing them to be absolutely certain. This certainty the atheist has apart from any belief in the existence of God. Even if God existed the atheist cannot conceive of himself as being deceived about such matters by God (*Objections*, VI, *ibid.*, pp. 235-36).

This fact about atheists is related to still another way in which the problems we are discussing is put in the sixth set of objections. The question is asked: "How can the truths of geometry or metaphysics such as you mention be immutable and eternal, and yet not be independent of God?" (*Ibid.*, p. 238). The point is here being made that if truths are eternal they cannot really depend for their truth on God, or if they really do depend on God they cannot be eternal.

The problem that is being posed for discussion in this essay has been long-standing in the criticism of Cartesian philosophy. Not only was it posed by those critics who were contemporaries of Descartes, it is posed by more recent critics of Descartes. H. A. Prichard focuses on this problem in his book *Knowledge and Perception.* First, he presents Descartes' doubt in what he considers to be its most fundamental form. He does not view the possibility of there being an evil genius as crucial to the doubt to which Descartes is giving expression when he doubts mathematical truths. From his point of view in calling attention to the possibility of our being deceived, Descartes is raising the question of whether our capacity for thought is such that it can enable us to attain a state in which we cannot be mistaken. He is raising the question of whether our intelligence is capable of giving us knowledge.

Having so characterized Descartes' doubt Prichard goes on to observe that Descartes' idea of how this doubt is to be put to rest is "obviously mistaken." It is mistaken because it requires the mind in proving the existence of God not only to complete such a proof, but to perceive clearly and distinctly that in completing this proof it is not mistaken. But given the general character of Descartes' doubt, this is precisely what is placed in doubt – whether the mind can complete a proof without being deceived in the process. To try to remove this doubt by any process of proof is, therefore, impossible given the extent of the doubt which Descartes has expressed. (This discussion is based on a reprint of this portion of Prichard's book in *Descartes: A Collection of Critical Essays,* ed. Willis Doney [Garden City, N. Y., 1967] pp. 146-147.)

There is much in Descartes' *Meditations* to support putting this problem in this almost insoluble form. Descartes urges that certainty with respect to everything hinges upon establishing that God, and not an evil genius able to deceive us, exists. In speaking of the truth that God exists Descartes writes

> At present I not only feel myself to be as assured of it as of all that I hold as most certain, but I also remark that the certainty of all other things depends on it so absolutely, that without this knowledge it is impossible ever to know anything perfectly (Haldane and Ross, *op. cit.,* vol. I, p. 183).

He also goes on to characterize the proposition that "What I perceive clearly and distinctly cannot fail to be true" as an inference from the proposition that there is a God. Both of these points suggest that no knowledge or certainty is possible prior to a proof that God exists. And yet, proving that God exists is itself only possible if one can have some prior certainty as to the reliability of one's intelligence – of one's mind and its processes. If the mind must engage in proof before it can be certain of its capacity to prove, the problem of removing doubts does indeed seem to be an insoluble one.

Prichard's discussion of the above problem has been included in the volume entitled *Descartes: A Collection of Critical Essays* edited by Willis Doney. In this volume, including the selection from Prichard's book *Knowledge and Perception,* there are a total of four essays in which the main problem of this paper is explicitly discussed. A. K. Stout, in an essay originally published in *Mind,* discusses this problem as one of appropriately relating "three main grounds of certainty" which Descartes reaches in the *Meditations.*

These are (1) the intuition of the necessity of his own existence, stated in the rather misleading form "*cogito ergo sum*;" (2) the general rule that all that is clearly and distinctly perceived is true; and (3) the veracity of God (A. K. Stout, "The Basis of Knowledge in Descartes" [Doney, *op. cit.,* p. 169]).

In an essay entitled "The Creation of the Eternal Truths in Descartes's System" Emile Brehier argues that Descartes viewed eternal truths as created, so as to account at once for their independence as eternal truths and their dependence on God. He relates this view of the eternal truths in Descartes directly to the criticisms of Descartes' contemporaries who maintained that if truths were eternal they could be known with certainty apart from God. In his essay entitled "Descartes' Validation of Reason" Harry G. Frankfurt sets out to clarify "just what question about reason Descartes found it necessary to ask in the *Meditations* and how he thought it possible to give a reasonable answer to it." This he sets out to do in order to make it "easier to judge fairly whether or not his reasoning is free of vicious circularity and other defects" (Doney, *op. cit.,* p. 209).

The above essays are mentioned only to provide some indication of the prominence in current discussions of Descartes' philosophy of the problem that forms the topic of this paper. The fact that this problem continues to have prominence in current discussions of Cartesian philosophy suggests two things: first, that the problem has not yet been finally resolved and, secondly, that it is a problem that is of central importance in the philosophy of Descartes.

III

The first attempts to resolve the problem of the relation of the certainty of the *Cogito* to the proof for the existence of God were made by Descartes himself in response to the criticisms of his contemporaries. Father Mersenne asked how Descartes could have certainty concerning the *Cogito* when he had not yet proved the existence of God, since the main purpose for proving the existence of God was to make certainty possible. In response to this question Descartes wrote as follows:

When I said that we could know nothing with certainty unless we were first aware that God existed, I announced in express terms that I referred only to the science apprehending such conclusions as can recur in memory without attending further to the proofs which led me to make them. Further, knowledge of first principles is not usually called science by dialecticians. But when we become aware that we are thinking beings, this is a primitive act of knowledge derived from no syllogistic reasoning (Haldane and Ross, *op. cit.*, vol. II, p. 38).

In this response Descartes is quite concerned to distinguish between the first principles and propositions which are known as the conclusions of proofs. He is equally concerned to distinguish between the manner in which first principles are known and the manner in which the propositions which constitute conclusions of proofs are known. First principles are essentially nonderivative propositions. We become aware of them through what he calls "a primitive act of knowledge derived from no syllogistic reasoning." Propositions which form conclusions of proofs, on the other hand, are derivative, and are known by means of a process of reasoning. Using this distinction to solve the problem raised by Father Mersenne, Descartes suggests that the dependence of certainty upon the existence of God applies to those propositions which are grasped as the conclusions of proofs. The certainty of the *Cogito* is not dependent upon the existence of God because the proposition "I think, therefore I am" is not the conclusion of an inference but a first principle. Thus, one can achieve certainty with respect to this proposition prior to achieving certainty as to the existence of God.

The proposition which Descartes develops in response to Father Mersenne is the one by which he stands in responding to his other critics. He refers Father Arnauld to this response and says "There I distinguished those matters that in actual truth we clearly perceive from those we remember to have formerly perceived" (*Ibid.*, p. 115).

In his "Letter to Clerselier" in which he discusses the fifth set of objections he refers both to his reply to Father Mersenne and to his reply to Father Arnauld. In his reply to the fifth set of objections he passes rather lightly over the objection that the eternal truths of geometry can be known independently of knowledge that God exists and considers his previous replies sufficient response to any charge of circularity in his reasoning (*Ibid.*, p. 229). In a later discussion of the atheists' knowledge of such truths as geometrical truths Descartes asserts that "It is easy to prove thus it is not immutable and certain" (*Reply to Objections*, VI, *ibid.*, p. 245). The atheist cannot claim to have as the source of his nature a perfect being. Consequently, he has the greater reason to doubt "whether he may not be of such an imperfect nature as to be deceived in matters which appear most evident to him: and he cannot be set free from that doubt unless he first acknowledges that he has been created by the true God, a God who has no intention to deceive" (*Idem*). In the reply to the same set of objections Descartes sees no conflict in allowing both that truths are eternal and that they depend on God. He does not regard the fact that truths are eternal as in any sense an indication of their dependence on something other than God, or presumably, of their independence of God. (See *ibid.*, p. 251).

In summary, then, Descartes never appears to waver from the view that certainty in human knowledge depends upon certainty concerning the existence of God. If the certainty of the *Cogito* is an exception to this, it is because it is itself a first principle. But human knowledge is not simply a set of first principles, it is science, *i.e.*, a worked-out body of propositions derived by logical principles of reasoning. As such, human knowledge requires something more than the primitive acts whereby first principles are known. It requires reasoning. But such reasoning is only regarded by Descartes as reliable to the extent that the mind originates with God, rather than an arch-deceiver.

There is a significant respect in which Descartes' solution to the problem posed by Father Mersenne and others is very unsatisfactory. Descartes' reply to Mersenne may explain how one can be certain of the *Cogito* prior to achieving certainty as to the existence of God. If the *Cogito* is a first principle known through a primitive act of knowledge, it in some meaningful sense cannot depend on knowledge of the existence of God for its certainty. But if this reply explains how certainty with respect to the *Cogito* is possible prior to knowledge that God exists, it does not explain how one can proceed from that certainty to the knowledge that God exists. Indeed, the reply poses a serious complication of the problem. As arising from a nonderivative primitive act of knowledge the *Cogito* itself must be a simple proposition. As a simple proposition, however, it does not itself imply the existence of God. Indeed, Descartes speaks of a proof as necessary for knowing that God exists. This in itself is sufficient to make clear that the existence of God cannot immediately be inferred from the certainty of the *Cogito*. But if knowledge of the existence of God itself requires a proof, and no proofs can be regarded as reliable until the existence of God is established, then it is not clear how one can ever proceed from the certainty of the *Cogito* to knowledge of the existence of God. Thus, it is not clear how one can move from the certainty of the *Cogito* to the certainty of any other proposition that requires that it be proved in order to be known.

Before any further discussion of this problem it is well to consider what some others have said by way of a solution to Descartes's problem. In this way we may place before ourselves some additional options for solving Descartes' problem. As noted above, H. A. Prichard judges that Descartes has confronted himself with an insoluble problem. From Prichard's point of view Descartes imposes impossible demands upon the process of knowledge. Descartes in seeking for certainty in human knowledge requires not only that I clearly and distinctly perceive that X is the case, but also that by an independent act of the mind I clearly and distinctly perceive that I clearly and distinctly perceive that X is the case. From this it is possible for me to infer both that "X is the case" is true and that X exists. It is the requirement of this latter act of the mind which makes it possible to direct doubt toward our knowledge that X is the case. If in the same act of knowing that X is the case we grasp that we know that X is the case, such doubt is not possible and Descartes' problem never arises.

Since Prichard's solution to Descartes' problem requires a recasting of the entire problem of knowledge, there is a sense in which it is not really a solution. It does not represent an option among a range of options for solving the problem of relating the certainty of the *Cogito* to the existence of God within Descartes' philosophy. It rather constitutes a way by which this problem can be avoided altogether.

A. K. Stout first discusses the relation between what he refers to as the "three main grounds of certainty" in Descartes *Meditations* from the point of view of the structure of the *Meditations*. These three main grounds are (1) the intuition of the necessity of his own existence; (2) the general rule that all that is clearly and distinctly perceived is true; (3) the veracity of God. The structure of the *Meditations* suggests that Descartes first found himself in possession of the intuition of the necessity of his own existence. From this intuition, he derived the general rule that all that is clearly and distinctly perceived is true. But, then, he found that there were instances in which he had thought that he had grasped propositions with clarity and distinctness, and thus, with certainty, only to find that later he was uncertain about these propositions – or, at least, only to find that later he was uncertain as to what had made him certain. On these occasions it was not as clear to him that the general rule "Whatever I clearly and distinctly perceive is true" is reliable since deception seemed to be a possibility. Thus, in order to remove this possibility of deception he proceeds to demonstrate the existence and veracity of God and, thus, the reliability of his understanding.

Stout maintains that however much Descartes may at times have suggested that this is the appropriate relation between the three grounds of certainty, this is not in fact how Descartes viewed their relationship. His reasons are as follows. The first reason involves the relation of the general rule to the *Cogito*. It would be logically incorrect to derive the general rule "What I clearly and distinctly perceive is true" from a single instance. Thus, Stout does not believe that this is what Descartes does. For Stout the *Cogito* is an instance which as an instance exemplifies the rule. But in such an instance reference to the rule is unnecessary. In such an instance, as in any in which one clearly and distinctly perceives a specific proposition, no reference to the rule is necessary – *i.e.*, the rule itself is not an issue. Thus, while Descartes does *note* the rule in connection with the certainty of the *Cogito*, he does not derive the rule from it.

The second reason for setting aside the above account of the relation of the three main grounds of certainty involves the relation of the general rule "Whatever I clearly and distinctly perceive is true" to the existence of God. The use of this rule cannot depend upon establishing the veracity of God because there is no way in which the existence and veracity of God could be established without its use. And if this were the case, Descartes could not be defended against a vicious circularity.

In defense of Descartes, Stout suggests the following relationship between the three main grounds of certainty. First, as already noted, the general rule "Whatever I clearly and distinctly perceive is true" is a rule that Descartes never places in question. He does not place it in question because in those instances which exemplify the rule one cannot doubt either the specific instance or the rule. One's state of mind, in short, is one of certainty, not doubt, in all such instances. Descartes' problem, however is not with such instances. His problem is with developing a system of knowledge out of what by themselves seem to be fragmentary insights. The development of a system of knowledge requires the use of memory since it involves deriving propositions one from another in logical sequence. It is in this reliance on memory that deception is possible. Thus, the veracity of God must be established so as to establish the reliability of the mind, so to speak, "between the acts," when memory holds before the mind the previous steps of a proof.

In order to stave off the charge of circularity that may still be presented against Descartes on the above relationships of the three grounds of certainty, Stout distinguishes between two different types of memory. The proof of the existence of God, as a proof, involves more than one step. Thus, memory is involved in it. If God's existence and veracity were thus demonstrated in order to establish the reliability of memory, there would be circularity in using memory to establish its own reliability. But Stout distinguishes between "retentiveness" and "reminiscence." "Retentiveness" involves keeping before the mind several steps of a proof "all at once," so to speak, so that the conclusion can be seen as an immediate consequence of these steps. "Reminiscence" involves remembering that a proposition has been proved, and thus, taking for certain, without recalling the concrete, detailed steps of the proof. Stout bases this distinction on several passages in the *Meditations* and suggests that it is to establish the reliability of the latter, not the former, that the existence of God is proved. In the proof itself, however, it is retentiveness that is involved. In this way no circularity is presumably involved.

In his paper "Descartes' Validation of Reason," Harry G. Frankfurt takes exception to such an interpretation of Descartes as that made by Stout. Frankfurt argues that what Descartes is really placing in question is not simply the reliability of memory, but the reliability of the mind even in its acts of intuition when that which is grasped presents itself as indubitable. In this view Frankfurt is in agreement with Emile Brehier. In his essay "The Creation of Eternal Truth" Brehier writes that it would be wrong

> to say that, according to Descartes, the divine guarantee is necessary only for reasoning that cannot be grasped in its entirety by intuition. On the contrary, the guarantee bears on actual intuition, though it is also related to time and memory. By the very nature of human reason it would be useless at the moment of intuition: for "as soon as I understand something very clearly and very distinctly, I cannot prevent myself from believing it to be true." The only problem is to know how I can foresee with certainty that, my intuition being, as it were, detached, what is intuited will continue to be true (Doney, *op. cit.*, p. 201).

Brehier does not himself in this essay relate this discussion to any attempts to solve the problem of circularity in Descartes. Frankfurt, however, does.

Frankfurt suggests that unless one sees the metaphysical doubt as directed toward the reliability of the mind in its very acts of intuition, one cannot fully appreciate just how Descartes is able to remove that doubt through establishing the existence of God. A key point in the development of Frankfurt's view is that it is not seen by Descartes as necessarily the case that what is indubitable is as such true. All that is needed is a lapse of time, some distance of the mind from its own acts of intuition, in order for the mind to begin to suspect that a proposition that previously presented itself as indubitable may be false. It may be false if indeed an evil genius so manipulated our minds that in every act in which something presented itself to the mind as indubitable, this something is in fact false.

When Descartes' doubt is put in this radical form, two points may seem to follow. First, it may seem as if there were no way in which such a doubt could ever be removed. Second, it may seem as if any use of reason to remove such doubt would involve reason in circularity. With respect to the first point, Frankfurt observes that it is extremely important to keep in mind that Descartes' metaphysical doubt is itself a creation of reason. Descartes never establishes the principle that what is indubitable is true. His concern extends no further than to deal with those "reasons" on the basis of which one might doubt that the indubitable is true. The reason in particular with which he deals is the evil genius. And what Descartes shows is that the most careful use of reason establishes the existence not of an evil genius, but rather of God. Once the existence of God is established, no ground remains any longer for doubting that what presents itself as indubitable is true. Since reason must be used in the process of establishing the existence of God, there is circularity involved in the process. But this circularity is the less vicious if one notes two points: first, that it is a most careful exercise of reason that establishes the existence of God, and second, that it is reason itself which also gave rise to the possibility of there being an evil genius and, hence, the metaphysical doubt.

IV

The above views suggest some of the options by means of which the main problem of this paper – that of relating the certainty of the *Cogito* to the existence of God – may be resolved. In the concluding portions of this paper, I would like to review these options, and through this review arrive at some further speculations as to the relation of the certainty of the *Cogito* to the existence of God in Cartesian philosophy. In the above discussions there are three main options set forth. The first is that Descartes' problem is insoluble, because it is ill-formed. The second is that the problem is to be solved by limiting the scope of metaphysical doubt to the reliability of memory. The third is to solve the problem in a limited way in the context of the widest possible doubt – one which ultimately encompasses the *Cogito* itself along with other propositions that seem to present themselves to the mind as eternal truths.

The first option is that of Prichard. For purposes of this paper, this option is the least interesting of the three, even though in the long run it may be the most relevant. Before setting this option aside, it should be noted that Prichard may not have correctly interpreted Descartes. Prichard suggests that for Descartes the problem of knowledge is that of clearly and distinctly perceiving that in knowing that X exists I clearly and distinctly perceive that X exists. As such, knowledge involves three levels: first, that of clearly and distinctly perceiving that X exists; second, that of clearly and distinctly perceiving that I clearly and distinctly perceive that X exists; and third, inferring from this that I know that X exists, and that X exists. Prichard regards these three levels as necessary to account for the possibility of doubt. It is not in its first act of clear and distinct perception that the mind doubts, but rather in the second act, and in the inferences that are based on it, that the mind doubts. That is to say, the mind doubts that its clear and distinct perception of its own clear and distinct perception that X exists is really sufficient to establish that X exists.

In this interpretation of Descartes, Prichard may be mistaken. It may well be the case that doubt requires a double act of the mind. That is to say, doubt may be possible only as an act of the mind which is directed toward an act of the mind. It may also be the case that removal of a specific doubt requires a double act of the mind. That is to say, to remove a doubt "that X exists" I may have to direct the mind to that act of the mind whereby I affirm that X exists. But it is not clear that in Descartes' philosophy the absence of doubt in making a judgment, *i.e.*, a judgment's presence before the mind as indubitable, requires a double act of mind. What presents itself as indubitable cannot be doubted. What I clearly and distinctly perceive is for Descartes indubitable. It is only through reflection on such acts that I can come to doubt their reliability. But this reflection need not be an immediate accompaniment of every judgment. It is a reflection that can occur at a later time. Indeed, it must occur at a later time in order for it to exist at all. It does indeed require Descartes to retire to his room in his dressing gown. This is a presupposition of the effectiveness of an evil genius. For the evil genius to be effective I must regard as indubitable whatever I clearly and distinctly perceive without any possibility for reflection upon my state of mind. Thus, Prichard is misinterpreting Descartes when he suggests that for Descartes the problem of knowledge is one of achieving certainty concerning one's own state of mind when apprehending whatever it is that one has certainty about. Thus, Prichard's judgment that the Cartesian problem is ill-formed and, therefore, insoluble, may also be mistaken.

The second option for consideration is that of Descartes himself and of Stout. As Descartes develops this option, metaphysical doubt is directed only to those propositions which are not first principles. It is extended to those propositions which are presented to the mind as conclusions of proofs. First principles such as the *Cogito* are objects of intuition and as such are indubitable. Propositions presented to the mind as conclusions of proofs are dubitable. They are dubitable because their certainty depends on correctly remembering the series of steps by which they have been derived from first principles. The removal of doubt is possible once it is established that there is a God who does not deceive us. Given the existence of God, the operations of the mind including memory are reliable, and that metaphysical doubt rooted in the possibility of deception is eliminated. Stout modifies this view so as to make it possible to speak of proof in connection with establishing the existence of God without an obvious circularity. According to Stout, the unreliability of memory does not extend to that type of memory which he has characterized as "retentiveness," but only to what he characterizes as "reminiscence."

Many considerations can be advanced in support of this option. One of the most obvious considerations is the extent to which Descartes himself stands on this option in defending himself against charges of circularity. This has already been noted above. A second consideration is that it explains how Descartes could regard as certain many other propositions besides the *Cogito* and never call these propositions into question. In his *Principles of Philosophy*, Part I, Principle X, Descartes writes:

> And when I stated that this proposition *I think, therefore I am* is the first and most certain which presents itself to those who philosophize in orderly fashion, I did not for all that deny that we must first of all know *what is knowledge, what is existence,* and *what is certainty,* and that *in order to think we must be,* and such like; but because these are notions of the simplest possible kind, which of themselves give us no knowledge of anything that exists, I did not think them worthy of being put on record (*Principles of Philosophy,* I, X, Haldane and Ross, *op. cit.,* vol. I, p. 222).

He is very careful in this passage to speak of these as "notions" rather than "propositions." Nevertheless, the contrast between "notions" and "propositions" may not be what is important in this passage. More important may be his concern to distinguish propositions that involve no more than the linking of concepts from judgments about what exists. Clearly, the *Cogito* is the first proposition as to what does or does not exist that Descartes is prepared to accept following his adoption of the method of doubt. But this does not rule out the possibility of his having previously assumed many propositions which are in effect definitions without which it would not even be possible to discuss knowledge. The list of "notions" which he presents includes at least one such proposition: "In order to think we must be." The proposition that "No qualities or properties pertain to nothing; and that where some are perceived there must necessarily be some thing or substance on which they depend" (*Principles,* I, XI, *ibid.,* p. 223) is another example of a proposition which he uses in the development of our knowledge. In the context of his reply to the second set of objections, Descartes presents his proof for the existence of God in a geometrical form. Before he proves any propositions about God he sets down a lengthy list of definitions, postulates, and axioms. All of these are "propositions" as distinct from "notions." And the certainty of all of these is assumed apart from any application of the method of doubt. This is understandable, however, if the method of doubt is not at all directed at first principles, or self-evident propositions, but only at those propositions which can only be affirmed as the conclusions of proofs.

There is a third consideration which supports the view that Descartes restricts his doubt to propositions resulting from proofs and thus relying on memory. This view explains why Descartes was insistent upon maintaining that the *Cogito* is not an inference. This insistence has already been noted in citing his replies to his critics above.

A fourth consideration which supports the above view is that it provides a possible explanation of the status of the general principle that whatever is clearly and distinctly perceived is true. This principle may be regarded by Descartes as one of those general propositions which defines what knowledge is prior to any actual acquisition. Descartes does advance this principle after he has achieved certainty with respect to the *Cogito*. But as we have already discussed, this does not necessarily imply that it was derived from the *Cogito*. The *Cogito* may be the first instance in which this principle is applied with the result of yielding knowledge of reality that cannot be doubted. But the principle itself may depend for its truth on nothing more than those notions which constitute in part the mind with which we think.

There is one final consideration to be advanced in favor of the option under discussion. This view explains Descartes' attempts to reduce the proof for the existence of God to its simplest form. Indeed, although initially in the *Meditations*, III, Descartes presents what appears to be a proof for the existence of God, *i.e.*, God's existence is affirmed as a conclusion following from a series of propositions, in *Meditations*, V, Descartes enters a new discussion of the existence of God. In this discussion, Descartes makes every effort to support the traditional ontological argument according to which the existence of God is implied by the very concept of God, an argument such that this nature cannot be thought at all without being thought of as including existence. This effort on the part of Descartes can be viewed as an effort to make the existence of God itself a first principle, a self-evident truth. Indeed in this context Descartes does go so far as to say

> And as regards God, if my mind were not preoccupied with prejudices, and if my thought did not find itself on all hands diverted by the continual pressure of sensible things, there would be nothing which I could know more immediately and more easily than him. For is there anything more manifest than that there is a God, that is to say a Supreme Being, to whose essence alone existence pertains? (*Meditations*, V, Haldane and Ross, *op. cit.*, vol. I, p. 183).

Although all of the above considerations support the view that for Descartes the method of doubt is restricted to those propositions which are known as the conclusions of proofs, there are also considerations which can be urged against this view. First, this view reduces the whole method of doubt to what may be called "a test of memory." This view suggests that of all the operations of which the mind is capable and of all the operations which are involved in the process of knowledge, it is primarily the memory which leads us into error. This seems to cast the entire system of Cartesian philosophy into a very different light. Descartes becomes not so much a philosopher in search of rules and principles for the right conduct of reason, but a philosopher in search of rules and principles for the correct use of memory.

This distortion of the entire system of Cartesian philosophy can be brought out in the additional considerations which can be urged against the option under discussion. In his defense of this option Stout uses the distinction between "retention" and "reminiscence." This distinction is indeed one which can be traced back to Descartes. Descartes does regard it as important to distinguish between viewing a proposition as an immediate inference from the premisses which precede it in a proof and recalling that proposition apart from its premisses. In the former case the proposition presents itself as certain in a way in which it does not in the latter case. But if this distinction is pushed, the entire method of doubt becomes a test of memory in only one type of its operations. Nor is it clear that this is the most important type of operation of memory – for, as it has been pointed out, the system of human knowledge is not thought by Descartes to be a collection of fragmented propositions. Moreover, if this distinction is pushed as crucial to the possibility of knowledge, there are two alternative points that would have to be considered. One point is that we would have to restrict the concept of "retention" only to those instances in which premisses and conclusions could be thought simultaneously. This would be a most limited set of arguments, for the mind can only retain before itself a small fragment of time. Empirically, the present constitutes but a small fraction of time. If one did not push the simultaneity in the mind of premisses and conclusion to this extent, one would have to consider an alternative point. This point is that there would be no way in principle by which "retention" could be limited to any given finite segment of our knowledge. In principle there is no reason within the Cartesian system why one could not present every conclusion in close conjunction with its premisses. Thus, there is in principle no reason why all memory could not take the form of retention. But if this were the case, the entire method of doubt would be unnecessary. This last observation leads to a third consideration that can be urged against the option under discussion. It may be granted that in principle the method of doubt is unnecessary. It may be urged that this method is advanced only to provide a test of memory in those instances involving reminiscence. But if this were the case, and in principle all of our knowledge could be constructed with certainty using only retention, then the existence of God would become much less central to the Cartesian system of philosophy. If God is needed only to assure the certainty of knowledge in cases involving reminiscence, his existence would be practically very important, but theoretically rather insignificant.

There is one final consideration to be urged against the option under discussion. As a test of memory the method of doubt would not extend to certainty as to the *Cogito* itself. The *Cogito* as a self-evident first principle would stand on equal footing with all of the other propositions presupposed by the possibility of knowledge. It would be no less certain than these, and no more certain than these. If this were the case, however, there would be little reason to single it out as a starting point of our knowledge. There would be no reason to regard this proposition as in any way unique. In short, the option under discussion would not only fail to do justice to the importance of the existence of God, it would also fail to do justice to the importance of the certainty of the *Cogito*.

Having found the two previous options posed for our consideration wanting, we are left with the third option for dealing with the problem of the relation of the certainty of the *Cogito* to the existence of God. The third option provides only a limited solution to the problem of circularity in proving the existence of God to establish the reliability of reason, but it provides that solution in the context of the widest possible doubt – one which extends to the *Cogito* itself along with all the other propositions which present themselves to the mind as eternal truths. This option is represented above in the view of Frankfurt. It is also represented in the view of Brehier. According to both of these views Cartesian doubt is so thoroughgoing as to extend even to those propositions which the mind grasps as indubitable. It extends to these propositions as well as all others precisely because it is directed to the reliability of the operations of the mind by which propositions are grasped. According to this view, if there is a circularity involved in using reason to prove the existence of God, this circularity is unavoidable. What is required by this view is some explanation of this circularity which does not render it vicious.

To speak of an explanation of circularity which does not render it vicious suggests that there is a meaningful distinction between vicious and nonvicious circularity. Rather than try to articulate formally what the distinction between vicious and nonvicious circularity is, I will do no more than specify with reference to Cartesian philosophy what vicious circularity would consist of. Cartesian philosophy would move in a vicious circle if

1) reason contained within itself the sufficient basis for doubting the reliability of reason;
2) reason were the only reality of which immediate certainty was possible;
3) reason were the only means of establishing its reliability to move beyond that immediate certainty.

under the above conditions, once reason found within itself a basis for doubting its reliability two consequences would follow: first, its certainty as to its own existence would be for it no more than a gratuity; secondly, there would be no means by which it could pass from the certainty of its own existence to the certainty of anything else.

Having given some suggestion as to what it would be like for Cartesian philosophy to be caught up in a vicious circularity, it is necessary to ask whether Descartes is indeed caught up in such circularity. There is much to suggest that this is the kind of circularity in which Descartes is caught up. First, it is reason itself which seems to provide the basis for doubt. Reason sifts the senses and finds that the senses do deceive us – deceive us to a point where waking life and the substance of dreams are scarcely distinguishable. And reason also seems capable of recognizing within itself the possibility of its being deceived by an evil genius. The difficulty as has been noted above is that this capacity does not seem to be present within reason when reason is confronted with propositions which seem indubitable, *i.e.*, with self-evident propositions. But all that one has to do is allow these acts of intuition to pass into one's memory in order to discover that even in these acts of intuition there is the possibility of deceit. It is because of this that the certainty of the *Cogito* presents itself to reason as a gratuity. It is the one proposition about which there is such certainty that it can never be so much as conceived without its being indubitable. Its very conception establishes its certainty. To think "I think" is to know that I exist. But this knowledge is a gratuity. It is a gratuity for it can never be grasped without being grasped in immediacy. And so grasped, however clearly and distinctly it presents itself, what is grasped is simply it, *i.e.*, the "I think" and nothing more. Given the purity of the grasp of the *Cogito* there seems no way in which one can proceed from this grasp to a certainty of anything else. If reason is such as to carry within it a sufficient basis for doubting its own reliability, it is not clear how reason can move beyond the pure thought of itself by means of its own efforts to certainty about anything, let alone certainty about God or the world.

But is this somewhat Hegelian reminiscence about Cartesian philosophy an accurate representation of it? There are several considerations to suggest that it is not. First, for Descartes, reason does not carry within itself the sufficient basis for doubting the reliability of reason. One can see that this is the case in the first instance by noting the deception that is related to the senses. This deception is not possible without ideas. Ideas for Descartes are essentially representations of things. To be deceived by the senses is, for Descartes, to make judgments which attribute to things that which is found only in our ideas. Such deception therefore already presupposes the possibility that there are things other than ourselves. But this possibility is not found within the mind itself: it is found in the ideas by which the mind thinks.

One can also see that reason does not carry within itself sufficient basis for doubting the reliability of reason by considering those instances in which reason regards itself as possibly deceived about those propositions which present themselves to reason as indubitable. While the mind is actually presented with such propositions, any doubt with respect to these propositions is impossible. It is only afterward that the mind becomes aware of the possibility of being deceived in such instances. In these instances there is nothing within reason itself which gives rise to the possibility of its deception. The possibility of its being deceived and, hence, of its being unreliable, lies entirely outside itself within the evil genius. The evil genius is simply an imaginary representation of something that must be quite separate from the mind itself if it is to function effectively in deceiving the mind. It is an imaginary representation of a reality that is unrelated to the ideas of reason, *i.e.*, those ideas which the mind is incapable of doubting so long as they are before the mind, *i.e.*, those ideas out of which self-evident propositions are formed.

Having seen that reason for Descartes does not contain within itself the sufficient basis for doubting the reliability of reason, it is necessary to ask whether reason is the only reality of which immediate certainty is possible. In one sense the answer of this question is affirmative. It is essential for the certainty of the *Cogito* that absolutely no more should be implied as regards the existence of the "I" than that which is expressed in the two words "I think." Concerning anything else which may be implied as regards the existence of the "I," no evidence is presented by the "I think." But this answer is not by itself complete. It is not complete because it does not make clear just how it is that the "I" which thinks has been reduced to this clear point of certainty. But more importantly it does not make clear that the "I" which in this instance thinks, is the finite, fallible "I" which is subject to deception. It is in this that the proposition *"Cogito ergo sum"* is unique, In any other judgments that reason makes, it might be possible on subsequent reflection to isolate at least in thought the act by which one thinks from the thought itself and, thus, place both it and the thought in question. But the *Cogito* is the one judgment in which the act of judgment and its content are inseparable. Not only are they inseparable, but inseparable in such a way that just what is present in either by itself is not known. The point is, therefore, that to the extent that the *Cogito* is a judgment to which certainty attaches in any unique fashion, the "I" which forms the subject of that judgment cannot be identified with any "I" that exists in a narrow circle of subjectivity and doubt. It is conceivable, therefore, that the "I" which is the subject of the absolutely certain judgment *"Cogito ergo sum"* is no less than God himself. The only basis for excluding this possibility would be to deny the certainty attaching to this judgment.

This leads to a consideration of the final question. Is reason for Descartes the only means of establishing the reliability of reason to move beyond the immediate certainty of the self? The answer to this question must be somewhat two-sided. On the one hand, there is no other means available for Descartes, or anyone else, by which to think other than one's mind. The only alternative to thinking is to remain at a level of immediacy, *i.e.*, not to think at all. In the sense that one is faced with the option of staying with immediacy, of living in piety, or the mysticism of the senses, etc., or of engaging in thought, reason is the only means of establishing its reliability to move beyond the immediate certainty of the "I." But for Descartes it is not reason itself which does in the last analysis establish by itself its own reliability. From the beginning Descartes regards reason as in possession of a number of ideas. As already noted, these ideas are essentially representative of things. Whether there are things or not, other than the *Cogito,* these ideas are representations of things distinct from the *Cogito* as it is grasped in the certainty of its pure self. Chief among these ideas for Descartes is the idea of God. For Descartes this idea is an idea of a being that is quite different from himself. It is different from himself in that all of the attributes which it possesses are greater than (while encompassing) all those which Descartes finds within himself. This idea he finds it necessary to posit as an idea of a being other than himself, *i.e.,* as an idea that must move him beyond the narrow circle of his own doubting subjectivity. In the last analysis, then, for Descartes it is not his own reason, *i.e.,* his reason as shaped by his own subjectivity, which establishes the reliability of reason to move beyond the immediate certainty of the *Cogito.* It is rather reason driven by a divine idea that moves beyond the certainty of itself.

RECONCILIATION OF FREEDOM AND NATURE IN KANT'S THIRD CRITIQUE

by

HEIMO E. M. HOFMEISTER

I

No work of Kant has so persistently influenced the development of German Idealism after Fichte as the *Critique of Judgment*. Nevertheless, compared with the other two Critiques, it has attracted little attention outside the area where German is spoken.[1] It is the task of this article to work out the status and the role of the *Critique of Judgment* in its relation to the critiques of theoretical and practical reason, and to show that by writing this book Kant did not intend simply to make a contribution to philosophical aesthetic "in reference to the formation or the culture of taste (for this will take its course in the future as in the past without any such investigations), but merely in a transcendental point of view." [2] That the *Critique of Judgment* (published

[1] See M. J. Scott-Taggart, "Recent Work on the Philosophy of Kant," in *Kant Studies Today*, ed. L. W. Beck (La Salle, Illinois, 1969), pp. 1-71.

There are however a few exceptions, as for example: G. Schrader, "The Status of Teleological Judgment in the Critical Philosophy," *Kant-Studien,* XLV (1953-54), 204-235; A. C. Genova, "Kant's Complex Problem of Reflective Judgment," *The Review of Metaphysics,* XXIII (1970), 452-480 (see footnote 22). Whereas these two articles deal with the *Critique of Judgment* in general or with large parts of it, the following two papers are concerned with particular issues: R. L. Zimmerman, "Kant: The Aesthetic Judgment," *Journal of Aesthetics and Art Criticism* (1962-63), 333-344 (reprinted in *Kant, A Collection of Critical Essays,* ed. R. P. Wolff, pp. 385-406); I. Stadler, "Perception and Perfection in Kant's Aesthetics," in Wolff, *op. cit.*, pp. 339-384.

French literature on this topic: M. Souriau, *Le Jugement réfléchissant dans la Philosophie Critique de Kant* (Paris, 1926); V. Basch, *Essai critique sur l'Esthétique de Kant* (Paris, 1927); V. Delbos, *De Kant aux Postkantiennes* (Paris, 1940); G. Mottier, *L'Esthétique et le subjectivisme issu de Kant* (Paris, 1941); J. Hyppolite, "La Critique Hégélienne de la Réflexion Kantienne," *Kant-Studien*, XLV (1953-54), 83-95.

[2] Kant, V, 170 (6). Kant's *Critique of Pure Reason* will be quoted according to the editions A and B. I use either the translation of Norman Kemp Smith (New York, 1965), or the one of F. M. Müller (Garden City, New York, 1966), whichever seems to be more faithful to the original text. All other citations taken from Kant refer to the Edition of the Prussian Academy of Science (Berlin, 1902 et sequ.). Since L. W.

in 1790) should be understood as completing a whole – comprising itself, the *Critique of Pure Reason* (published in 1781) and the *Critique of Practical Reason* (published in 1788) – is supported by a hint given by Kant himself. Kant himself announced his intention to turn towards metaphysics after the completion of the "critical business." He himself pointed out the trichotomous character of his philosophy, and he appealed to the concept of synthesis to justify this trichotomy.[3]

Already the choice of the topic indicates that Kant has taken up in the *Critique of Judgment* one of the most important problems of philosophy. He asks if there is a realm which combines in itself the principles of theoretical and practical philosophy, namely the natural concept and the concept of freedom, and raises the question how this combination can be thought. Understanding, as the legislator of nature, and reason, as the lawgiver of itself, although operative in the same territory (*territorium*), with respect to their realms (*ditio*) are still separated from one another by an "immeasurable gulf." [4] The possibility of the "coexistence of both legislations" has been shown in the Transcendental Dialectic, which "has annulled the objections to this (theory) by exposing the dialectical illusion which they contain." [5] This kind of connection is not sufficient from the point of view of the *Critique of Practical Reason* however, since from that view it is necessary that the concept of freedom influence the realm of the natural concept. The

Beck's translation of the *Critique of Practical Reason* (Indianapolis, Indiana, 1956) includes the Academy pagination, it is not necessary to cite pages in this edition. The page numbers of J. H. Bernard's translation of the *Critique of Judgment* (New York, 1961) are indicated in parentheses. Citations taken from a text not originally written in English may be modified. These modifications will not be indicated.

[3] "Although, then, philosophy can be divided only into two main parts, the theoretical and the practical, and although all that we may be able to say of the special principles of judgment must be counted as belonging in it to the theoretical part, *i.e.*, to rational cognition in accordance with natural concepts, yet the critique of pure reason, which must decide all this, as regards the possibility of the system before undertaking it, consists of three parts: the critique of pure understanding, of pure judgment, and of pure reason, which faculties are called pure because they are legislative *a priori*" Kant, V, 179 (15). Compare also: "It has been thought a doubtful point that my divisions in pure philosophy should always be threefold. But that lies in the nature of the thing. If there is to be an *a priori* division, it must be either *analytical*, according to the law of contradiction, which is always twofold (*quotlibet ens est aut A aut non A*), or it is *synthetical*. And if in this latter case it is to be derived from *a priori concepts* (not as in mathematics from the intuition corresponding to the concept), the division must necessarily be trichotomy. For according to what is requisite for synthetical unity in general, there must be (1) a condition, (2) a conditioned, and (3) the concept which arises from the union of the conditioned with its condition" Kant, V, 197 (34), footnote.

[4] Kant, V, 175 (12).

[5] Kant, V, 175 (11).

concept of freedom is meant "to actualize in the world of sense the purpose proposed by its laws, and consequently nature must be so thought that the conformity to law of its form at least harmonizes with the possibility of the purposes to be effected in it according to laws of freedom." But if there is no "peculiar realm" [6] which embraces both, so to speak, and if practical reason does not have a determining power in respect to the natural law, as understanding does not have in respect of the practical laws of freedom, and if it is not possible "to throw a bridge from the one realm to the other" [7] – nevertheless there must be another way of "transition." [8]

II

The *Critique of Pure Reason* has shown the understanding as the ground of the *a priori* principles of the cognitive faculty as the *Critique of Practical Reason* has shown reason as the ground of the *a priori* principles of the faculty of desire. In the "family of the supreme cognitive faculties" [9] there can be found a middle term between understanding and reason, namely, judgment. Its territory is the feeling of pleasure and pain. Whereas understanding and reason relate to objects to produce concepts of them, judgment is related to the subject only and does not produce concepts about the object at all. It is this relation to the subject which constitutes the feeling of pleasure and pain. Judgment does not have, like understanding and reason, a realm of its own for its laws; nevertheless, it still has principles which mediate between pure understanding and pure reason. It is necessary to "think nature" not only in accordance with the law of causality but at the same time in accordance with the law of purposiveness, which is the basic concept of the realm of freedom. That is exactly what judgment does. As we will see, judgment views nature in such a way that it imputes to it the concept of purposiveness. This principle of purposiveness is for reflective judgment not a constitutive but a regulative one.

Through judgment nature is brought into the perspective of purposiveness and thus reflective judgment is supposed to mediate the transition from the realm of freedom to the realm of nature. The concept of purposiveness arises in this transition from the causality of freedom to the final purpose, the causality of nature. Through the concept of purposiveness the possibility of the operation of the concept of freedom within the realm of nature shall be made understandable.

[6] Kant, V, 176 (12).
[7] Kant, V, 195 (32).
[8] Kant, V, 176 (12).
[9] Kant, V, 177 (13).

The concept and status of judgment already came up for discussion in the two other *Critiques*. In the *Critique of Pure Reason* there is a short passage devoted to it in the first book, "The Analytic of Principles." In an introductory way Kant points out that the division of the supreme cognitive faculties into understanding, judgment, and reason corresponds to the division of general formal logic into the doctrine of concepts, judgments, and inferences. And he shows why reason has to be excluded from this section ("The Analytic of Principles").[10] Transcendental logic refers to a determinate content: pure *a priori* knowledge; and this distinguishes it from formal logic. Therefore the transcendental employment of reason cannot be "objectively valid, and cannot therefore belong to the *logic of truth*, that is, to Analytic. As a *logic of illusion*, it calls for separate location in the scholastic edifice, under the title of Transcendental Dialectic." [11] Within the realm of analytic there remain only the concepts of understanding and judgment. The statements which are made here about the latter are very scarce, and it may be necessary therefore to dispense with Kant's direct references to judgment and instead to watch it in its "business" within the second section of Transcendental Analytic, which is the canon of judgment and therefore named the "Doctrine of Judgment."

Kant introduces judgment as a talent which cannot be taught but only practiced. It is therefore a natural talent. Understanding is the same in all men; we think or we don't think at all. We cannot think more or less well. But we can judge more or less well. Understanding "is the faculty of rules" which may be trained through study. On the other side, judgment is the faculty of the application of these rules. Someone may possess an excellent understanding and nevertheless may have a limited judgment. The scholar and the teacher have a special need for the faculty of understanding, whereas the physician, the judge, and the politician need excellent judgment. If they lack this specific talent, they may comprehend the universal *in abstracto* but will not be able to determine whether a concrete case falls under it or not. They are in the possession of a lot of important rules but unable to apply them in the right way. Judgment is viewed here as a faculty subordinate to understanding because it uses only the rules of understanding. We have heard that transcendental logic deals with concepts which relate *a priori* to an object and give the general conditions to the rules. Because of this it is

[10] Since formal logic abstracts from all content of knowledge it "may well contain in its analytical portion the canon of reason also. For the form of reason possesses its definite rules which can be discovered *a priori*, simply by analyzing the actions of reason into their components without reference to the particular nature of the knowledge to which they are applied . . ." Kant, A 131, B 170.

[11] *Idem.*

its task to "correct and secure by definite rules judgment in the use of the pure understanding," and to prevent mistakes "in its use of the few pure concepts of the understanding which we possess." [12] It is the advantage of transcendental philosophy that it can indicate *a priori* the case to which the rule which is contained in the pure concept of understanding may be applied and at the same time show "by means of general but sufficient marks the conditions under which objects can be given in correspondence to those concepts." [13]

What then is the task and the status of judgment? Understanding offers to the categories the pure forms of connection of the sensuous manifold. To apply these forms understanding needs the sensuous material which is provided by intuition as its complement. Between the appearances and the categories the schemata intervene. The schemata are homogeneous on the one hand with the categories and on the other hand with the appearances and thus make "the application of the former to the latter possible." Transcendental schematism is supposed to mediate between pure thinking and pure form (of intuition) and by this gives "sense and meaning" to the categories and a categorical structure to intuition. "This mediating representation must be pure, that is, void of all empirical content, and yet at the same time, while it must in one respect be *intellectual*, it must in another be *sensuous*." [14] The schema brings about the synthesis between the forms of thinking and the form of intuition that is time. Itself the schema is "a product of the faculty of imagination" but of a very restricted one. And it proceeds in accordance with the rules of judgment because only there the instructions of transcendental logic may be found. To be very exact, it is judgment which constitutes the synthesis between understanding and sensibility by the means of the schemata. In this synthetic way of functioning, judgment is determinant because it subsumes a particular under a universal and in doing so it has to proceed according to prescribed rules.

> The schemata of judgment are "thus nothing but *a priori* determinations of time in accordance with rules. These rules relate in the order of the categories to the *time-series,* the *time-content,* the *time-order,* and lastly to the *scope of time* in respect of all possible objects." [15]

By means of the temporal concepts of the schemata, judgment here introduces reason in the synthesis between understanding and sensibility. Reason is introduced because the forms of time and space, insofar as they occur as

[12] Kant, A 135, B 174.
[13] Kant, A 136, B 175.
[14] Kant, A 138, B 177.
[15] Kant, A 145, B 184-85.

infinite given magnitudes, are concepts of reason. The inner sense, as time is also called by Kant, grants to the cognitive faculty this correspondence and harmony, which it needs but which did not become a philosophical theme prior to the *Critique of Judgment*. In the *Critique of Pure Reason* the categories have an *a priori* character only as far as they relate to objects of appearances. Only in such a way can metaphysics be established as a science. The issue of the sense and purposiveness of that harmony and correspondence is only postulated in the *Critique of Pure Reason* but cannot be justified there. The *a-priority* of the teleological principle, as this issue can also be formulated, must therefore remain excluded from this *Critique*. This is possible for Kant since the universality and necessity of this principle does not refer to the organism's purposiveness as object or as appearance, but is based on the way of thinking of our discursive understanding. According to this Kant can state in the *Critique of Judgment*:

Now the concept of an object, so far as it contains the ground of the actuality of this object, is the *purpose*; and the agreement of a thing with that constitution of things which is only possible according to purposes is called the *purposiveness* of its form. Thus the principle of judgment, in respect of the form of things of nature under empirical laws generally, is the *purposiveness of nature* in its variety. That is, nature is represented by means of this concept as if an understanding contained the ground of the unity of the variety of its empirical laws. The purposiveness of nature is therefore a particular concept, *a priori,* which has its origin solely in the reflective judgment. For we cannot ascribe to natural products anything like a reference of nature in them to purposes; we can only use this concept to reflect upon such products in respect of the connection of phenomena which is given in them according to empirical laws.[16]

I should like to clarify this train of thought, stated here in brief, and supported by several other citations given above. It is the task of the determinant judgment to subsume the particular under the universal and to bring the multiplicity of reality to the unity of the concept. In the *Critique of Pure Reason* understanding proves itself to be capable by means of determinant judgment of thinking the universal in the form of a natural law and by doing this to "determine" the particular (the empirical). Understanding determines nature by bringing its appearances under legislating forms. In doing this we experience our inability to constitute the necessary unity sought by understanding. We find we cannot exclude the contingent. General natural laws of course make up a system which aims toward a necessary unity of possible *a priori* experience, but the "particular" laws of nature fit together in a comprehensive unity only contingently. Consequently we can call it a contingency, and not a necessity which is based on the immediate insight

[16] Kant, V 180-81 (17).

of understanding, that the first law of Kepler, which asserts the elliptical figure of the motion of the planets, can be comprehended in a general law of gravitation to which also the falling stone of Galileo is subjected.[17] For this reason we find ourselves forced to view the occurrence of the systematic unity of experience as contingent. Since our interest is not directed towards an aggregate of experience but a systematic whole, reason has to introduce a subjective principle. Reason does this in the form of reflective judgment. That means judgment has to extend its task of determining and subsuming the manifold under general laws in such a way that it makes it a maxim to judge nature according to the principle of a thoroughgoing purposiveness. Consequently reflective judgment has a synthetic function. Reflective judgment is distinguished from determinant judgment insofar as it does not prescribe a given universal of which we seek the particular instance, but seeks through reflection the universal in the particular. "It is a mandate of our judgment to proceed according to the principle of the harmony of nature with our cognitive faculty." [18] Consequently its kind of synthesis is not the one between intuition and understanding but between freedom and nature.

The question put forward above as to the position and task of judgment in the *Critique of Pure Reason* can now be answered. The judgment fulfills from the perspective of reason two different tasks: (1) Through the schemata it makes possible the synthesis between the understanding and sensibility. (2) As a principle of reason judgment poses the question as to the sense and purposiveness of that synthesis and by this it points out its conditioned and historical character.

III

In the field of ethics too we find that judgment has a synthesizing function. A particular possible action is subsumed under a general law by practical judgment. Ethical quality rests on the kind of relation which the empirical will has to unconditionally commanding law whereby the good is not to be thought as independent of all relation to the circumstances but only as a special way of apprehending them. Only the form and, as Kant expresses it, not its matter ought to be the determining ground of a moral will. The law given by practical reason (categorical imperative) shows the *type* of all lawfulness and does not allow an exception.

That the law mediates a given sensible content is not the source of its

[17] F. Kaulbach, *Immanuel Kant* (Berlin, 1969), p. 269.
[18] Kant, V, 188 (25).

immediate objectivity; rather this objectivity is based on the fact that reason itself lays the ground for practical knowledge and thought. Here there is no need for intuition as in the case of theoretical philosophy. Therefore we have to renounce our claim for a transcendental intuitional schema which would make the application of the moral law possible. In the *Critique of Pure Reason* we were able by means of judgment and its schemata to deduce the principles of pure understanding. In the *Critique of Practical Reason* we take an opposite approach. This *Critique* starts out with the principles of practical reason and proceeds to the concept of good and evil "as the consequences of the *a priori* determination of the will." [19] The demonstration is based on the distinction between the sensible nature of man, which is "necessarily subject to the laws of causality," and his intelligible nature, according to which man is conscious in another "aspect as a being in itself . . . of his existence as determinable in an intelligible order of things." [20] The being which belongs at the same time to the sensible and to the intelligible world ought to integrate the moral law into nature, i.e., the system (*Inbegriff*) of appearances in accordance to natural laws, by means of acting. That is to say that by means of human acts, the "supersensible" nature shall be made present in sensible nature. "Intelligible nature" is no reality of experiences but belongs to the practical idea. On one side it is not permissible to eliminate the lawfulness of appearances; on the other side, acting has to function as effectiveness in the realm of nature, and it can find its concrete content only in sensible nature (desires, inclinations, etc.). Therefore Kant has to ask how it is possible that the pure law, namely, the categorical imperative, comes into relation to concrete content. The response to this is that it has to be "schematized" so that it will not remain inapplicable to practical experience. For that the schema as we find it in the *Critique of Practical Reason* can serve only partly as a model. There we were dealing with the synthesis between understanding and intuition, whereas here we are dealing with the application of the moral law, namely, the "factum of reason," to the sensible world whereby intuition as a moment for this synthesis is not available. Kant explains that point by writing:

To the law of freedom (which is a causality not sensuously conditioned), and consequently to the concept of the absolutely good, no intuition and hence no schema can be supplied for the purpose of applying it *in concreto*. Thus the moral law has no other cognitive faculty to mediate its application to objects of nature than the understanding (not the imagination); and the understanding can supply to an idea of reason not a schema of sensibility but a law. This law, as one which can be exhibited *in concreto* in objects of the senses, is a natural

[19] Kant, V, 65.
[20] Kant, V, 42.

law. But this natural law can, for the purpose of judgment, be used only in its formal aspect, and it may, therefore, be called the *type* of the moral law.[21]

Again it is judgment which performs the synthesis; but this time it is not imagination which serves for that purpose, but understanding. As judgment mediated in theoretical philosophy between intuition and understanding, it mediates in practical philosophy between reason and understanding. From that point of view we can again formulate the task of judgment, namely, to mediate between nature and freedom, and by doing this to make possible the concretization of the moral good. This task of judgment, as we already emphasized once, is not discussed prior to the *Critique of Judgment.*

IV

We have seen that Kant distinguishes between reflecting and determinant judgment, and we have tried to define this distinction. Determinant judgment is not legislative, either for the realm of nature or for the realm of freedom. Legislation for the first realm is understanding, and for the second it is reason.[22] Determinant judgment carries out the synthesis between tran-

[21] Kant, V, 69. On this topic see my "The Ethical Problem of the Lie in Kant," *Kant-Studien,* forthcoming 1972.

[22] Since determinant judgment is not legislative it does not need to be criticized and the *Third Critique* consequently deals with reflecting judgment only. *Cf.* Walter Biemel, *Die Bedeutung von Kants Begründung der Ästhetik für die Philosophie der Kunst,* Kantstudien, Ergänzungshefte, 77 (Köln, 1959), p. 12; also Kant's remark to the First Introduction to the *Critique of Judgment*:

A subdivision of a critique of judgment (. . .) has to be based on the distinction between determinant and reflecting judgment, whereby it is necessary to consider that only reflecting judgment possesses *a priori* principles of its own and the first one proceeds merely schematically under the guidance of another faculty (the understanding), whereas the second one proceeds merely technically (according to laws of its own . . ." Kant, XX, 248.

In the light of the facts I cannot agree with the view that "Kant's need for a third *Critique* is actually necessitated by the aesthetical judgment and not the logical reflection on nature." (Genova, *op. cit.,* p. 471). The mutual relation between intuition and understanding can be judged as purposive either in respect to intuition or in respect to understanding. In the first case a sensuous representation regardless of its concept seems to be well proportioned to understanding in respect to its intuitionable character. Here we judge a representation to be beautiful. In the second case the actuality of an object seems to be totally adequate, which is considered to be the reason for the actuality of this concept. Here we judge, the object is an organized product of nature. The beautiful and the organism represent the territory where reflecting judgment can unfold its principle of purposiveness and at the same time be legislative. It is wrong to assume that "for Kant a critique is needed whenever an *a priori* principle claims to be constitutive . . ." (*Idem*). Rather a critique is necessary whenever an *a priori* principle has a legislative function.

Cf.: Of judgment, "we have cause for supposing according to analogy that it may scendental universality and the empirical manifold, between concepts of understanding and their intuitional contents, as the doctrine of principles in the *Critique of Pure Reason* shows. Nevertheless judgment does not explain the peculiarity of an object with respect to the transcendental conditions of its possibility, namely, that it is an object at all, that it can be experienced. This peculiarity remains a "contingency" which cannot be deduced from the transcendental universal sense of constitution. This contingency is purposive insofar as it can be universalized, and insofar as it brings the disjunction between the transcendental conditions of possibility and the empirical manifold to synthesis. The purposiveness of the object insofar as the judging subject reflects on the object does not concern the object as such, but rather it expresses the relation in which it can be found towards purpose-setting reason. The judgment of reflecting judgment does not concern the object *qua* object but rather the characteristics which it has in respect to the judging subject: it is signified as a reflecting judgment because its form of existence is reflexive towards the subject.[23] In the *Critique of Pure Reason* this synthesis remains external and unmediated. A reflective

contain in itself, if not a special legislation, yet a special principle of its own to be sought according to laws, though merely subjective *a priori*" Kant, V, 177 (13).

"A transcendental principle [purposiveness], then, the reflective judgment can only give as a law from and to itself" Kant, V, 180 (16).

Concerning determinant judgment Kant explains that it "only subsumes under universal transcendental laws given by the understanding; the law is marked out for it, *a priori*, and it has therefore no need to seek a law for itself in order to be able to subordinate the particular in nature to the universal" Kant, V, 179 (15-16). "Although our concept of a subjective purposiveness of nature in its forms according to empirical laws is not a concept, but only a principle of the judgment for furnishing itself with concepts amid the immense variety of nature (and thus being able to ascertain its own position), yet we thus ascribe to nature, as it were, a regard to our cognitive faculty according to the analogy of purpose. Thus we can regard *natural beauty* as the *presentation* of the concept of the formal (merely subjective) purposiveness, and *natural purposes* as the presentation of the concept of a real (objective) purposiveness. The former of these we judge of by taste (aesthetical, by the medium of the feeling of pleasure), the latter by understanding and reason (logical, according to concepts)" Kant, V, 193 (29-30).

See also footnote 3.

[23] Reflecting judgment introduces another issue in addition to the two already mentioned. This third one confronts us with the question as to methodic philosophical self-reflection. Kant did not, at any time, refer to this problem, but it became of ultimate importance for the German Idealists following Kant. This issue can already be found implicitly in Kant's train of thought, especially where he attempts to think one common origin of the different kinds of faculties (*Vermögen*). Besides, this question is unavoidable with respect to the issue we are currently discussing. If the judging subject reflects the adequateness of the object to the purpose of reason and thereby to reason itself, the subject not only judges about the purposiveness of the object, but also about itself. By reflecting about the purposiveness of the object, it necessarily reflects also about its own adequateness to the object.

judgment considers the purposive relation between contingency and necessity by referring this relation to the meaning of the constitutive universality and by "having the obligation to ascend from the particular to the universal." [24] In doing this judgment is effective, in accordance with the abstraction of the particular in respect to its intuitional or conceptual sense, either as aesthetic judgment or as teleological judgment. To express the same in the words of Kant:

> The aesthetical judgment is . . . a special faculty for judging of things according to a rule but not according to concepts. The teleological judgment is not a special faculty, but only the reflective judgment in general.[25]

In our investigation we turn first to the aesthetical judgment. Kant subdivided the first part of his third *Critique* into two sections: first the analytic of aesthetic judgment, and second the dialectic of aesthetic judgment. The first section is divided again into a book on the analytic of the beautiful and one on the analytic of the sublime. In reference to a remark that Kant made in the *Critique of Pure Reason*, the question may be asked what place the beautiful and the sublime have in this context. In that remark Kant criticizes Baumgarten's use of the word "aesthetic" to signify the "critique of taste." [26] He himself proposed to reserve this name for the doctrine of sensibility. The usage of this word in both *Critiques* has in common that it points to something which seems to be at first merely subjective.[27] Kant explains in the *Critique of Judgment* that

> that which in the representation of an object is merely subjective . . . is its aesthetical character . . . in the sense representation of external things, the quality of space wherein we intuit them is the merely subjective [element] of my representation (by which it remains undecided what they may be in themselves as objects), on account of which reference the object is thought thereby merely as phenomenon.[28]

In our context we are dealing with the feeling of pain and pleasure, that is, we are dealing with the "aesthetical representation of purposiveness." [29] For through pleasure or pain I recognize nothing in the object of representation and no characteristics of the object itself but the subjective [element] of our representation, which cannot be an ingredient of cognition.

[24] Kant, V, 180 (16).
[25] Kant, V, 194 (31).
[26] Kant, A 21, B 35, footnote.
[27] *Cf.* P. Heintel, "Die Stellung der transzendentalen Ästhetik in der '*Kritik der reinen Vernunft*,'" *Wiener Zeitschrift für Philosophie, Psychologie und Pädagogik*, VIII (1965), 65 ff.
[28] Kant, V, 188-189 (25).
[29] Kant, V, 189 (26).

In the following I plan to sketch out the main train of thought of such sections which are of particular interest for our analysis. Following this I will try to throw light on the position and task of these sections in their systematic context.

The purposiveness of the beautiful does not seem to be real and objective, as does that of the teleological, since the first one lacks any relation to a concept of purpose. In a judgment in which something is called beautiful, the representation is not related by the help of understanding to an object of cognition but by the means of imagination to the judging subject and its feeling of pleasure and pain. The purposiveness of the beautiful is not comprehended by the means of reason teleologically, but rather we feel it immediately. Since the fulfillment of the purpose generates pleasure we find it pleasurable and can even "taste" it. The feeling of pleasure and pain signifies nothing in the object; rather it is the expression of a reference "in that the subject feels itself as it is affected by the representation." [30] Pleasure and pain here are not the result of the faculty of desire but they are "a reflective perception." Consequently the aesthetical judgment is grounded on the feeling of pleasure alone and is a judgment of taste.[31] So far in our explanations we have based the judgment of taste on the relation of the object to the subject, and we spoke about "a purposiveness of the objects in relation to the reflective judgment, conformably to the concept of nature in the subject;" but we also can, conversely, "in virtue of the concept of freedom" view the purposiveness "of the subject in respect of the objects according to their form or even their formlessness." [32] The reason is,

the aesthetical judgment is not only related as a judgment of taste to the beautiful, but is also as springing from a spiritual feeling related to the *sublime*; and thus the "Critique of the Aesthetical Judgment" must be divided into two corresponding sections.[33]

I return again to the analytic of the beautiful. Here we find four explanations of the beautiful in accordance with the four categories. At first aesthetical pleasure, which is also defined as satisfaction in the beautiful, is distinguished from any other kind of pleasure. Under the title of Quality, taste is determined as "the faculty of judging of an object or a method of representing it by an *entirely disinterested* satisfaction or dissatisfaction. The

[30] Kant, V, 204 (38).
[31] Its subjective character supplies to intuition the character of spontaneity.
[32] Kant, V, 192 (28-29).
[33] *Idem.*

object of such satisfaction is called *beautiful*." [34] Excluded are the pleasant (the useful) and the good, since the pleasant is that which "gratifies," and the beautiful is that which merely "pleases" (*gefällt*).[35] The gratifying is excluded because it is based on empirical purposes and has a reference to our desires. Satisfaction in the good arises of course from practical reason, but in such a way that practical reason attributes esteem (a moral value) to an object or an action. Just as Kant tries to distinguish the judgment of taste from the objectifying understanding, he also distinguishes it from practical reason and its faculties of desire, since their "satisfaction" always signifies a reference to the "faculty of desire, either as its determining ground or as necessarily connected with its determining ground." [36] This is because pleasure in the beautiful is neither a pleasure of enjoyment nor of law-abiding activity "but of mere reflection." [37]

Guided by the second category, Quantity, we find the second explanation of the beautiful: "The beautiful is that which pleases universally without [requiring] a concept." [38] Our first determination of the judgment of taste has shown the beautiful as independent of theoretical and practical concepts, because in both cases an interest precedes a purposive relation. We could draw this result: Beautiful is what pleases without interest and is its own purpose. From this definition we can make a transition to the explanation in accordance with the category of Relation.

> Since satisfaction, as Kant explains, "does not rest on any inclination of the subject (nor upon any other premeditated interest), but since the person who judges feels himself quite *free* as regards the satisfaction which he attaches to the object, he cannot find the ground of this satisfaction in any private conditions connected with his own subject, and hence it must be regarded as grounded on what he can presuppose in every other person." [39]

Because of the independence of the beautiful from theoretical and practical concepts, Kant calls the harmony of the cognitive faculties a "free play." [40] Consequently there cannot be universal criteria for the beauty of an object. Nevertheless the judgment of taste is universally communicable, even though it is not possible to prove it in accordance with concepts because it is the expression of a mere state and not of an objective representation. The aesthetical universality, and Kant is just concerned with that one, neither

[34] Kant, V, 211 (45).
[35] Kant, V, 207 (41).
[36] Kant, V, 204 (38).
[37] Kant, V, 292 (134).
[38] Kant, V, 219 (54).
[39] Kant, V, 211 (46).
[40] Kant, V, 217 (52).

serves for the recognition of an object nor is it based on desires and inclinations. Rather it has to be comprehended as the result of "complete" freedom.[41] The explanation under the guidance of the category of Relation shows that the beautiful, in addition to the determinations we have already worked out, pleases without relation to an objective purpose. All singularities fit into one another in a piece of art as a purposive whole without there being, from the aesthetical point of view, a particular purpose in reference to the content. Kant expresses the same with the following words: "*Beauty* is the form of the *purposiveness* of an object, so far as this is perceived in it *without any representation of a purpose.*" [42]

Although the beautiful is without concept and independent of interest and of any relation to purposiveness with regard to the contents, the judgment of taste has inherent within it not only universality but also necessity. Exhibition under the category of Modality is supposed to make this clear. If a judgment of taste claims universality, the satisfaction it expresses must also claim necessity which is characterized by Kant as follows:

Now this necessity is of a peculiar kind. It is not a theoretical objective necessity, in which case it would be cognized *a priori* that everyone *will feel* this satisfaction in the object called beautiful by me. It is not a practical necessity, in which case, by concepts of a pure rational will serving as a rule for freely acting beings, the satisfaction is the necessary result of an objective law and only indicates that we absolutely (without any further intention) ought to act in a certain way.[43]

The necessity now

which is thought in an aesthetical judgment can only be called exemplary, *i.e.*, a necessity of the ascent of *all* to a judgment which is regarded as the example of a universal rule that we cannot state.[44]

It was already mentioned that Kant distinguished the sublime from the beautiful. It agrees with the beautiful in that both please in themselves and neither "presupposes a judgment of sense nor a judgment logically determined, but a judgment of reflection." [45] Concerning the beautiful it is based on a relation between imagination and understanding. In contrast to this in the realm of the sublime we have a relation between reason and imagination. Kant succeeded here in introducing the infinite and the unconditioned. The beauty of nature concerns, according to Kant,

[41] Kant, V, 211 (46).
[42] Kant, V, 236 (73).
[43] Kant, V, 236-37 (73-74).
[44] Kant, V, 237 (74). Italics added.
[45] Kant, V, 244 (82).

the form of the object, which consists in having [definite] boundaries. The sublime, on the other hand, is to be found in a formless object, so far as in it or by occasion of it *boundlessness* is represented, and yet its totality is also present to thought. Thus the beautiful seems to be regarded as the presentation of an indefinite concept of understanding, the sublime as that of a like concept of reason.[46]

The feeling of the sublime does not presuppose like the beautiful a mind of silent contemplation. Rather it brings with it "a movement of the mind bound up with the judging of the object." [47] This movement is related through imagination either to the faculty of cognition or to the faculty of desire and consequently we have to distinguish between the mathematical or the dynamical sublime. The feeling of sublimity may arise in us in two different ways. We compare either the magnitude or the might of the appearance with either the absolute magnitude or the absolute might which our reason represents in the idea.

The determination of the beautiful as being without interest shall preclude each attempt to bring it in relation with the practical or theoretical interest and at the same time enable the surpassing of these two kinds of interest. In a judgment of taste, and for that reason it is called contemplative judgment, there is no question of any knowledge of the object or the subject but merely of the relation of these to one another. This relation is supposed to constitute the agreement between freedom and nature. The judgment of taste is, to use Kant's words, "merely *contemplative*; *i.e.*, it is a judgment which, indifferent as regards the existence of an object, compares its character with the feeling of pleasure and pain." [48] Based on its determination a special task can be attributed to the beautiful, a task for which the pleasurable is not appropriate because it just "gratifies" and therefore is also a part of the "irrational animals" and for which the good also is not appropriate because it esteems and approves and therefore belongs to every rational being in general. But within the beautiful, because it pleases and "concerns men, *i.e.*, animal, but still rational, beings," [49] judgment can find its mediating role between nature and freedom. The reason of the animal man expresses itself in the beautiful without interest, not only as pure reason, as it does in the good, but also as the intuitable picture. Therefore the synthesis of freedom and nature finds its eternal realization in the beauty of art and nature since only here the satisfaction is not restricted by the sensibility of inclinations and also not subject to the law of reason; rather

[46] *Idem.*
[47] Kant, V, 247 (85).
[48] Kant, V, 209 (43-44).
[49] Kant, V, 210 (44).

satisfaction is "*free* satisfaction." [50] The universality of the judgment of taste is, as we already know, neither conceptual nor comparative.[51] Rather it is "of a particular kind, because it does not unite the predicate of beauty with the concept of the object, considered in its whole logical sphere, and yet extends it to the whole sphere of judging persons." [52] The aesthetical judgments of taste are subjective, but an "agreement" [53] is imputed to everyone. By this Kant attempts within aesthetic universality to mediate the moment of the particular individual (nature) with the absolute universal (freedom and reason). Thereby the following has to be taken into consideration:

> The judgment of taste itself does not *postulate* the agreement of everyone (for that can only be done by a logically universal judgment because it can adduce reasons); it only *imputes* this agreement to everyone, as a case of the rule in respect of which it expects, not confirmation by concepts, but assent from others. The universal voice is, therefore, only an idea (we do not yet inquire upon what it rests).[54]

The universality of the synthesis between nature and freedom as it is exhibited in the beautiful is not absolute and can also not be an exhaustive exhibition of the idea. *Its completion always remains as a task set before us.*

Formal purposiveness, as it confronts us under the name of the category of Relation, is dealing with this just-mentioned synthesis between nature and freedom. Here Kant also points out the mediating role of judgment. The judgment of taste, because it is an aesthetical and not a cognitive judgment, concerns only the relation of the representative powers to one another. There is no underlying subjective purpose of sensibility, nor is there any representation of an objective purpose. Rather we find in a judgment of taste a "subjective purposiveness ... without any purpose (either objective or subjective)." [55] In theoretical philosophy as in practical we always find purposes bound to a concept. There we are always dealing with particular individual purposes. Judgment does not stop here but aims toward final purpose in general, *i.e.*, it always supersedes the particular theoretical or

[50] Kant, V, 210 (44); and compare Kant's remark: "An object of inclination and one that is proposed to our desire by a law of reason leave us no freedom in forming for ourselves anywhere an object of pleasure. All interest presupposes or generates a want, and, as the determining ground of assent, it leaves the judgment about the object no longer free" (*Idem*).

[51] For the difference between comparative and conceptual universality see Kant, B 3-4.

[52] Kant, V, 215 (49).

[53] Kant, V, 216 (51).

[54] Kant, V, 216 (50-51).

[55] Kant, V, 221 (56).

practical purposes and focuses on their conditional character. Only as formal purposiveness can judgment fulfill its task without getting lost in a particular synthesis. The explanation of the possibility of formal purposiveness we can make intelligible only by deriving it from a will. There can be "purposiveness without purpose, so far as we do not place the causes of this form in a will" because what we observe

> we are not always forced to regard (in respect of its possibility) from the point of view of reason. Thus we can at least observe a purposiveness according to form without basing it on a purpose (as the material of the *nexus finalis*), and remark it in objects, although only by reflection.[56]

The consciousness of the mere formal purposiveness in the play of the subject's cognitive powers is pleasure itself. This pleasure "has to maintain the occupation of the cognitive powers without further intention."[57] It is therefore the force driving us from synthesis to synthesis without the intention of this progress being immediately given. The intention of this progress, namely, to reach the perfect synthesis between freedom and nature, is not the motive and may therefore be excluded since the beautiful is not identical with perfection. Because of this distinction between the beautiful and the good, formal purposiveness can be exhibited in the first one. We already referred to the determination of necessity as the fourth mode of the judgment of taste. It remains only to add that exemplary necessity shall provide the mediation between theoretical and practical necessity. Thereby also in respect to the fourth category the task of judgment, namely to mediate between nature and freedom, has been pointed out.

In the beautiful, the synthesis of judgment finds its exhibition in a picture. In the sublime synthesis shall break out of this restricted frame, and the historicity of an exhibition of the synthesis in its pictorial character shall become the motive.[58] The pictorial way of exhibiting the synthesis of freedom and nature in the beautiful is reflected within the sublime with respect

[56] Kant, V, 220 (55-56).

[57] Kant, V, 222 (58).

[58] Kant comments on the inner and most important distinction between the sublime and beautiful, that if "we only bring under consideration in the first instance the sublime in natural objects (for the sublime of art is always limited by the conditions of agreement with nature," we can say: "Natural beauty (which is independent) brings with it a purposiveness in its form by which the object seems to be, as it were, preadapted to our judgment, and thus constitutes in itself an object of satisfaction. On the other hand, that which excites in us, without any reasoning about it, but in the mere apprehension of it, the feeling of the sublime may appear, as regards its form, to violate purpose in respect of the judgment, to be unsuited to our presentative faculty, and as it were to do violence to the imagination; and yet it is judged to be only the more sublime" Kant, V, 245 (83).

to its conditionedness. For the sublime, properly so-called, cannot be contained in a sensible form. It "concerns only ideas of the reason which, although no adequate presentation is possible for them, by this inadequateness that admits of sensible presentation are aroused and summoned into the mind." [59] Reason demands from imagination an adequate sensuous (pictorial) exhibition of its idea of the unrestricted. Since imagination is not in the position to solve the task imposed upon it, the disharmony of the faculties of the mind (idea, sensibility, reason, imagination) causes in us a feeling of pain. Only the reflection that this disproportion of the restricted and unrestricted is adequate to the relation between nature and freedom is able to generate a feeling of pleasure, which Kant calls "a negative pleasure." [60] In the contrast between idea and sensibility the harmony is established. It is in fact "the very unpurposiveness of the faculty of imagination ... for ideas of reason and the arousing of them" which is judged as purposive. Thus the object is comprehended as a "sublime pleasure, which is only possible through the medium of a pain." [61] As a sensible magnitude cannot exhaustively demonstrate the absolute magnitude, in the same way the synthesis between freedom and nature cannot catch up with its own historicity. The inadequacy of each particular synthesis to its guiding idea finds its reflective expression within the sublime. The sublime therefore does not ask, like the beautiful, as to the agreement between freedom and nature but as to the sense of agreement. Thereby it reveals that it has a very particular *praxis*. It is not the landscape or a natural phenomenon like the "threatening rocks; clouds piled up in the sky, moving with lightning flashes and thunder peals" [62] which are sublime, but rather it is the mood caused by them which makes us feel our "physical impotence" [63] and at the same time makes us conscious of the superiority of "humanity in our person" [64] over nature. This is so because the "sublime is what pleases immediately through its opposition to the interest of sense." [65]

In this context I regret we cannot discuss Kant's "Critique of Aesthetical Judgment" in full detail as it will be necessary to omit the sections on deduction and dialectic. After having attempted to work out the status of aesthetical judgment and to point out its mediating role, the question has to be asked what status the teleological judgment has. If our assertion is

[59] Kant, V, 245 (84).
[60] Kant, V, 245 (83).
[61] Kant, V, 260 (99).
[62] Kant, V, 261 (100).
[63] Kant, V, 261 (101).
[64] Kant, V, 262 (101).
[65] Kant, V, 267 (107).

correct that the synthesis between freedom and nature will be established through aesthetical judgment, it seems necessary to ask what status is occupied by teleological judgment.

Aesthetic judgment is able to think a subjective purposiveness, whereas teleological judgment thinks an objective purposiveness in nature. Its topic is the judging of the organic which is an object of judgment additional to that of the beautiful and the sublime. Reflective judgment considers nature as systematically composed by regarding it as if it were created according to a plan.[66] Thereby it is necessary for reflective judgment that nature not only be thought in accordance with an external purposiveness, but also to suppose in nature itself an internal purposiveness, *i.e.*, means and purpose have to exist in it at the same time. The organ of a product of nature, for example, of a tree, "is thought as existing by means of others, but also for the sake of others and the whole, that is, as an (organic) instrument." [67] It is thought in such a way that each organ has to be apprehended as one that is producing the other parts. The organism is the whole of its organs, and organism and organs are mutually means and goal as the individual organs are to each other. From this, Kant explains, it must follow that there is nothing vain in nature and "that nothing happens by chance." [68] It makes a difference if a thing is judged as a natural purpose because of its internal form or if the existence of a thing is considered as a purpose of nature:

> For the latter assertion we require, not merely the concept of a possible purpose, but the knowledge of the final purpose (*scopus*) of nature. But this requires a reference of such knowledge to something supersensible far transcending all our teleological knowledge of nature, for the purpose of [the existence of] nature must itself be sought beyond nature.[69]

In this case it is not the form but the matter that carries necessarily with it a concept of its natural purpose "because this its specific form is at the same time a product of nature." [70] According to the concept of nature as organism, we are forced to convert the principle of a formal purposiveness into a principle of objective purposiveness. The principle of reflective judgment is itself only subjective and says:

> Everything in the world is some way good for something; nothing is vain in it. By the example that nature gives us in its organic products we are justified, nay called upon, to expect of it and of its laws nothing that is not purposive on the whole.[71]

[66] *Cf.* Schrader, *op. cit.*, p. 220.
[67] Kant, V, 373 (220).
[68] Kant, V, 376 (223).
[69] Kant, V, 378 (225).
[70] *Idem.*
[71] Kant, V, 379 (225-26).

The maxim of reflective judgment is regulative and is a clue for us

> by which we consider natural things in reference to an already given ground of determination according to a new law-abiding order, and extend our natural science according to a different principle, *viz.*, that of final causes, but yet without prejudice to the principle of mechanical causality.[72]

The product of nature which is at the same time self-purpose must be considered as the "final purpose" of nature. In the eyes of reflective judgment, the position of the final purpose is taken up in the nature by man.

We saw earlier that aesthetical purposiveness had nothing to do with the self-purpose of an object: an "aesthetical judgment upon the purposiveness of the object" is a judgment "which does not base itself upon any present concept of the object nor does it furnish any such." [73] Through the object the cognitive powers shall only become conscious of their *agreement*. In a teleological judgment on the other hand, purposiveness is represented, for an objective reason, in an object given in experience. That is, it is represented "as the agreement of the form of the object with the possibility of the thing itself, according to a concept of it which precedes and contains the ground of this form." [74] Here we are dealing with the agreement of the form of an object as it is apprehended by us and the possibility of the thing itself. The business of judgment consists in setting a corresponding intuition beside the concept of the object, where the concept is given. This may take place "through nature in its technique (as in organized bodies) when we supply to it our concept of its purpose in order to judge of its products." [75] We therefore do not represent its products merely as purposiveness of nature but rather as natural purpose. The product of nature which is self-purpose is man, and as such he is also the final purpose. The final purpose is unconditioned insofar as it needs no other purpose as the condition of its possibility. This is only possible insofar as it is based on a principle which is external to nature, namely, that of freedom. The question of teleological judgment, how the agreement of the forms of the thing with the possibility of the thing itself may be possible, is therefore the question how nature can be in itself purpose and also the purpose of freedom. The answer to this question Kant attempts to give in the Critique of Teleological Judgment by demonstrating the relation between the self-purpose of nature and the purpose of freedom. The question of the affinity between nature and free-

[72] Kant, V, 379 (226).
[73] Kant, V, 190 (27).
[74] Kant, V, 192 (29).
[75] Kant, V, 193 (29).

dom has been developed here from the viewpoint of nature, whereas this affinity has been viewed in the Critique of Aesthetical Judgment from the aspect of the subject, that is, from the viewpoint of freedom. Both parts of the Third Critique therefore are complementary by dealing with the same topic but by attempting to conceive the issue from different aspects.

EXPLANATION AND RELIGION

EXISTENTIAL INTERPRETATION AND THE PROBLEM OF GOD IN THE THEOLOGY OF FRITZ BURI

by

CHARLEY D. HARDWICK

The major unresolved issue bequeathed to contemporary theology by the immense influence of existentialism is the problem of an adequate doctrine of God in a fully existential theology. This problem emerged with sharpness only after such thinkers as Rudolf Bultmann and Fritz Buri demonstrated that the promise of existentialism for theology requires taking up the hermeneutical question in its full range, that is, only when they showed that it is necessary to apply a rigorous existential methodology not merely to the *fides qua creditur* but to the *fides quae creditur* as well. This move is summed up by Bultmann and Buri's claim that the objective, mythological content of all theological doctrines must be interpreted as expressions for a non-objective self-understanding, as expressions of existential possibilities. The problem is self-evident. If the notion of existential possibilities is not just a heuristic device helpful for a random illumination of various doctrines but a rigorous methodology to be carried through exhaustively, is the content of "God" to be reduced without remainder to certain human possibilities of existential self-actualization? [1] If not, is there any way of preserving the independent reality of God without violating the limits of an existential methodology?

The difficulty of the problem is indicated by the paucity of attention given it in the major works of Bultmann and Buri. Bultmann, for instance, has never succeeded in giving an answer, or at least a fully analyzed answer, to his own question whether the concept of an act of God is mythological in principle.[2] And the crucial unclarified concepts in Buri's theology are

[1] It might be thought that the same problem occurs with Christology. Here, however, I shall take it as well established by the "left-wing" commentators on the demythologizing controversy that Christology can receive an adequate analysis within the limits of an existential methodology.

See Schubert M. Ogden, *Christ Without Myth* (New York, 1961) and William O. Walker, Jr., "Demythologizing and Christology," *Religion in Life*, XXXV (1965-66).

[2] Rudolf Bultmann, "New Testament and Mythology," in *Kerygma and Myth*, ed. Hans Werner Bartsch, trans. Reginald H. Fuller (New York, 1961), pp. 32 f.

those of "Transcendence" and the "personhood of God." [3] Unlike Bultmann, however, Buri is engaged in developing a full systematic theology, and in the third, as yet uncompleted, volume of his massive undertaking, it will be impossible for him to avoid confronting the doctrine of God directly. It is of some importance, therefore, that in *Der Pantokrator: Ontologie und Eschatologie als Grundlage der Lehre von Gott* Buri has given sustained attention to the doctrine of God for the first time in his career and given a foretaste of how he thinks an existential theology can deal with this doctrine. Since Buri's work is both the most consistent and the most ambitious of the existential theologies, it is worth looking more closely at this book to see if he is successful in meeting this most crucial problem for an existential theology.

I

Buri's problem in *Der Pantokrator* is to provide an interpretation of the Christian doctrine of God that is consistent with primitive Christian eschatology and with the eschatological crisis created by the delay of the parousia. He takes as his clue the Pantokrator concept. "Pantokrator" is the term used in the ancient creeds to confess God as Father Almighty, but it is also the iconographic designation for the majestic Christ figure on the vault of Byzantine cathedrals. In a detailed historical-critical analysis of the Biblical and Patristic foundations of Christian theology, Buri argues that a unity can be found between the creation/providence motif (*i.e.*, God, Trinity, traditional person of Christ issuing into ontology) in classical theology and the eschatological/apocalyptic motif (*i.e.*, primitive Christology) in the New Testament when each is seen to articulate the same structure of faith, namely, the victory of God over the powers of chaos and evil in creation and the turn of the aeons. The Pantokrator symbol with its ambivalence between God and Christ can then serve to express this mythological unity of motif which, from an historical perspective according to Buri, underlies all Christian theology.

Assuming the validity of this historical thesis, Buri's more important question concerns the demythologized and existentially interpreted meaning that can be given to this mythological structure. Here he takes as the basis of an existential interpretation (i) a criticism of objectivity and (ii) an existential dialectic. Criticizing on both epistemological and religious grounds the adequacy of any purely objective statement of theological con-

[3] See Fritz Buri, *Dogmatik als Selbstverständnis des christlichen Glaubens*, vol. I: *Vernunft und Offenbarung* (Bern, 1956), pp. 138-141, 151-154, 296-299.

tent, he argues that the content of faith must be interpreted solely in terms of the non-objective act of the self in which self-actualization in freedom and responsibility occurs. This act is a transcending of all objective (*i.e.*, "worldly") conditions, and it has the structure of a choosing and a being chosen. In contrast to losing oneself objectively in the world, it is the actualization of authentic existence by freely taking responsibility for oneself; yet in this same act one finds himself mysteriously given or "gifted" to himself. The term of this donative character of existence is bound, however, to the non-objective dialectic. To articulate it objectively is to lose it and to lose the existential dialectic wherein alone it is intelligible. It can be articulated, consequently, only by a limiting concept such as "Transcendence" (Buri's term) the content of which cannot be specified beyond the existential dialectic itself. From this non-objective dialectic of existence, Buri then develops the existential possibilities which constitute an authentic human existence. Because this limiting concept (the "term" of being chosen) is bound to the non-objective dialectic, it cannot immediately be identified with an objective concept of God. The meaning of "Transcendence" must itself be a function of the total structure or the internal dynamics of the non-objective, existential dialectic. It is for this reason that the existential dialectic supports the full hermeneutical force of the claim that theology must become existential interpretation. To put this differently, God cannot interpret "Transcendence;" rather, Transcendence must interpret "God."

Buri proceeds to show how the objective, mythological language of Christian theology serves to express this existential dialectic. He gives a detailed analysis of the Christian language of creation, providence, governance, sin, redemption, and consummation, in every case showing how this ostensibly objective language expresses the structure of non-objective self-actualization in which meaning, purpose, and community are actualized in a world where they are not objectively demonstrable apart from such non-objective actualizations and where the contrary possibilities of relinquishing responsibility and merely losing oneself in objectivity is at every moment present. In this way, Buri gives a Christological interpretation to God dictated by the unity of the Pantokrator symbol. The interpretation is controlled throughout by the norm that objective theological language has its content solely in existential possibilities. And the Pantokrator symbol of Christ and God shows that these possibilities are symbolized in Christianity as the existential actualization of meaning and purpose in a world where meaning and purpose are not objectively evident. In the last section of the book, Buri turns directly to the traditional theological assertions about God and the Trinity, but again, the primary purpose of this discussion is not to develop an independent doctrine of God but to show how "God language" serves to articulate symbolically the unity of existential possibilities in the non-objective existential act.[4]

In a certain sense, the question whether Buri's existential interpretation of the Pantokrator thesis constitutes a doctrine of God is misplaced. Given the historical-critical interpretation of the structural unity at the basis of all Christian theology and his argument that religious language is intelligible only in its existential meaning, his existential interpretation of the elements in the Pantokrator is his doctrine of God. His analysis amounts to a philosophical account of the only meaning that language about "God" can have once the hermeneutical intention of such language is uncovered. The real question is whether his interpretation of "God" does not reduce theistic language totally to the anthropological circle of human subjectivity. With his assumptions, can Buri establish the reality of God *pro se, extra nos, et contra nos* or does "God talk" reduce to an allegory for the structures and relations of an existential dialectic? [5] When Buri comes in the last section of the book to discuss how the traditional categories about God and the trinity can be existentially interpreted via the Pantokrator structure, he does not hesitate himself to raise precisely the same question:

> If the Pantokrator is an expression for the special possibility of human existence, how, then, is it possible for God to receive any ontological relevance independent of man and his self-understanding? . . . Outside his revelation as creator and consummator in the Pantokrator, has he any being which is anything other than an inexpressible mystery? But can this mystery then represent anything else than a structure and function of man's being – especially when the Pantokrator performs its function as a symbol for the possibility of actualizing authentic human existence in community? [6]

As has been suggested by the above sketch of Buri's thesis in *Der Pantokrator,* such an allegorization does occur with the Christian language about Christ, and this interpretation, in turn, constitutes the content of Buri's doctrine of God. But ironically, it is precisely this Christological interpretation of "God" which makes the necessity of affirming the reality of God *pro se, extra nos, et contra nos* absolutely central to Buri's project. This follows from the fact that both here and throughout his other writings Buri has made quite evident his willingness to surrender any soteriologically constitutive character for the particular events of the life and death of Jesus

[4] For a more detailed analysis of Buri's argument in *Der Pantokrator,* see my "God and the Christian Self-Understanding," *The Journal of Religion,* L (1970).

[5] The word "allegory" is used here quite advisedly.

[6] *Der Pantokrator: Ontologie und Eschatologie als Grundlage der Lehre von Gott* (Hamburg, 1969), p. 108.

of Nazareth because the only way such a soteriology can be established is irreducibly mythological.[7] Consequently, the only way Christ can maintain any reality *extra nos* is if "Christ" is grounded in the reality of God *pro se et extra nos*. If "Christ" can be grounded this way, then the existential allegorization of "Christ" is not debilitating because theology is not thereby reduced without remainder to anthropology. This does require, however, that the allegorization of theistic language in terms of the existential dialectic not reduce the reference of that language entirely to the dialectic.

In *Der Pantokrator* Buri makes it quite clear for the first time in his career that he does not regard a reductionistic conclusion to follow from existential interpretation.[8] The important question concerns Buri's success in escaping what appears to be the logic of a fully consistent existential position which from another perspective is the strength of his thought. Because of the initially problematic character of Buri's intentions regarding the status of "God language," the question of adequacy must be posed in two different ways. It is necessary, first, to examine how adequately he is able to establish the claim that it is possible to avoid the reduction of "God" to human subjectivity in a fully existential theology. Only then will it be possible, second, to enquire concerning the adequacy of what he actually has to say about God.

II

Buri's position turns on what might be called "the classical existentialist move" in theology. This move rests on an analysis of objectivity in which it is concluded that intrinsic selfhood is non-objective (in the sense of transcending objective specification) and, consequently, can be "pointed to" only under categories of act and decision. It follows from this move that one can speak appropriately of God only from the perspective of an event in one's personal existence. To speak objectively of God is to turn the reality of God into an idea toward which it is possible to take a neutral stance. Unlike objective observation of events in the world which requires no change in my understanding of myself, properly to understand the meaning of God is to see that I cannot speak of God at all except from the standpoint of a self-involving change in my self-understanding. Buri combines this classical

[7] See, *e.g.*, Fritz Buri, "Entmythologisierung oder Entkerygmatizierung der Theologie," in *Kerygma und Mythos*, ed. Hans-Werner Bartsch (Hamburg, 1952) and "Die hermeneutische Funktion der Lehre vom prophetischen Heilswerk Christi" in *Der historische Jesus und der kerygmatische Christus*, ed. Helmut Ristow and Karl Matthiae (Berlin, 1960).

[8] *Der Pantokrator*, pp. 122-124.

move with another analysis of objectivity and non-objectivity having to do with the limits of consciousness in which he concludes that God may not be objectified because to do so is to relativize God's unconditionedness into the subject-object structure of human consciousness. But it is important to realize that for Buri this analysis of consciousness is controlled by and receives its theological significance from the logically prior existential move. That is, the hermeneutical meaning of God in the existential dialectic provides the criteria for rejecting the relativization of concepts of God in the subject-object structure.

One result which seems to follow from this move initially is the limitation of language about God to God *pro nobis*. But this does not necessarily entail that theology is thereby subjectivized. In fact, some existentialist theologians simply develop a theology of "faith seeking understanding" from this move. Here the independent objective reality of God is never in question. Such a theology simply assumes a starting point within the theological circle, and existentialism then becomes a resource (i) for articulating the meaning of faith and (ii) for showing the proper way of understanding traditional Christian language about cross, resurrection, sin, atonement, etc.[9]

This understanding of existential theology is not available to Buri, however, and consequently, his position is more problematic from the beginning. It is not available because the hermeneutic he develops out of the classical move requires that the *meaning* of *all* theological concepts be explicated entirely in terms of the existential dialectic. With Buri, unlike the former position, one cannot start within the theological circle of faith for which the independent existence of God is never in question because the very meanings of "faith" and "God" are evident only when they are translated into structures of the existential dialectic; one doesn't know what "God" means except in an allegory, so to speak, where the literal term is the structure of selfhood. For this reason Buri's interpretation of the problem of objectivity and of the classical move represents their radicalization and makes it possible to describe him as the only theologian prepared to apply the existential method with full consistency. But this also means that he

[9] Despite the existential ambiguity that runs through his thought, Bultmann at times seems to assume this understanding of existential theology. For this ambiguity and for Bultmann's struggle, now on one side now on the other, to overcome it, see his two essays on God from different periods in his career: "What Does It Mean To Speak Of God?" in *Faith and Understanding*, vol. I, ed. Robert W. Funk, trans. Louise Pettibone Smith (New York, 1969) and "The Idea of God and Modern Man," in *Translating Theology into the Modern Age*, vol. II: *Journal for Theology and the Church*, ed. by Robert W. Funk, essay trans. Robert W. Funk (New York, 1965). *Cf.* Helmut Gollwitzer, *The Existence of God as Confessed by Faith*, trans. James W. Leitch (London, 1965), pp. 15-24, 30-34.

can maintain the reality of God in the full and proper sense only if he can show reflexively that such reality is required to account fully for the existential dialectic (which dialectic is itself the final hermeneutical term for "Christ," "creation," "providence," "sin," "redemption," *and* "God").

Buri does seem to give such a reflexive justification, something like a transcendental deduction, in several places in *Der Pantokrator* and, less clearly, in his other writings. Since what Buri says here is central not merely to his claim that he has preserved the reality of God but also to the way he then proceeds to discuss the doctrine of God, it must be examined rather closely. One of his most direct statements of the reflexive justification occurs when he is introducing his interpretation of the trinitarian symbol:

> The statement of the three-in-oneness of God articulates not merely the summation of that which we have said about being and fulfillment in relation to personhood in community. Rather, for the sake of their [full and proper] meaning, these assertions about the possibility and the realization of our personhood in the community of unconditioned responsibility also require the use of the trinitarian symbol of God. The significance of the reality therein brought to expression is, to be sure, nothing capable of demonstration; it occurs, rather, only in the enactment of faithful self-understanding. *But the enactment of faithful self-understanding is a reality. If its meaning cannot be expressed otherwise than by using these theological concepts, then we will be able to deny reality to what is therein intended and designated no less than we can deny it to the enactment of our faithful self-understanding.* As little as the enactment is an illusion for the one enacting it, constituting rather the fulfillment of his vocation to responsible personhood in community, just as little is the trinity as the appropriate form for articulating this self-understanding an illusion. Form and content belong together as appearances of one and the same reality.[10]

While this statement makes clear the *form* of Buri's argument, it does not yet say what the *content* is that is required in order to account for the indubitable actuality of a non-objective act of personal existence. Later, however, this content is partially specified in another version of the same argument. When Buri treats the predicates of God's essence he uses the classical schema of the threefold way (the *via causalitatis, eminentiae*, and *negationis*) to organize his discussion. The *via causalitatis,* developed in dependence on the cosmological argument, is used to articulate the aseity, the unity, and the *actus purus* of God. After criticizing the conundrums to which the falsely objectifying cosmological argument leads, Buri then presents his own existential interpretation:

> What is unattainable through discursive thought or collapses into pantheism, nevertheless reveals itself as the unconditionedness of the trinitarian God before

[10] *Der Pantokrator*, pp. 110 f. My italics.

whom the believer knows himself called to responsibility. That unconditionedness befits this God is an assertion of faith which in this way expresses the experience of its own unconditionedness. In the act (*Vollzug*) of faith, aseity is not just a limiting concept; rather, in the act of faith this unconditioned of *ens a se* occurs, represents a unity, and at one and the same time is an *actus purus*. But this is so not as a postulate of our thinking, not as something generally demonstrable; it occurs, rather, as a reality in the act of the self-understanding of faith which documents its character as faith precisely by not claiming these moments for itself but reserves them for that before which it knows itself responsible. Just because faith is in its enactment (*Vollzug*) an unconditioned, self-enclosed act of spirit, it does not claim that which occurs in its enactment for itself but speaks here of the aseity, the unity and the *actus purus* as the attributes of God.[11]

By "self-enclosed" Buri does not mean that the act is self-positing but simply that it is fully an act of man's freedom that requires no mysterious, objective, supernatural powers to account for it. At the same time, however, the existential act of deciding for oneself is a "being chosen," a being gifted to oneself that cannot be accounted for objectively but is given only in and with the non-objective act itself. Thus, the unity of this act correlates with the unity of God, its unconditionedness with the unconditionedness of God, and its character as non-objective act, as reality only in act, with the *actus purus*. In this way, Buri shows how he believes that the existential dialectic demands the content of particular predications of a reality independent of selfhood if that dialectic itself is to be accounted for.

What Buri is claiming in these statements seems relatively clear, but how he develops his case is highly confused both in terms of the adequacy of his claim and its consistency with the rest of his position. Several different issues have to be sorted out.

(1) In the first place, the appeal to faith is confusing. He seems to be saying that, because they are incapable of demonstration, the truth of such concepts as the trinity, unity, unconditionedness, etc. of God can be affirmed only by believing them to be true. But for Buri this appeal to faith would be inconsistent because it would presuppose a falsely objective understanding of faith and its content. Furthermore, the meaning of "faith" can be translated entirely as "non-objective act of responsible freedom." The appeal to faith, consequently, seems to commit Buri to a curious *non sequitur*. To say that to account for "faith" (in the sense of the act of responsible freedom) requires positing the reality of God which, however, can only be known in the act of "faith" (again as the act of responsible freedom) is to beg precisely the question that is at issue. That question concerns nothing other

[11] *Ibid.*, p. 130.

than the conditions of faith as an existential dialectic, but when faith cannot mean the affirmation of an objective proposition, it is circular to warrant the necessary requirements for the proper meaning of an act of faith by an appeal to that act itself.

(2) What Buri means by this appeal is probably closely tied up with his statements about the impossibility of demonstration. But this too is confusing. What is it that cannot be demonstrated? Either it is the truth of the proposition that God is a trinity, unconditioned, etc. or it is the act of faith itself. The first possibility must be rejected because it simply reduces to the former falsely objective understanding of faith. It would assume that we already knew *objectively* the *meaning* of the terms which cannot be demonstrated. The second possibility, however, will not accomplish Buri's purpose, to say nothing of the fact that it adds further confusion. To say that the act of faith cannot be demonstrated is to say that the act of responsible freedom (the *that* of its occurrence) cannot be reduced to an objective approximation process. But this is never at issue. The question is: Given the act of faith (the *that* of its unconditioned actualization) what must be assumed to account for the structures of its existential dialectic?

(3) It thus appears that despite his appeal to faith and to the impossibility of demonstration, Buri can only be understood as presenting something like an argument (*i.e.*, a demonstration). It is, to be sure, an argument that depends for its cogency on a proper recognition of the character of faith as a non-objective act and of the indemonstrability of this act, but it is an argument nonetheless. Buri is *arguing* that what is given in, with, and under the existential act to which he has reduced the meaning of theological concepts can only be accounted for by a transcendent reality irreducible to that act but inaccessible apart from it. But if this is the conclusion to which we are forced, then a host of additional problems are raised in regard to Buri's understanding of the limits of objectification. We can only get at these problems, however, by first sorting out some of the other issues raised by the passages above.

(4) Granting for the moment that Buri is presenting an argument, the question naturally arises whether it is adequate to establish his case. We may assume that Buri's analysis of the existential dialectic as a process of choosing and being chosen (of freedom and grace) is correct. Of the three predications of God we have before us (*i.e.*, unconditioned, unity, and *actus purus*) we can exclude unity and *actus purus* as too ambiguous because with them Buri might only be making a proposal about how to understand these ascriptions existentially. (*E.g.*, with *actus purus* he may be saying that it is not a predication about God but properly should henceforth be understood to

mean the act character of faith in and with which faith knows itself referred to an other.) But at least with "unconditioned" his claim seems much stronger. He appears to say that the unconditioned character of our own acts of responsible freedom requires a truly unconditioned reality as their term. But surely this claim requires additional support. My own acts are unconditioned only in the sense that neither their "that" nor their explanation can be reduced to a series of objective (*i.e.*, relative) observations. But this meaning of unconditioned in no way requires that my acts be posited in a relation to an unconditioned term unless further reasons are brought forward. This remains true even when the dialectic of choosing and being chosen is introduced, for this dialectic can be acknowledged and yet still accounted for in purely existential terms – *e.g.*, by Heidegger's account of "facticity" and "conscience" or Bultmann's understanding of the historicity of human existence. As attractive as it would be, Buri cannot avoid the problem by saying that precisely the meaning of faith is the ascription of the dialectic to a relation with God because that would be to fall back into either the falsely objective understanding of faith or the illicit circularity discussed above.

The same problem comes out clearly in another version of the argument Buri often uses.[12] He says that because we receive our own personhood in the transcending act of the existential dialectic, we must speak of the relational term in the dialectic as personal and that any philosophical or theological position that fails to speak of the final context of human existence in personal terms cannot account for human selfhood. But without additional support, this argument, if it is an argument, is clearly false. The very most that can be concluded alone from any relationship in which I become a self is that in a figurative sense the relationship was personal but not that all the ultimate terms of the relationship must be personal.

(5) It seems evident, therefore, that Buri must bring forth additional reasons to establish his case. And this brings us back to the qualifications in the meaning of objectivity and its limits mentioned above (3). The only way Buri could adduce the reasons his position requires would be by some form of a metaphysics of selfhood or, at least, by some form of reasoning that would seriously endanger his understanding of the limits of objectivity. Despite the inadequacy of his argument, it may even be asked whether this has not already occurred. We have seen that if Buri is not presenting an argument it is difficult to know what he is doing and that, in any case, the appeal to faith and indemonstrability will not accomplish his purpose. If he is presenting an argument, however, inadequate as it may be, it is still an

[12] *Cf.* Buri's defense of the personal character of God, *ibid.*, pp. 107, 127 f., and *Dogmatik . . .*, vol. II: *Der Mensch und die Gnade* (Bern, 1962), pp. 102-104.

objective presentation quite independent of any particular act of faith (even if it depends on being clear about what is going on in such acts). To the extent that Buri is forced to qualify his position this much, then no further harm could be done by the more extensive use of objectifying thinking needed to establish his case.

Of course, it must be asked whether this conclusion does not destroy the whole rationale for an existential theology, especially Buri's which represents a radicalization of the problem of objectivity. Yet there are good reasons for saying that it does not. The real strength of Buri's position on the non-objectivity of faith is the way it allows him to analyze the proper meaning of faith in terms of the existential categories of act and decision. The radicalization of his program then occurs in the brilliance with which he succeeds in explicating the meaning of all theological concepts in terms of the dynamics of this non-objective process. But to say that the "that" of faith is inaccessible to objective determination and that the meaning of theological concepts must be explicated in terms of this non-objective process and nothing beyond it in no way means that to speak objectively about these meanings is illicit. It only means (i) that to be a theologian is not necessarily to be a man of faith and (ii) that what one says objectively as a theologian must be controlled by the act of faith understood as a non-objective process. This much can even be drawn rather directly from the classical existential move. We have seen that this move means that one can speak appropriately of God only from the perspective of an event in one's personal existence which requires a change of self-understanding. If we now allow the possibility of objectifying language in theology but acknowledge that is must be controlled by the existential understanding of faith, we have said no more than that the *objective* categories which we use to speak about God must be categories appropriate to the existential and, thus, non-objective acts in which God and man are related. This point will be taken up again in the concluding section. But first it is necessary to take up the second question concerning the adequacy of what Buri actually says about God.

III

Buri begins his discussion of God by criticizing the false objectivity he claims has characterized the traditional theological approach to God. This objectivism, its formality and detachment from the existential situation of the believer, is nowhere more evident than in the scheme of topics under discussion. First in order comes the being or existence of God, usually treated under the proofs for the existence of God. Next the essence of God is discussed, and the abstract attributes which apply directly and properly to God are developed. A common method for developing these attributes was the threefold way mentioned above. Only after this are the truly Biblical attributes such as God's love, wisdom, holiness, justice, etc. brought forward. Indicative that perhaps something has gone wrong is the tinge of embarrassment with which these attributes are mentioned as *attributa positiva, operativa, metaphorica,* or *relativa* and developed analogically so as to suggest that they do not apply fully and properly. Finally, and oftentimes unrelated to the prior discussion, the trinity is introduced.

In contrast to this, Buri completely reverses this order beginning with the trinity, then the attributes, the essence, and the being of God. As always, the Pantokrator motif developed earlier controls the development of ideas. Buri argues that one cannot begin with the question of the existence of God because treated in isolation this question not only leads to a merely formal answer unrelated to the existential character of the act of faith in which alone it can have meaning, but its objectivity also falsifies the very meaning of God in that dialectic. If we start, on the other hand, with the act of faith itself, we have already seen that the Pantokrator motif provides an ontologically meaningful interpretation of creation and eschatology as "the meaning of human existence in history and its possible fulfillment." [13] The doctrine of God in the proper sense is legitimate if, as Buri tries to establish in the argument above, it is necessary to affirm that the existential dialectic points beyond itself and is not self-positing. The trinity then receives primacy if it can be shown that it articulates the "structural schema of the fullness of God revealed in the Pantokrator." [14] In this sense and consistent with the way Buri treats other theological concepts, the trinity exposits the "trinitarian structure of our personhood and its fulfillment." [15] The attributes, the essence, and the existence of God receive a place in the theological system only to the extent that they provide further definition to the trinitarian structure.

Buri's existential interpretation of the *Pantokrator* is divided according to the threefold structure of the kingly office of Christ, the *regnum potentiae, gratiae,* and *gloriae.* (The concept of original creation has a unique status because existentially it symbolizes the objectively underivable character of the act of selfhood.) The structure of mediate creation, *i.e.,* providence, *creatio conservatio, concursus,* and *gubernatio Dei,* correlates directly with the threefold structure of the kingly office of Christ and thereby,

[13] *Der Pantokrator,* p. 108.
[14] *Ibid.,* p. 111.
[15] *Idem.*

under the Pantokrator motif, provides the structure for an existential interpretation of God which is intrinsically christological. The significance of the trinity is that it articulates this same threefold structure. It only adds something new to the previous existential structure to the extent that it explicitly says that the existential dialectic points beyond the anthropological circle, *i.e.*, cannot be comprehended apart from the doctrine of God in the full and proper sense.

The *conservatio* correlates with the Father by expressing the "wonder" of the givenness of being in which the victory over chaos not only can occur but in which the struggle and the victory is meaningful. That *conservatio* occurs, however, cannot be derived objectively from a natural theology but is given only in and with the non-objective act of personal responsibility. For this reason the meaning of the Father in the trinity is controlled by the christological motif. For the same reason, the *conservatio* requires the *regnum gratiae* and *concursus* and, consequently, the Son. Because the givenness of a world in which the victory over chaos occurs and is meaningful cannot be derived from an objective examination of the world itself, its occurrence must be understood from within the "gift" structure of the existential dialectic. At the same time, this "giftedness" occurs only in the ever to be renewed acts of personal responsibility. In this way the *concursus* as *regnum gratiae* and Son brings to expression the meaning of redemption, atonement, and covenant in the sense of ever new possibilities of taking responsibility for oneself. Finally, the Holy Spirit correlates with the *regnum gloriae* and the *gubernatio Dei in christo* in terms of the manifestation of the reconciled community of responsible selves in history. It thereby grounds the theological interpretation of the problem of evil, the church, and hope. The unity of the trinity is then grounded, as we would expect, by the unitary character of the act of self-understanding which, despite "the diversity of aspects of self-understanding, is still always just one self-understanding of faith in its unconditionedness and its communal character." [16]

Buri begins his discussion of the attributes by noting that they can be known only in the act of self-understanding and not objectively. This principle leads him to ground the actual content of his doctrine of God on a concept of analogy derived from the act of faithful existence itself. The existential character of faith, that is, requires a particular kind of *analogia fidei* based on the dialectic of existence. The analogical mode of predication must be an *analogia fidei* because God is given only in and with the non-objective act of faith itself. Buri opposes Barth, however, who grounds the *analogia relationis* in the fact "that God 'determines his own predicate

[16] *Ibid.*, p. 114.

(*sich prädiziert*)' prior to and independent of the act of self-understanding." [17] This would again be an illicit objectification. For Buri the analogy can be grounded only in the fact that "he allows us to experience our personal being in that he judges our failures to attain it and helps us in its realization." [18] Thus, in line with the above argument for the necessity of God, we can speak of God only "in order to bring to expression the character of grace and judgment in man's becoming authentic or inauthentic." [19] Buri goes on to argue that after one has established the principle of the *analogia fidei*, it is appropriate to go on to speak of an *analogia entis* in the sense that "the manifestation of a particular kind of being occurs in this faith." [20] But because Buri is prepared to speak of ontology only in relation to the existential dialectic which is itself a non-objective act, this is not an analogy between God and being as such that could be established independently but an "*analogia entis in Christo.*" [21]

On the basis of this interpretation of analogy (which, it should be noted, is nothing more than a restatement of the classical existential move), Buri then proceeds to develop the attributes of God according to the distinction between essence and existence. The attributes of God's essence are derived from those aspects of the existential structure that warrant the positing of God as such. These are, in particular, the unconditionedness of faith and the non-objectivity of its actualization. The attributes of God's essence thus recapitulate the argument discussed above. In this respect they are the existential correlates of what was traditionally known as *attributa immanentia*. As we saw above, the *attributa immanentia* of the *via causalitatis* are the unconditionedness, the unity, and the *actus purus* of God. Parallel with the same argument and in every case existentially interpreted, the attributes derived from the *via eminentiae* are immutability, eternity, and omnipresence and from the *via negationis* simplicity, spirituality, inconceivability, and invisibility.

In contrast to these attributes that warrant God in the existential dialectic, the attributes of God's being or existence express the actual structure of the existential dialectic itself – the being-called-out-into-responsible-selfhood (*Gerufensein*), the being-enabled in the gift structure of existence (*Instandgesetzt-sein*), and the being-judged by the failure to take responsibility for ourselves (*Gerichtet-sein*). Over against the traditional treatment of the existence of God which attempts to demonstrate *that* he exists, Buri's argu-

[17] *Ibid.*, p. 123.
[18] *Idem.*
[19] *Idem.*
[20] *Idem.*
[21] *Idem.*

ment is that one can speak of the existence of God only out of the structure in which God is actually given in faith. In this sense, one cannot speak of the existence of God objectively apart from faith but only in that act itself; consequently, God's being is not merely "is" but is only *in actu*. Thus, Buri develops an extremely interesting twist on the traditional treatment of the existence of God in the proofs, which are the most formal part of the traditional division of topics relating to God. He argues that the existence of God should only be discussed under the least formal of the attributes, namely, the attributes of God's relatedness, the *attributa transeuntia*, which express God's being as essentially a being that comes out from itself. In this way, the ontological argument is used to develop God's life, omnipotence, and wisdom; the cosmological argument, his love, righteousness, and faithfulness; and the teleological argument, his wisdom, holiness, and glory. In all these cases, both with the *Wesensfülle* and the *Seinsfülle*, the threefold structure is interpreted in terms of the trinitarian structure of creation and providence *in Christo* and, thus, in terms of the Pantokrator.

There can be little question that Buri presents here an extremely imaginative and suggestive re-interpretation of the doctrine of God. This is true not merely of his proposal to restructure the order of development to bring it more into line with the real content of the tradition of the Christian self-understanding but also in the detail of, for instance, his re-interpretation of analogy and his presentation of the *Seinsfülle* in terms of the *attributa transeuntia*. But running through his whole discussion is a decisive problem which threatens to call the whole program into question.

This problem is directly parallel to the one discussed above regarding the ambiguities in his attempt to establish the necessity of God in his theology. Though he does not solve it, Buri brings it out clearly in the following statement:

> The unconditionedness which is at stake in faith is not a reality outside of faith but occurs in its enactment. As something to be asserted, there is, outside this enactment only the conditioned or, at any rate, the unconditioned only as that which presents itself to conceptual thought as nothingness [*i.e.*, because of the subject-object schema]. But within this sphere of the conditioned and against the background of nothingness there occurs in the act of faith the reality of the unconditioned. Just as this act is possible only by means of objective concepts, so is this conceptual objectivity ... also now the foundation for an analogical speaking about God which corresponds to that act. In its assertions, faith relates itself to the reality of its enactment. The content of its assertions stands in relation to the reality which occurs in its enactment. These assertions are not this reality but stand in relation to it. This relation does not belong to an ontological order independent of faith but occurs likewise only in the act of faith. In its assertions, it is thus not a matter of an *analogia entis* but of an

analogia fidei. Other than in this relatedness to the act of faith, they become false objectifications of something essentially non-objectifiable. But as assertions of faith concerning its unconditionedness, they correspond to its reality. . . . Through the function which belongs to them in faith, they bring faith to appropriate assertions about God *as the symbol of its unconditionedness.*[22]

The problem here, of course, concerns getting clear on precisely what the analogy refers to and what warrants the reference. There is no question that Buri intends the *analogia fidei* to warrant attributes of God. But the actual content of those attributes only refers to the structures of faith. For instance, the immutability, eternity, and unchangeability in the *via eminentiae* refer respectively to the unchanging, exceptionless character of the demand placed upon us that we be responsible selves, to the *Augenblick* of decision in which "eternity" occurs in time, and thereby to the fact that every moment can become a moment of grace in which in our acts of responsibility we are given to ourselves.[23] Or again, we know of love, righteousness, and faithfulness, according to Buri, only in the encounter with others in which we are called to responsible selfhood. These become attributes of God by bringing to expression that we are the kind of beings who become true selves only by responding to these encounters, are judged in our being when we fail, and yet may constantly actualize the possibility of atonement by assuming responsibility for ourselves in the context of judgment.[24] In every case here, the attributes of God refer to structures of selfhood. Or to put it another way, the attributes of God *as Buri discusses them* refer to or require other attributes which themselves remain unknown. It is difficult, in other words, to know whether we have a doctrine of God here at all.

It is possible, of course, to avoid this conclusion by saying that precisely the meaning of "act of responsible selfhood" *as faith* is to believe that the structures of our existential selfhood are grounded in God. But this has problems too. In the first place, this interpretation would seem to commit Buri to the falsely objective understanding of faith discussed above. And in the second place, even if this alternative were possible, the attributes as Buri discusses them still do not refer to God, and they provide no warrants in and of themselves for saying "this" rather than "that" about God – something presumably of some importance even for a falsely objective understanding of the faith move.

It is, consequently, difficult to comprehend precisely what gain there is in grounding the *analogia fidei* in the *act* of faith as Buri does in the

[22] *Ibid.*, pp. 126 f. My italics.
[23] See *ibid.*, pp. 130 f.
[24] See *ibid.*, pp. 140 f.

passage quoted above. While the proper intelligibility of analogical predication may be grounded in the existential dialectic, that ground does not work unless in some sense it allows predication of God. It is possible, of course, that Buri sees his theology as nothing more than a development of the recurrent theme in modern theology since Schleiermacher of treating the attributes of God only as attributes *pro nobis*. But aside from the fact that such a move condemns him to the same subjectivizing criticism that has been the bane of all such theologies, this interpretation is particularly problematic in his case. Because he refuses to move outside the existential dialectic alone, he cannot, unlike Schleiermacher, ground even the *pro nobis* in a reality transcendent to the dialectic either by an appeal to belief or by an ontology independent of the "positivity" of any particular act of faith.

IV

If this is the last word to be said about Buri's doctrine of God, it would appear that a fully existential theology cannot in fact meet the minimal criterion for an adequate theology, namely, an ability to state a doctrine of God independent of human subjectivity. Despite his most strenuous efforts – either in establishing the necessity of a relation to God or in existentially interpreting "God language" – Buri cannot move beyond the internal structure of an existential dialectic. It would be a mistake, however, to think that this conclusion should be drawn in any straightforward way as though it once and for all demonstrates the inherent failure of an existential theological method. To draw such a conclusion would ignore the fact that the issue of existential interpretation arose out of the most serious effort to take seriously the hermeneutical crisis of contemporary theology. We saw this repeatedly above when we noted the unfruitfulness of simply applying a quasi-existential method to beliefs the *meaning* of which were themselves accepted as unproblematic. It is precisely the meaning of, for instance, "God" which is at stake today, and to pretend that one can retreat to a theological method which fails to acknowledge this is to fall short of the theological demands of the present situation. It is the radicality of the hermeneutical commitment of existential theology which has attempted to meet this situation. If there is a way out of the problem, therefore, it must be one that proceeds through existential interpretation, not one that pretends that it is possible to go behind it.

Can Buri's approach be revised, then, without surrendering its existential character? There is not space here to propose such a complete revision, but we can make a beginning by looking more carefully at the essential reason why Buri ends with the problems we have uncovered. This reason would seem to be Buri's attempt to reduce the entire scope of theological hermeneutics to the act (or the character in act) of faith. By consistently refusing to allow any theological assertions which are not a function of this act, Buri cannot avoid confusing the hermeneutical question and the ontological question with the result that his interpretation of the meaning of theological concepts prevents him, despite himself, from making or implying any ontological assertions (assertions about what is believed to be the case) beyond the existential structure of the self. While, that is to say, his method allows him to succeed brilliantly in the hermeneutical task of explicating the meaning of theological concepts *in human existence,* this same method prevents him from explicating the equally important question of the ontological ground of just these existential meanings. The question, then, is whether the ontological question can be compatible with an existential method whose hermeneutical fruitfulness is beyond dispute.

The problem here centers on the existentialist position on objectivity which is the methodological background for Buri's inability to move outside the non-objective act of existence and for his consequent failure to combine the hermeneutical and the ontological tasks. Here Buri is faced with a particularly acute form of what might be called "the dilemma of objectivity in existential thought." [25] If, on the one hand, Buri maintains the limits of objectivity in a fully consistent way, he is forced back into the non-objective dialectic without hope of escape, and there is little question that he cannot avoid the reduction of theology to anthropology, or at least, he cannot provide warrants for an alternative. If, on the other hand, he does provide warrants, he can only do so by qualifying the restrictions placed on objective description. Can this latter restriction occur in an existential theology?

Such a qualification would have to occur in relation to each of the two major points of our discussion of Buri in this paper. Admitting the possibility of these qualifications the only problem is to show, contrary to the supposition of many existentialists, that they are not really incompatible with the hermeneutical task of existential interpretation. As we saw above, Buri would first have to show how the dialectic of existence, as articulated in the assertions of the Christian self-understanding, itself requires positing the reality of God. This qualification would in no way alter the non-objective character of the structure of faith itself, but the *argument* warranting the

[25] For a detailed analysis of this dilemma, see my book, *Faith and Objectivity: Fritz Buri and the Hermeneutical Foundations of a Radical Theology,* Martinus Nijhoff, 1972.

claim would have to be objectively independent of the non-objective act. The act would simply provide the theological basis for developing the claim and then, in correlation with the claim, would hermeneutically clarify the meaning of its terms *pro nobis, i.e.,* in the existential life of faith. As was argued above, however, there is no reason to think that this distinction between the existential act of faith and an argument warranting its ontological basis need debilitate the contribution the classical existential move has made to the hermeneutical problem as long as the point of reference and the norm for *what* the theologian has to say continues to be the proviso that the act of faith itself is non-objective.

The second kind of qualification would require a further step in the discussion of the attributes of God. It would have to be shown how the meaning of the attributes in the existential act of faith correlates with the attributes of God in the full and proper sense. One would have to show, for example, not only why Buri's meaning of the "love of God" as the articulation of existential possibilities properly correlates with the love of God in the full and proper sense, but warrants would also have to be provided for saying just one thing about the love of God rather than something else.

While the first kind of qualification of the limits of objectivity would require, given just the assumptions Buri makes, something like a metaphysics of selfhood, there is no reason to think that the second kind of qualification would need to be either a demonstration of faith or a full-blown speculative system. All that is required is to make clear that Christian faith (even in the sense of *anima humana naturaliter christiana*) rests on or implies certain belief claims about what is the case. This is true even if access to and the content of those claims must be controlled by a non-objective understanding of faith as an act of responsible selfhood. In the same respect, it is not necessary for such an objectifying analysis to be a demonstration that the content of those claims is true. There need be nothing more than a description of precisely what is belieffully implied by existential acts and the theological language used to express them (*i.e.*, the hermeneutical level of interpretation). The only demonstration would be one internal to this description. The analysis, that is, might take the form of an argument showing why just these claims are made, how they are consistent with one another, and how their consistency requires the exclusion of other claims. While such an ontological explication would be a function of the hermeneutical structure of theological assertions as existentially interpreted, the warrants for the intelligibility and the coherence of these ontological claims would have to be objective in character and would have to be assessed on their own terms independently of the existential dialectic of faith alone. But as long as the task is properly theological and is hence controlled by an interpretation of Christian assertions seen as expressions for certain existential possibilities, there is no reason to think that this further ontological level would do violence to the essential task of an existential theology.

It might be replied that violence would indeed be done because the qualifications which I am suggesting would necessarily require re-introducing the false conception of belief spoken of above and would thus destroy the hermeneutical relevance of existential interpretation. It will be recalled that this false conception resulted from viewing the existential method on the model of "faith seeking understanding" and using existentialism to address the problem of the appropriation of belief contents the meaning of which was seen to be essentially unproblematic. The position I am advocating does not, however, entail this position. The question of ontology can legitimately be raised provided the hermeneutical question is allowed its full force, and this is precisely what the above qualifications allow. The ontological question, that is, need not be a retreat behind the hermeneutical problem but can be an extension of it. To put this another way, existentially interpreted theological assertions themselves require ontological explication. The problem is whether they admit it, and here the problem centers on the problem of objectivity. But we have seen that *if properly qualified by the hermeneutical content of faith as existentially interpreted,* ontological explication need do no violence either to the non-object act of faith or to the non-objective character of its content. This violence is done only when the full hermeneutical force of the existential method is not first given its due.

There can be little question that the intelligibility of faith assertions today requires a radical hermeneutical reconstruction. There is also no question that the existential method as employed by a man like Buri has been immensely productive in essaying this task in detail – instead, as with most, merely at the level of methodology or of promissory notes. The only point to be made here is that this use of the existential method need in no way prevent us from asking what God must be like such that the existential possibilities of the Christian self-understanding are an appropriate response to the reality we encounter. Unless this is a question which can legitimately be appended to the hermeneutical task, then, as we have seen, Buri's method cannot avoid falling of its own weight into the trap of human subjectivity.

* *
*